VIRTUAL WAR AND MAGICAL DEATH

THE CULTURES AND PRACTICE OF VIOLENCE SERIES

SERIES EDITORS:

Neil L. Whitehead, University of Wisconsin, Madison
Jo Ellen Fair, University of Wisconsin, Madison
Leigh Payne, University of Wisconsin, Madison

The study of violence has often focused on the political and economic conditions under which violence is generated, the suffering of victims, and the psychology of its interpersonal dynamics. Less familiar are the role of perpetrators, their motivations, and the social conditions under which they are able to operate. In the context of postcolonial state building and more latterly the collapse and implosion of society, community violence, state repression, and the phenomena of judicial inquiries in the aftermath of civil conflict, there is a need to better comprehend the role of those who actually do the work of violence—torturers, assassins, and terrorists—as much as the role of those who suffer its consequences.

When atrocity and murder take place, they feed the world of the iconic imagination that transcends reality and its rational articulation; but in doing so imagination can bring further violent realities into being. This series encourages authors who build on traditional disciplines and break out of their constraints and boundaries, incorporating media and performance studies and literary and cultural studies as much as anthropology, sociology, and history.

VIRTUAL WAR

Technologies and Imaginaries for Terror and Killing

AND MAGICAL DEATH

NEIL L. WHITEHEAD AND
SVERKER FINNSTRÖM, EDS.

Duke University Press
Durham and London
2013

© 2013 Duke University Press

All rights reserved

Printed in the United States of America on acid-free paper ∞

Designed by Heather Hensley

Typeset in Warnock by Tseng Information Systems, Inc.

Library of Congress Cataloging-in-Publication Data appear on
the last printed page of this book.

FOR NEIL (1956–2012)

Deep sorrow in our hearts
Paralyzing
This cannot be the end
This is some kind of beginning
We have to carry on
And we shall meet

Don't know where, don't know how
Just don't know

So much remains unsaid
So much remains to be done
Life is unfinished
You are life
Life is everywhere

Bewilderness, so hard to swallow
Yet gardens will again grow and blossom
Your fight is over
We continue
Together

CONTENTS

ACKNOWLEDGMENTS

The chapters in this volume were first presented at the American Anthropological Association's annual meetings in Philadelphia in 2009, on a panel organized by Neil L. Whitehead, Koen Stroeken, and me called "Virtual War and Magical Death," a title we kept for the book. This discussion followed up on a panel called "Ethnographies of Violence," organized by Neil at the American Anthropological Association's annual meetings in San Jose in 2006, to which he had invited me, and which eventually was published as a special issue of *Anthropology and Humanism* (2009, vol. 34, no. 1). The San Jose panel was sponsored by the Society for Humanistic Anthropology. In 2010 I visited Neil in Madison to plan the current anthology with him. We also invited David Price to contribute a paper. He attended the discussions in Philadelphia but was not a panel participant.

To work with Neil on this anthology was a true dialogue, immensely inspiring, with draft versions endlessly traveling the cyberspace between me and Neil, between Uppsala and Madison. Following up on our anthology, a number of panels were planned for the American Anthropological Association's annual meetings in San Francisco in 2012, when Neil's untimely death disrupted everything. So it felt. Only slowly did we get back on track again. Warm thanks to Erika Robb Larkins, Neil's friend and former student, whom I first met on Neil's panel in San Jose, who was instrumental during these final stages.

I want to thank all contributors for encouragement and patience, and I extend this gratitude to everyone at Duke University Press, including the anonymous reviewers who unquestionably helped us improve our spinning thoughts. Special thanks to Valerie Millholland, Miriam Angress, and Liz Smith, who helped me finalize the book in times when everything suddenly was up in the air. Thanks also to Laura Poole, who copyedited our texts.

Neil was a mentor, inspiring, a guide to the galaxy. He is missed greatly. Thanks, Neil, for everything. With this anthology, we hope to honor your legacy.

SVERKER FINNSTRÖM, UPPSALA, APRIL 2012

VIRTUAL WAR AND MAGICAL DEATH

This book was inspired by a number of considerations: the limits of ethnographic participation in war zones, the way in which the imaginary becomes significant in creating meaning in the chaotic context of war zones, and how a space of virtual conflict and war emerges from these conjunctions. Such a virtual space is not separate from the physical battlefield, although for most Euro-Americans the battles are something "out there" in the presumably dangerous spaces of Africa, Middle East, or south of the Mexico–United States border. However, we contend in the volume that the actual killings on the battlefields, wherever they happen to be located, are intimately linked to an emerging virtual space created by news and cinematic and gaming media as well as the mediating and mapping technologies of contemporary military violence—such as airborne attack drones, satellite surveillance from space, stealth airplanes and helicopters, night-vision equipment, and the associated use of politically covert assassination operations. This is the character of war today, which has definitively moved beyond the confines of nation-states and through mechanisms such as "peacekeeping" or terrorist interdiction, and now has a global and increasingly permanent character. Ethnographic fieldwork in these contexts of deep political entanglements between corporate interests, military planning, and government decision making (see Nordstrom 2004a) clearly suggests that the production of war as a cultural and social phenomenon now extends far from any particular battlefield and must be understood through considering the virtual technologies that mediate both combat and decision making. The vast investment by Euro-American militaries in virtual technologies for combat and a simultaneous political reworking of the meaning and purpose of "war" following the events of September 11, 2001, in the United States demand a critical assessment of them as cultural phenomena that deeply affect the lives of all of us.[1]

If *modern* warfare evinces an increasing expansion into the realm of everyday life as a result of its highly mediated character, both for observers and participants, then it is important to note that anthropological examinations of *modernity* itself often stress the reemergence of the magical as an aspect of quotidian understandings worldwide of technology and the global political order (Meyer and Pels 2003; West and Sanders 2003). For these reasons, we think it useful to extend the notion of "virtual war" to include the realm of magic, sorcery, and witchcraft. Just as the label "tribal" has most often been used to reference the threatening, if anachronistic, alterity of the non-Western world, paradoxically implying a global phenomenon coeval with and connected to a liberal progressive modernity, then this is also the case with the term *magic* (Fabian 1983; Ferguson and Whitehead 2000). Magic and cyberspace are both "virtual realities," as Jeffrey A. Sluka remarks in this volume. "In tribal societies," he writes with reference to Whitehead, "war shamans were believed to be capable of physical assassination by remote means—killing their enemies at a distance by occult methods." Here we wish to call attention to how killing one's enemies through secretive and hidden methods, such as high-altitude bombing, covert operations ("black ops") that shapeshift the identities of killers, or the simple darkness of night, perfectly reproduce the imaginative worlds and subjective experience manifested in forms of witchcraft, magic, and assault sorcery known from the anthropological literature.[2] As the chapters will show (some more than others), the virtuality of the concept of culture and the virtuality of war have become mutually implicated. Sorcery is not just analogous with virtual war, it is continuous with it—it even "is" it.

This is not really a matter of semantics only. Rather, from our contributors' respective horizons of ethnographic insight, we intend to indicate that the "techno-modern" and "magico-primitive" in fact blend into each other and thus need to be addressed through a *symmetrical* anthropology that challenges the military doctrine of "asymmetric warfare" in which the magical technologies of night vision, aircraft drone attacks, and online battle worlds would otherwise appear as unrelated phenomena. The military doctrine of asymmetry serves to mark off a "modern" practice of war and violence from a supposedly more "primitive" world of war magic, shamanic attack, and assault sorcery. But the claim of such a distinction is a telling illustration of Bruno Latour's (1993) classic conclusion that "we," the self-declared modern, paradoxically "have never been modern." The asymmetry of today's warfare, we argue instead, is to be located in the very process of bracketing off the allegedly modern from the allegedly premodern or even primitive, by which dominant groups readily ascribe themselves the role of the modern civilizer and defender of democracy, while at the same time identifying the enemy as primitive, somehow less human, or anyway in need of education. As the contributions to the volume illustrate, such a Manichaean process follows a faulty epistemological tradition of thought. It conceals the complex global realities of war, where the modern cannot really be separated from the premodern.

Rather than one set framework, our contributors address the asymmetry of today's warfare by way of very different case studies, differently structured and collected from the heart of America to the assumed peripheries of Latin America, Africa, and the Middle East. Here we encourage different anthropological positionalities, allowing for various focuses and individual tones. Our passion for difference will still indicate a general trend of similarity and sameness. Again, in placing the cases on a par with each other, heterogeneous as they may be, we aim to promote a symmetrical anthropology in the critique of the idea of asymmetrical warfare.

So in understanding "virtuality" as magical, we build on a range of anthropological work that has not just ethnographically reconsidered the ritual practices of non-Western societies but sought to pursue an important analogy between the exercise of power and the practices of sorcery. To examine practices of violence and power in militarized social contexts is the recognition that the cultural meaning of virtual experience is readily assimilated to discourses of magic and witchcraft. The stress here is on the intersubjective experience of violence and power and how that often stands in contrast to the highly rationalistic formulation of governments and their military institutions as to what we should understand as "really" happening. As we discuss later, this has become a very well evidenced theoretical component of contemporary anthropology. What is new in this volume is to extend those insights to the particular realm of military and police violence and signal how important the apparatus of military secrecy and occlusion has become in sustaining the wider Western political order. As Bruce Kapferer (2002:22–23) writes, "the very force of magic" is a "phantasmagoric space" and an "imaginal field" whose significance derives "not so much by what it is representative of external to itself" but how it creates "a dynamic space entirely to itself and subject to its own emergent logics," a kind of self-proclaiming and self-generating truth. Kapferer acknowledges the influence of Gilles Deleuze and Félix Guattari's (1987) notion of "virtuality." This is the notion we wish to call attention to as present for the Western users of military technology we will discuss, especially in the chapters by Robertson Allen, Antonius C. G. M. Robben, Jeffrey A. Sluka, and Matthew Sumera. At the same time, the phantasmagorical world of remote killings, black ops, death squads, and spaces of militarized chaos are encoded by the non-Western inhabitants of such worlds and the objects of these forms of violence, as likewise phantasmagorical and magical and as sketched ethnographically by Sverker Finnström and by Koen Stroeken in this volume. The difference is that the cultural process of such encoding produces very different discourses that are, without anthropological interpretation, occult and opaque to Western observers, because they are not reducible to some universal idea of Reason, however rational their application may be to their practitioners. Here "rationality" becomes merely another reassuring example of the reduction of the magical to the rational, an intellectual colonialism that was a key part of the wider program of the Western Enlightenment, as discussed in Neil L. Whitehead's chapter.

In comparing and relating magic to the deployment of high-tech weapons and surveillance systems, we are also inspired by Harry G. West and Todd Sanders's (2003) collection of ethnographic accounts of transparency and conspiracy in a new world order. Conspiratorial thinking about power is not confined to the West but appears in different forms globally. Thus, Western conspiracy theories often do analogous cultural work to occult cosmologies in non-Western contexts. As West and Sanders point out: "Suspicion of IMF claims to produce a transparent economic environment in places like Korea or Tanzania may be expressed in the form of consultation with shamans . . . or seers. . . . Beliefs that power continues to conspire even under a regime of electoral democracy may be expressed in Mozambique or in Indonesia in the form of reference to the dark world of sorcery" (2003:5). However, as West and Sanders (2003:6) recognize—as with our contention that sorcery and magic are aspects of contemporary Western militarism, even if understood by the military through other concepts—initial reactions may be that "we are comparing conceptual apples and oranges." This is due in part to how magic and assault sorcery have been understood by anthropologists and others as atavistic or expressions of primitive thinking. Nonetheless, as West and Sanders (2003:13) say, a similarity between the cultural work of science and rationality and the occult cosmologies is precisely that both "explained happenings that direct observation and common sense could not, ordering an otherwise disorderly world of human experience." Both are ways of understanding power. In turn Kapferer (1997), and more recently Danny Hoffman (2011)—again, they both follow the works of Deleuze and Guattari (1987)—characterize state governance and the ever-growing young workforce of decentralized and highly flexible "war machines" as interdependent practices of power. Kapferer and Hoffman productively reference both governance and war machines as forms of sorcery, seen as quintessentially operating both outside and inside the normal relations of modern capitalism—in Hoffman's analysis a hallmark of post-Fordism that disrupts established hierarchies of value and perpetually transforms material realities (Hoffman 2011; see also Kapferer 1997:274–85). Particularly relevant to the analysis of West and Sanders (2003) is Kapferer's identification of the International Monetary Fund and global corporations as being like sorcerers, forever destabilizing established markets and existing distributions of capital.

Other anthropologists have both foreshadowed and expanded this insightful analysis of increasingly globalized realities (see, e.g., Comaroff and Comaroff 1993; Geertz 1980; Geschiere 1997; Meyer and Pels 2003; Vidal and Whitehead 2004), whereas Giorgio Agamben's (2005) work on states of exception likewise, although not with an anthropological vocabulary, delineated how occult unseen enemies and visionary prophecies of crisis and social breakdown have become a permanent part of the constitution of political authority, as seen from many dictatorships all over the world but also from the everyday workings of the self-declared liberal democracies of the West. All of this comes together precisely in such phenomenon as the U.S.-directed war on terror against a shadowy network of terrorist-witches that constantly threaten the very foundation of "civilization," which then require exceptional measures of the exercise of surveillance and violence to ensure the security and peace of the Euro-American homeland. Moreover, as the essays prepared for this volume demonstrate, this model of contemporary political power and leadership is globally evident from the Israeli invasion of the Gaza Strip to the warscapes of Africa, from the borders of Afghanistan and Pakistan to the streets of Guatemala City where the armed *narco-traficante* shape-shifts into the figure of a criminal terrorist.

This "War of Shadows" (Brown and Fernández 1991) or these "Shadows of War" (Nordstrom 2004a) are the prime focus of this volume not just because we simply wish to make transparent that which is occluded but, more important, because these kinds of occluded relationships define power and powerlessness in the new world order. Also, such "a veil of transparency" (West and Sanders 2003:20) defines global war. The virtual worlds of advanced military technique and planning cannot be understood or, more important, politically and democratically controlled without appreciating their cultural logic and how they are a conscious part of military purposes and strategies.

The blending of the "techno-modern" and "magico-primitive" is also evident in the very nature of technology, especially virtual technologies in which the apparent simplicities of binary code result in the magical complexities of an online experience. Some chapters herein take up this aspect of virtual war more than others. When this dimension is left tacit, as in Roberto González's, R. Brian Ferguson's, and Victoria Sanford's contributions, their discussions of the wider political context of new military technologies and their interface with both social control and policing still provide important insights into the ways military technology and practice is brought "back home."[3] On the other hand, Robben directly draws out the nature of mediation and immediation in contemporary warfare with regard to optics in his chapter, but it is also salient to note that the hypertext which fundamentally constitutes online virtual worlds is itself magically produced.[4] As discussed by Robertson Allen and Matthew Sumera in their respective contributions, bodies of hypertext contain not just simply streaming text but various forms of interactive multimedia ranging from graphics to sound and video. It is, in essence, the *text* with which we interact whenever we use the Internet. However, the text provided is a collaboration, a real-time performance of many "authors," and in this way it is a mimetic analog to ritual performance. As with movies and theater, the techno-modern and the magico-primitive here merge in a ritualized drama of "public liminality" (Turner 1979). Thus, hypertext is also analog to how magic or sorcery are practically realized. The micro-technology of a computer, the hypertexts that constitute connections between computers, and the ways hypertexts both mediate and constitute virtual experiences as interactive performance can seem to be something miraculous to those who are not "tech-savvy."

Via media technologies, the simulacra of violence that circulate through all of us as news, online videos and games, photos, fashion, and even smartphone applications, create subjectivities unwittingly harnessed to the project that globalizes war. In his chapter on the making of the video game *America's Army* for military and civilian use, Allen makes the important point that there is a connection between the cultural depictions of the enemy in these media and the normalization of war through consumption, just as David Price's discussion of how weaponizing culture more generally enables a whole range of ways that "War, Inc." can market its product inside and outside of the material kill zone. This underscores the growing cultural and commercial relevance of magic and virtuality to understanding the practice of contemporary war, as well as how the formation of individual subjectivities may be profoundly affected through this constant engagement with the chaos of the techno-imaginary of combat, as indicated in Robben's essay. The disabled empathy, crippled compassion, and anxious search for security thus enables the practice of war and violence to appear as a means of salvation, redemption, and therapy that will cure the world of "our" fear and "their" terrorism. At the same time, intricate global commodity chains, unceasing industrial production, and a merciless search for corporate profits combine to disgorge weaponry, vehicles, electronics, fuel, food, ammunition, AK-47s that ten-year-olds can operate, and military clothing into the sites of war. All this, if anything, constitutes the weapons of mass destruction.

As Carolyn Nordstrom (2004a) has pointed out, the "shadows of war"—those apparently background or occluded processes that stand in contrast to the realities of actual battlefields with gunfire, explosions, rockets, and dismembered bodies—are a central part of the material aspect of that set of cultural and social relationships and practices that constitute "war." In short, "war" is not an aggregation of violent acts that finally reaches a given threshold of carnage to become war rather than armed conflict, counterinsurgency, or peacekeeping, but is the invocation and creation of a particular political reality that engages allies and enemies, civilians and soldiers in a particular style of violent interaction. As battlegrounds are international, even global, the kind of ethnography we want to sketch here needs to be pieced together across long distances and over extended stretches of time. The question therefore is not "What is war?" but rather, "When is war?" How that latter question is answered is precisely what goes on to legitimate and order the expectations, attitudes, and experiences of affect that consume both those with guns and those without in the space of war. In addition, having the indefinite horizons of the virtual in mind, we also ask *where* war is. For this reason, there is a seamless continuity between virtual and material war, or more properly between war online and offline.[5] War is always global.

Equally, this potentially infinite and immaterial space of violence, no less than material violence itself, poses critical questions for anthropological knowledge, for the purposes and possible forms of ethnographic engagement, and for research more generally. This is not just to raise the well-rehearsed issue of the continuities between colonial and neocolonial epistemologies and their unexamined presence in ongoing ethnographic practice (indeed, some of the key ethnographic contributions to such issues over the past decade or so were developed by contributors to this volume) but also to ask, in the words of one reviewer for this volume, whether anthropology's historical "association with coloniality has morphed into an association with 'Empire.'" In view of the cogent arguments made in the chapters that follow, with regard to the use of social sciences for the prosecution of war by Euro-American militaries from Northern Ireland to Afghanistan, the answer given here is a resounding "yes." Thus, the legacy of colonial complicity and today's global wars talks directly to the demands—may they be creative, interpretive, epistemological, or pragmatic—of our current research ethics, in anthropology and beyond.

Global war, if we are to define the concept, is basically a cycle of violence without any certain ending, to reference Stroeken's contribution to this volume. In no conflict are there clear distinctions between combatants and noncombatants or easily defined front lines. Instead, the destruction of communities and forced displacement, terror and sexual abuse, fear and brutality, and perhaps most importantly chaos, unpredictability, virtuality, and the absurd are tools by which all kinds of actors try to establish control. This arsenal of terror, from the very local to the most global, which both insurgents and counterinsurgents seem to share, "focuses less on killing the physical body than on terrifying the population as a whole into, the military strategists hope, cowed acquiescence" (Nordstrom 2002:275–76).

Through global networks, physical and cyber, the space of virtuality connects directly and lethally to the space of materiality, as Sluka demonstrates in his contribution to this volume, which is a truly scary assessment of remote drone killing. So, too, the imaginaries of soldiers, rebels, insurgents, civilians, and the "innocent" are all suffused with the myriad representations of war, both past and present, which as cultural and historical actors we all bring to our unfolding experience. Price also points this out in his careful examination of the advocates of the use of anthropology by the military. "The military's needs for low-tech human ethnographic knowledge," he writes in his chapter, "grow in proportion to the reliance on futuristic war tools like drones and satellite-based systems." For this reason the potential of ethnography and the forms of cultural analysis practiced by anthropologists are currently central to the U.S. military's hopes for its Human Terrain System (HTS) program. As discussed by Roberto González in his contribution, the HTS program itself is a first step toward implanting the "software" of cultural analysis into the "hardware" of cybernetic military systems of targeting that might even predict sites of resistance or insurgency. Such a technological development will be magical in essence, in the sense that magic works as a dehumanizing device here, whereby the enemies' humanity is replaced with a stereotypical and mechanical otherness, as is illustrated by the contributions of Allen, Sumera, and Finnström. But also, as they note, inward-facing representations are part of such magical developments. Here the human terrain mapping exercise projects an idealized version of "us" (or U.S.), which anyway seems to cohere only in relation to a stereotypical Other (the not-U.S.).

When such virtual modeling moves from active target acquisition to prophetic identification of enemies, the intertwining of the magical and virtual becomes complete. Enemies are made through processes of cultural and ideological production, as Alexander Hinton (2005) has showed with regard to the Cambodian and other genocidal discourses. The fluid and uncertain nature of those processes of identification lead to the hyperreality of the war zone, or the fear that witches, sorcerers, insurgents, enemies, and terrorists are everywhere, all the time. What these magical and genocidal scenarios share is the way they are linked through the global connections of economy and politics that can create immiseration in Papua New Guinea or West Africa, even as the apparatus of Homeland Security in the United States disciplines its own citizens lest they become vulnerable to the "hate" and "terrorism" of those whose immiseration they have been implicated in creating. In a somehow related development, and in the wake of the Arab Spring, the Khartoum regime announced the creation of a special battalion of "cyber-jihadists" that would swiftly identify and crush any online youth dissent groups. Asking whether the battalion was for real misses the point. What we want to stress is that the human terrain mapping by definition is a dehumanizing process, in Sudan as everywhere else.

González and Price both note that this in fact entails that the military imagines itself as being engaged in forms of social engineering, techniques that, as Sanford continues to show in her essay, might equally be deployed against the threat of burgeoning "drug wars" or "homegrown" terrorists and criminal networks. For these reasons, as Ferguson argues in his chapter, it is critical to appreciate not just the direct attempts to recruit anthropologists or "anthropology" to military purposes but also how the defense industry as a whole—the Pentagon, arms manufacturers, government, and police agencies—threaten to distort the programs of academic research across a broad range of the social sciences given the resources and intent to fund basic research over the coming decades. What may be quite resistible to a tenured professor becomes temptingly possible for a freshly minted out-of-work doctorate holder. Moreover, as Ferguson makes clear, such funding is not just for dedicated military programs but will seep into standard and basic forms of academic research. As twentieth-century-style government function is outsourced more and more to private contractors, the space of government as a civilian institution shrinks and the military as government expands. This point is also taken up by Allen, who notes that the assumed binary between civilian and military is becoming increasingly more problematically visible. The soldier mode of thinking and acting integrates with a civilian mode of thinking and acting and vice versa (Der Derian 2001; Maček 2009).

With such developments in mind, we intended this book to contribute to the ongoing ethical debates within the social sciences and anthropology in particular. Here we follow the call from Sanford and Angel-Ajani (2006) and their contributors that anthropologists must explore their positions as engaged observers and self-reflexive scholars. Several of our contributors are members of the Network of Concerned Anthropologists, and this volume also engages the debate on anthropology's colonial legacies.[6] As some of the authors show, in a time of global war it is more urgent than ever to assess past legacies. In revisiting the debate, we do not provide any final answers. Still, to quote Ferguson's contribution, "the military invasion of anthropology must be recognized in its scope and ambition." Every day anthropologists are approached by military or quasi-military organizations that seek their advice. Paired with past fieldwork engagements in politically volatile environments, personal experiences as coveted "cultural experts" have encouraged some of us to reflect continuously on what can be regarded as legitimate, ethical scholarship. Certainly this is a current concern of the American Anthropological Association, although the 2009 official Code of Ethics essentially sidesteps key questions as to the purpose of information gathering and whether this actually is the same thing as "scholarly knowledge," issues that are glossed over in the professional code of ethics and are at the core of the notion of "human terrain."[7] The kind of historical, socially and culturally decontextualized statistical and survey information needed for cybernetic battle systems, which anthropologists once gathered in such forms as the Human Relations Area Files in the hope of revealing etic "structures" or "processes," can now be seen as not only intellectually flawed but also culturally lethal.

We therefore propose that first and foremost, anthropologists need to repeatedly ask themselves what they are doing and why they are doing it. Anthropologists must remain engaged and self-reflexive observers who are aware of their own cultural regimes and how those regimes are expressive of differential power relations, both individually and within the wider global order. Thus, anthropology as such always needs to be theoretically and thus ideologically open-minded to the cultural nature of its own practice and ready to consider its negative as well as positive promise for those who are its subjects.

In contrast, we can see that human terrain mapping essentially works as a closed and highly ethnocentric system. Also, in looking for facts that seem to fit the theory, such mapping tends to be conspirational, even magical (see West and Sanders 2003:25). Contemporary anthropology is not innocent here, as González elaborates on in his chapter. In contrast to such reductive trends, old-timers such as E. E. Evans-Pritchard (1976) promoted a theoretical and methodological openness, sketched in a brief "reminiscences and reflections on fieldwork," an appendix to the abridged paperback edition of the famous book on Azande witchcraft. On the other hand, as his equally famous book about the Nuer attests to, he was also working as a representative of the colonial regime in Sudan. Even if Nuer poems of resistance and other subversive details found their way to the printed text, his "description of the modes of livelihood and political institutions of a Nilotic people" very much remains a report commissioned by the colonial authorities and directed to their purposes (Evans-Pritchard 1940).

Our point is that there is no black and white here; today's almost habitual dismissal of the Malinowskian legacy risks missing the fact that anthropology in those days was not simply a colonialist enterprise working under faulty epistemological premises. This scholarship sometimes paved the way for an engaged, reflexive, and global anthropology. For us, then, the potential of ethnography to overcome its torturous and colonialist legacies comes from recognizing that anthropologists must ask not just what they want to know but why they want to know it. As Whitehead discusses more fully in his contribution, with such a question in mind, the nature of fieldwork and the purposes of ethnography can resist the human terrain system or even the models of those missionaries, journalists, and aid workers who remain uncritical of their own cultural regimes. Moreover, as Whitehead points out, legitimate ethnography builds subjectivities that may, by being entailed in the field situation, be more and more useless to the project of colonial knowing. As we show in this book, the instrumentalist mapping of the human terrain by its very design is blind to these critical dimensions. It even represents a step backward from the well-known blindness of colonial and imperialist epistemologies because it lacks the methodological openness that encourages critical reflections that can actually be found with Evans-Pritchard and others of his time.

As the space of government as a civilian institution shrinks, the military as government expands, and the academic world is infiltrated by the military, such developments are in turn paralleled by processes of militarization of the cultural imagination, as outlined by Allen and Sumera in their respective chapters. We also see the militarization of cultural relationships as in the HTS program, a theme discussed by both Ferguson and González. Sluka and Robben, on the other hand, delineate from two different angles some radical changes in the mediation of combat experience. In short, the way of war seems set globally to define the emerging forms of human social experience in the twenty-first century.

This volume brings together a set of analyses of aspects of this burgeoning immaterial space of killing and death with the purpose of demonstrating not just how the political and subjective path to war is deployed and sustained by governments, corporations, and their enemies, since there is already an extensive literature from numerous academic disciplines on how ideology, belief, custom, and culture feed into the practice of war and violence. Rather, we aim to illustrate how war, no less than other forms of violence (Whitehead 2007), may be an integral and sustaining (rather than destroying) part of sociocultural reproduction as it is being practiced by national governments and international corporations. We have encouraged each contributor to follow his or her own track, still having in mind, explicitly or implicitly, a wider global context from which we want to locate today's technologies and imaginaries for terror and killing. As Price and González discuss, this understanding of today's global complexities is far from the dated 1950s anthropological notions of culture as personality writ large that are propagated in U.S. special forces manuals, which simply reproduced the idea of the primitive other as possessing a culture of the irrational and as being an essentially violent enemy. Yet as Ferguson notes in his contribution, however obsolete it may be from a perspective of contemporary anthropological debates, such an essentialization of cultural life is the only way out when the military experts generate models of cultures and cultural behavior from their "security" horizon. Writing on witchcraft violence among the Sukuma in Tanzania, Stroeken argues that such a cultural expression is not really anything that is essentially Sukuma, but a kind of violence that Tanzanians—dependent on the vagaries of the global economy and from their existential horizons—are most likely to resort to. These are people at the global peripheries whose lived experience fully demonstrates to them that external forces are occult and violent in their actions, as Finnström shows in his analysis of the magical discourse that seems to penetrate anything that has to do with the violence of the Lord's Resistance Army/ Movement (LRA). Moreover, as Sluka goes on to point out, for populations marginalized with regard to emerging global realities, the periphery is characteristically a field of exaggerated violence, with war as the means of control. Such emplacements of global war constitute the "tribal zone," as described by Ferguson and Whitehead (1992b:27), and it may easily "saturate the fabric of social life," even "consume a population, leading to major demographic losses."

Here it becomes acute not to see war as a thing in itself or as the outcome of any clash of civilizations, but rather, to allude to Sanford's contribution on Guatemala, as a social project among many other social projects (see also Richards 2005). Even more, and having in mind the virtual realities explored in several of the essays, it seems that war is increasingly becoming a never-ending social routine among other open-ended social routines. In his contribution, Stroeken talks about the magic of advertising by which the U.S. government seeks to keep its many war efforts going, which also was the subject of a satirical Hollywood movie, *War, Inc.*, directed by Joshua Seftel and starring John Cusack (2008). These tactics include scapegoating, wishful thinking, creating a demand for one's military supply, and promising big gains, as Stroeken notes, but they also tend to lump conflicts and opponents across the world into one war and one enemy. To reiterate, global war is a cycle of violence without any sure way of ending.

In expanding this argument, one might directly reference the idea of a "military-industrial complex," formulated by U.S. president Dwight D. Eisenhower as well as, from the other end of the political spectrum, the Trotskyist theory of a "permanent arms economy," which was forwarded to explain the sustained economic growth that occurred in the decades following World War II and which continues to allow late capitalism to reproduce itself despite the inherently contradictory nature of the capitalist growth cycle (see Hoffman 2011). In this way, Western liberal democracy can be seen to be dependent on its violent practices in "foreign" wars, yet its violence is nonetheless justified by presenting itself as a mere response to a violence that is generally located with the non-Western, nonmodern, irrational, and superstitious other, as we illustrate with this volume. Moreover, the iconic moment of "combat" in this culture of permanent global war is just a small part of the overall conflict and exercise of violence. This book therefore calls attention to the virtual war that itself drives the forms and occasions of combat and is no longer a mere reflection of those supposedly supervening realities. When Jean Baudrillard (1995) asked if the 1991 Gulf War really took place, the question was misunderstood as signaling an implosion of postmodernity as it finally lost any grip on meaningful realities "out there." In fact, as wars in the Gulf have raged on and spread to other places such as Afghanistan and Pakistan, the cultural production of combat has become as much through the home gaming consoles where future soldiers while away their teen years, as it has from the frontline reporting of embedded journalists, whose experiences seem to be filtered to almost conform to the expectations of the video gamers. After all, as Allen shows, quoting the candid admission of a civilian developer of the video game *America's Army*, "We like to play at being in the army." Moreover, as Sumera illustrates in the self-fashioning of soldiers through the medium of their YouTube videos, we also like to play at being in the army, even when we are in the army. Such play is exactly a component of the practice of virtual war just as prior regimes of "basic training" also shaped subjective embodiment of new recruits, as did militaristic children's games, or conventional printed literature and art illustration in comics.

Although the Pentagon might claim otherwise, this represents not an evolutionary advance in the practice of war but important changes in the relation between the military and society whereby war is increasingly seen as the normal routine. The new military has a social vision and mission, evident in these ongoing "asymmetric wars" where the lines between war and peace, collateral damage, civilian casualty, and "killed in combat" shape-shift groups of armed men ("armies") into agents of genocide or humanitarians with guns. Essential to such shape-shifting tendencies is the magic of numbers, and more, propaganda and the concealing of numbers, as Sluka's discussion on the Afghan and Pakistani "body counts" show. The child soldier who manages to escape from the LRA will be labeled a rescued child, whereas the one who is killed by the Ugandan army's helicopter gunships will be listed as yet another killed rebel, an enemy taken out.

Many enlisted soldiers, no less than patriotic civilians, dream of "real war" or "real peace," meanwhile filling the years of waiting with endless rehearsal of those possibilities in the "virtual" but certain space of "militainment," a conjunction of entertainment and military media. So if the modern gaze is the unbiased registering of the world as it is, then Sumera's chapter shows how the editing practices and technological mediation of music videos create representations of wartime realities that are anything but modern. Rather, this is sorcery at work.

Although the prominence of technology in the construction of this new military order might suggest that it will be the United States or European Union that would then hold the military edge in technical innovation, in fact perhaps this has made asymmetrical warfare more symmetrical. In the virtual battle space, Al-Qaeda can be as powerful and influential as the

Pentagon, while readily available, cheap software proves sufficient to hack the cameras of drones. Sophisticated protocols for accessing email accounts, appreciation of the tactics of using satellite-locatable cell phones, as well as the production of video and news bites, also indicate that this is a situation quite unlike the political and cultural frameworks that surrounded the control of nuclear technologies. WikiLeaks reconnected the ever-growing virtual archives with the political realities, a process of demagicalization that again exposes the self-proclaimed myth of the modern world as particularly transparent and democratic (see, e.g., West and Sanders 2003:7). Nonetheless, as Sanford's contribution on Guatemala reminds us, conventional nondigital media may be quite sufficient for the creation of a magico-virtual battle space. In her discussion of government and popular media representations of high homicide rates of young men in Guatemala as being gang-related, we are necessarily reminded of the "drug wars" currently raging along the Mexico–United States border. Whatever the "human terrain" might actually contain in terms of actors, intentions, motivations, subjectivities, and memories, to operationalize other aspects of established policies on "drugs" such a space must be produced as one of chaos and war, for which, as Sanford notes, the disciplined techno-imaginary of governmental forms of combat and killing will be the cure. Her ethnographic research findings indicate that the structural causes of violence, which implicate both governments and gangs, should also be historically linked to past and present policies that have long imagined violent social cleansing as the answer to delinquency and criminality. Yet the dehistoricizing tendency in the analysis of global war, which essentially is a depoliticizing tendency, points to the very magic of the dominant discourses. The collusion of the U.S. military and police agencies in the suppression of Mexico's current drug war, which has claimed more Mexican lives than U.S. combat deaths in Iraq and Afghanistan combined, thus seems to portend yet another route through which military forms of social engineering may become more prominent in the agendas of Western liberal democracies, no less than that of "failed states."

Such considerations are drawn out in Finnström's contribution on the LRA in east-central Africa and the role of media representations in the culturally entangled production of insurgency, counterinsurgency, and outside intervention. Whatever the local realities of extended fighting between the insurgents and the Ugandan army, peoples' lives (as Stroeken also shows for Tanzania) have become deeply entangled with larger regional and even global warscapes. It was thus not surprising that the long-standing U.S. logistical support to the Ugandan army in 2011 was supplemented with drone aircrafts as well as widely announced U.S. soldiers on the ground. It is a Faustian bargain. The critical point is not the form of mediation but the fact of it. Such mediation in the cultural imaginary of Uganda or the international system of human rights, military intervention, and aid thus emphasizes the rebels as a primitive and fanatical party to the conflict, a threat to modernity itself, as is so often the way that an atavistic Africa is imagined in the West. This is the vision of a bipolar world as magically mediated by the camera lenses of remote-controlled drones.

Certainly insurgent atrocities in Africa and elsewhere can be linked to witchcraft paradigms and the legacies of sacrificial logics. At the same time, for those victims and spectators to global war, it is also the case that international humanitarian and military intervention itself appears as part of the global sorcery of Western domination, humanitarianism, and exploitation, truly the nightmare of fetishized, vampiric capital that roams the land cannibalizing community and sucking the life-blood from human souls, something Chris Dolan (2009) has described in great detail as a process of extended "social torture." As a result, magical terror is produced not by any localized and historically bounded culture, but in the local emplacement of the global forces of a universally shared contemporary world. At the same time many insurgents, just like Al-Qaeda groups that are hiding in inaccessible caves of Afghanistan, have chosen to become exactly "the primitives" they have been labeled as. It has become standard "insurgent" or "terrorist" practice to carefully avoid detection by keeping satellite phones and electronic navigation devices switched off, instead using secret runners who bring communications between decentralized, fragmented, and highly mobile insurgent pockets operating over ever-widening geographical stretches.

Anthropology has also been a key player in the magical labeling of cultural otherness, which brings us back to the issues of the growing human terrain mapping and how to counter such mappings with legitimate forms of ethnography. In the context of deterritorialized, often immaterial cultural worlds, Whitehead argues that the standard anthropological approach of participant observation itself must be reexamined, as it is occurring more broadly with regard to the myriad forms of online worlds (see also Boellstorff 2008; Whitehead and Wesch 2012). Moreover, Whitehead argues that the epistemological basis of the creed of participant observation is flawed when it reproduces Western traditions of knowledge as necessarily based in agonistic process. The relevance of ethnography to military practice, as in the human terrain programs, stems not just from how the military imagines ethnographic information might be deployed but also from the logic of domination inherent in the ethnographic project itself—a logic it shares with the Western notion of interrogation and torture. Thus, the manner of our participation (rather than the limits and qualities of our observations) now need to be thought through more carefully. In both online contexts and socially occluded offline worlds, observation of any kind is by definition utterly dependent on the forms of participation that the ethnographer may choose or have available. Undoubtedly this has constrained prior ethnography in various ways as well, but what has changed, then, is the need for the ethnographer to explicitly theorize participation no less adequately than we have learned must be accomplished in the case of observation and representation. Robben, in this volume and in an earlier work (Robben 2010b), shows how the use of ethnographic imagination as a research tool to analyze the Iraq War through insightful comparisons with previous and current armed conflicts can provide a way out of the impasse of being theoretically reliant only on direct observation.

Robben's analysis is fundamentally different from that of the anthropologists working *within* the human terrain systems. Made manifest here are parallel anthropological worlds, and in hiring anthropologists on a scale comparative to that of the colonial days, perhaps the United States and other Western armies simply tap into an anthropological legacy that very much remains central to the discipline, despite much debate over the years. After all—and again having in mind pioneer anthropologists such as Evans-Pritchard (1940) and his work among the Sudanese Nuer under British military occupation—is not the work of militarily embedded anthropologists today an inevitable consequence of the whole idea of participant observation as it developed in the colonial context, and thus the rule rather than the exception? In his essay, González quotes Joseph Gallieni, a French army commander and colonial administrator, who clearly saw ethnographic intelligence as a tool of divide and rule. "An officer who succeeds in drawing a sufficiently exact ethnographic map of the territory he commands has almost reached its complete pacification," Gallieni argued.

"If there are customs and habits to respect, there are also rivalries which we have to untangle and utilize to our profit, by opposing the ones to the others, and by basing ourselves on the ones in order to defeat the others." Under these conditions, González notes, social science can easily become a martial art—a tool or a technique to be sold to the highest bidder. It is not just the issue of whether the results of ethnography might be ethically shared with all kinds of dubious agencies, military and nonmilitary. Again, we want to draw attention to the deeper question as to what extent the apparent facility of such information sharing represents a hidden history of the epistemology of ethnography itself, making it uncomfortably similar to the agonistic processes of torture, which then appears as a shortcut rather than a negation of ethnographic inquiry.

We have already indicated that this volume seeks to extend the critique of the human terrain mapping systems, both methodologically and conceptually, by simultaneously considering much more familiar and heavily researched categories in ethnography—witchcraft, magic, and sorcery. Several contributors show that the virtual world of witchcraft, sorcery, and magic is exactly that space of combat and killing that we now experience through discursive and technological (rather than only ritual and performative) modes. More specifically, Sluka takes up this thread of discussion in effective ways through comparison of the drone launches in Afghanistan and the ongoing practice of war magic as constituting for their practitioners equivalent cultural worlds of "death at a distance." U.S. Air Force drone operators experiencing battle fatigue and post-traumatic stress disorder as a result of killing in virtual spaces thus makes "real" for Westerners the same experience of silent, unseen, and unanticipated killing that is encoded in the discourse of magic among non-Westerners as described by the classic anthropological literature.

So, too, the Western shape-shifters roam both geographic and cybernetic battlefields just as the magic arrows of Amazonian shamans—appearing as jaguars, now anteaters, then were-baboons—create a chaotic and threatening space in which death may erupt unannounced and in unpredictable forms. Or to quote a Mozambican soldier, describing for Nordstrom the state of affairs in the Mozambique war: "Shape-shifters; people who walk among us we can't see—people say only we Africans practice such things. But don't believe it, there are plenty of shape-shifters in your country, throughout the world. The Europeans say this is witchcraft, but what nonsense. It is power, pure and simple." From the soldier's horizon, shape-shifting is about power, and the really powerful shape-shifters are from the West. He continues, "Now tell me these people aren't shape-shifters: these guys travel around from all over the world, working the night. And they say only Africans believe in this ability to turn invisible" (Nordstrom 2004a:25).

It seems that the virtual space of killing and war in cyberspace, television, and print media is akin to the magical realm. The similarity is in its subjective power, political presence, and the cultural frame created for meaning in killing. Witchcraft studies no longer have reason to differentiate themselves from these virtual realities. Mutilation murders in southern and eastern Africa appear to be colored by similar processes of national and international media production. Taking cultural labels such as "Africa" out of the occult might finally shed light on the occult itself, as Stroeken shows in his contribution. In this book, magic goes global, and this leads us to a consideration of virtual war and magical death as intertwined topics presenting new fields for ethnographic research and representation.

In many other areas of the globe, such as South America, sorcery engages and is a means of mediating the modern, not retreating from it (Whitehead and Wright 2004). As Sluka suggests here, the imaginaries, if not technologies, of terror and killing are lethally similar in the space of unseen death, be that by the drone aircrafts or the shape-shifting kanaimà sorcerers in Guyana (Whitehead 2002). But the connection of the techno-modern and magico-primitive is also the way the very occult nature of such acts allows them to speak loudly in wider cultural discourses, and how the global order itself, as viewed from the local context, is a transparency that hides forms of magical conspiracy. It seems like the liberal idea of transparency paradoxically encourages counterinsurgency violence by almost magically rendering such violence more invisible.

This is a theme that Sanford elaborates on in her contribution, which focuses on gang violence in relation to state structures. With the glasnost (openness) of the post–cold war era, power wished to be seen as more transparent than ever. Yet for those subject to the operation of a global system of economy, polity, and law, this situation often appears opaque, arbitrary, and unpredictable. Sometimes, it seems, you need a personal coach or a manager, basically a shaman of your own, to successfully navigate the bureaucracy and institutions of the contemporary modern state. Popular suspicion of power thus correctly and creatively deploys forms of shamanism, sorcery, conspiracy theory, and urban legend to illuminate and make sense of the occult operation of global power itself, a process compounded by the vastly uneven access to information and means of more direct political control.

For these reasons also the "shadow warriors" of popular TV series, the adulation ninjas, and a "zen" for war, as well as Hollywood representations of "men who stare at goats," are all mimetic military fantasies of the magical and unseen. But at the same time it is most real. So when Dana Priest and William M. Arkin wrote a revealing piece titled "Top Secret America," they quoted not Darth Vader but an officer of the U.S. military's Joint Special Operations Command: "We're the dark matter. We're the force that orders the universe but can't be seen" (*Washington Post*, September 2, 2011).

Alongside the techno-imaginary of the military, there is also a magico-imaginary. From psychological operations of the Vietnam era to the torture rooms of Abu Ghraib, the promise of, as Malinowski called it, "primitive man's most secret longing and wisdom"—the invocation of the tribal and magical—is a force multiplier in certain scenarios of combat and terror. The idea of ethnic soldiering (Ferguson and Whitehead 2000) is a historically well-established example of this melding of the techno-modern and warrior avatar, and it remains potent in the space of militainment production as Conan the Barbarian blends into a Rambo-style "Terminator," incidentally also a literal translation for the term kanaimà, the Amazonian sorcerer alluded to above.

The space of magical and military killing not only consumes the offline combatants and bystanders to material violence, it also replicates the subjectivities of war and violence through media and online computing technologies such that civilians can globally participate in the agon ($\dot{\alpha}\gamma\dot{\omega}\nu$) of war. Again, the very categories of soldier and civilian modes of life blur, and as Allen and Finnström suggest, this blurring produces "virtual soldiers." The bystanding witness is a participant, as several of our contributors show. In turn, the "collateral damage" of offline material war and violence is fed by the magical and virtual online cultural imaginary. This has provoked massive atrocities by groups like the LRA or the Janjaweed militias in east and central Africa, as well as more village-based episodes of inquisitions, scapegoat searches, and witch killings elsewhere. At the same time this perpetual cycle of the imagination of "terror" and the enactment of state-sponsored counterinsurgency campaigns as measures of "security" then enables the counteratrocities of Abu Ghraib, Guantánamo, or drone-delivered death in Afghanistan. Sooner or later, as is evident from many parts of the world, all this implodes into a self-sustaining business. Again global war, as we have claimed, becomes a cycle of violence without any certain ending.

The essays brought together here not only include discussions of such topics as virtual battlefields, social media as a context for both armies and insurgents, witchcraft tribunals, military technological ambition, and recruiting of social scientists, but also seek to draw attention to the overarching phenomenon of *spectacide*, wherein attacks are waged not only or even primarily to finish off the enemy but more as performative acts in front of the TV cameras, to be able to take and keep the propaganda initiative, which is a kind of magical logic.[8] Forms of virtual-visual killing, such as missile cameras and war games for training (which is a kind of spectacular killing as info- or militainment) follow a similar magical logic when it combines with the ahistorical production of news images for media outlets. At the same time, it is important to distinguish analytically the forms of such spectacide from the forms of the "immediation" of combat as discussed by Robben. Here the sensory world of the soldier, material, actual, and geographical in all the standard ways, is nonetheless an experience of the virtual. In a sustained comparison with the U.S. military experience in Vietnam, Robben shows how the current use of night vision goggles and cameras allows the military, as they are fond of saying, to "own the night."

Such a technological claim to ownership may be seen as the ultimate expression of modern warfare, but it is not without implications. The night is and will remain culturally ambivalent. Ideally it is the time for rest and peace, as the Ugandan anthropologist Okot p'Bitek (1971:155) once wrote. At night even nature is supposed to be at rest; still, the night is when human beings can be caught off-guard, and it is also the time when witches and other antisocial beings usually come to work. So those "working the night" who also claim control over the night may themselves be the actual witches. In East Africa, such witches would simply be called "night dancers." Even in conventional military thinking, the claim to own the night alone would be a massive change in the practice of warfare. As Robben puts it, "dehumanization by the mediated hostile gaze is preceded by the depersonalization of people in war zones," so that another layer of sensory mediation overlays the culturally mediated category of "enemy." The examples given by Robben show that this quickly leads to tragic and violent absurdities as the fleeting green images seen by goggled troops easily mistake water bottles for artillery shells and walking sticks for rifles. To the extent we fail to question not just the morality but even the practicality of "military solutions," that is, to distinguish the forms of immediation from their usages, we risk being caught up in a technophilia that seems to proffer the possibility of social engineering and surgical precision in killing, which has therefore become the military's political response to alternatives to military action in the first place. Again we see global war as a cycle of violence without any certain ending. Beguiled by the possibility of actually and accurately identifying and killing the "bad guys," we have forgotten that we must also examine, historicize, and deal in other ways with what made them the "bad guys" in the first place. That somebody's terrorist may be someone else's freedom fighter, even if an overused propaganda phrase, is of some relevance here.

On one hand, the technology of mimetic simulation inures soldiers to increasingly devastating forms of violence; on the other hand, the steady diet of video feeds from global battlefields hypnotizes a T V and computer-gazing public. The production of war as spectacle with images from Baghdad or Israel, or the production of terror through the virtual-visual, with players such as the L R A, Al-Qaeda, or albino killers in East Africa, rely on such spectacidal processes. There exists an urgent need to situate those technologies and imaginaries within the unfolding efforts of government to deliver cyberwar and cyberterror. But a note of hope may yet emerge, as for example Robben and Allen note in their respective chapters, when the use of virtual media has helped many deal with the traumas and memories of combat experiences, just as the realm of militainment and the gamers who create it offer examples of how such virtual reality may well be enough reality, and so obviate the need for the paradigm of war at all.

In the chapters that follow, we encourage the reader to contemplate the possibility, as we do, that the seemingly endless cycle of violence that we call global war is a fundamental aspect of liberal Western democracy itself, and as such it is an inbuilt tool in the development of the world, rather than something we can bracket off and conveniently dislocate to development processes of the West's cultural other and to faraway geographical distances. In this sense, the material here is most directly responding to recent developments, especially after the events of 9/11. However, this is not meant to limit our analysis in a topical and regional way because the arguments developed here will (unfortunately) continue to be relevant not only to the United States and its European allies but to the emergence of other militaries, such as in China, Brazil, and India, and also, as contributions to this volume indicate, in Latin America, Afghanistan, and Pakistan, as well as on the African continent. In historical terms as well, the notion of virtual war might be usefully brought to considerations of ritual and the magical in past warfare, for what is at stake here is the need for anthropology (and the social sciences more generally) to engage violence in a more sophisticated way that permits analysis and interpretation to avoid the fallacy of assigning material violence an instrumentality that is sufficient explanation for social science purposes and so relegating cultural meaning and its dynamics to a secondary effect. Immaterial though the virtual and magical appear, they obviously have tragic and continuing material consequences, as we show in this volume.

This is the historical legacy behind today's wars for democracy or on terror, and anthropology, both past and present, can provide a critical lens on all this. As the irony of history had it, the colonized subjects, rather than the oppressive colonialists, have been labeled as warlike. Michael Taussig's (1987:495) classic description of the construction of colonial culture describes this aspect of today's global war fought in the name of democracy—it is a "colonial mirror" that reflects back onto the conquerors the barbarity of their own social relations, but as imputed to the savage or evil figures they wish to dominate or even destroy. As in the realms of sorcery, the art of war, as famously summated by Sun-Tzu (2007:1,18, p. 7) 2,500 years ago, is a deception of others, but also of ourselves.

NOTES

1. According to the *Economist* (September 12, 2011), the U.S. Department of Defense is the world's largest employer, followed by the Chinese People's Liberation Army.
2. Evans-Pritchard (1937) famously saw witchcraft as different from magic and sorcery: witchcraft is said to be an inborn ability to harm and kill, whereas magic or sorcery is learned. Moreover, witchcraft can be unintentional, while magic, being deliberate, cannot. Finally, in contrast to magic, witchcraft does not involve the manipulation of substances. This model is perhaps more etic than emic, and even if its neatness has a certain pedagogic value, that very neatness can be questioned. In this volume, we do not really draw any firm line between witchcraft and magic but want to indicate their everyday entanglement. By the more specific phrase "assault sorcery" we mean forms of ritual mutilation and killing that are manifested materially in physical injury and death.

3. As noted by Radley Balko in his editorial "A Decade after 9/11, Police Departments Are Increasingly Militarized" in the *Huffington Post* (September 12, 2011): "Then-Secretary of Defense Dick Cheney declared in 1989, 'The detection and countering of the production, trafficking and use of illegal drugs is a high priority national security mission of the Department of Defense.'" This trend to militarize police operation has continued unabated since then. Balko also quotes Joseph McNamara, who served as a police chief in San Jose, California, and Kansas City, Missouri: "Simply put, the police culture in our country has changed. . . . An emphasis on 'officer safety' and paramilitary training pervades today's policing, in contrast to the older culture, which held that cops didn't shoot until they were about to be shot or stabbed."

4. *Hypertext* refers specifically to the electronic text found on computational devices that is connected directly inside the technological interface to other forms of hypertext, thus forming the most basic structure for the World Wide Web.

5. We also distinguish virtual war in the sense in which we have outlined it from "cyberwar," which is a narrower concept to describe disruption to computer and Internet systems using such means as hacking, viruses, and spam attacks.

6. For the Network of Concerned Anthropologists, see https://sites.google.com/site /concernedanthropologists.

7. For the 2009 Code of Ethics, see http://www.aaanet.org/_cs_upload/issues /policy-advocacy/27668_1.pdf.

8. *Spectacide* is a term to denote the production of war for its spectators not just (or even) for its instrumental political, military, and economic advantages (see also Virilio 2002). In a similar vein, Der Derian (2001) argues that America has created a mighty military, industrial, media, entertainment network (with the evocative acronym MIME-NET) that has replaced discernment with entertainment.

ETHNOGRAPHY, KNOWLEDGE, TORTURE, AND SILENCE

The "Ethnographer's Magic" was the phrase used as a title by George Stocking (1992) for a collection of essays that principally examined the work and influence of Franz Boas and Bronislaw Malinowski and anthropology's powerfully mythic qualities and persistent romanticism, established precisely through the "incorporative ritual" and often obscure occult procedures of "fieldwork" (1992:13). The "magic" of the ethnographer then, as Stocking shows (1992:12–59), refers both to the way the experience of fieldwork cannot be readily taught as a methodology and to the way penetrating the culturally mysterious and occult is the guiding ambition of ethnographic activity. This founding myth of anthropology has certainly become part of the popular cultural understanding of what fieldworkers do, and this volume has a number of essays precisely examining how the military seeks to operationalize that "magic" and use it to better understand the human terrain and cultural landscapes of those it would kill.

This chapter questions the basis of that "ethnographic magic," unveiling the occult mysteries of "fieldwork" as rooted in a far deeper and more troubling cultural tradition than that discussed by Stocking. It examines how the epistemological basis of ethnographic fieldwork is starkly revealed through its recruitment to recent military programs. In turn, this prompts questions as to how ethnography, as part of social science, is rooted in a Western view of truth and inquiry that is culturally validated through agonistic processes. For this reason, the convergence between ethnography and torture is also explored, which entails a critical examination of the methodology of narration and translation in fieldwork itself, a better acknowledgment of the persistent colonial role played by anthropology through its unsilencing of others, and a reevaluation of the resulting ethical imperatives of the ethnographer's own subject position.

The "weaponization" of culture discussed in this volume and the ways ethnographers engage with both sorcery and the burgeoning space of "virtual war" necessarily provoke new questions as to the place of observation and participation in ethnographic practice. Equally, a pressing need is to examine aspects of this relationship as part of the historical emergence of anthropology as a distinct academic discipline and to set that process within the broader context of post-Enlightenment ideas of scientific epistemology. In particular, and because this a potentially vast and unwieldy topic, the focus here is on the nature of ethnographic practice.

The suggestion will be that certain ways of conceiving ethnography, specifically that of ethnography as an objective or neutral mode of "data collection," represent an epistemological tradition that needs closer critical examination. Certainly, since its professional inception in the twentieth century, the colonial legacies of anthropology have been periodically discussed before by ethnographers. In such discussions (Asad 1973; Boas 1928; Bremen 1998; Dowie 2009; Fabian 1983; Herskovits 1938; Wolf 1982) varying degrees of unease as to the uses of anthropological knowledge and data have been raised by many other anthropologists. Indeed, the "literary turn" of the 1990s provoked by the analysis of such authors as George Marcus and Michael Fischer (1986) arguably led to a thorough reexamination of the purposes and forms of ethnographic writing. So why return to this topic now if it has already been repeatedly rehearsed within anthropology? First because the anthropological practice is engaged not just in the production of scholarly monographs but also in the production of more circumscribed and policy-driven forms of cultural knowledge in the form of "applied anthropology." However, as Melville Herskovits wrote of applied anthropology in 1938: "The uncritical tendency to see native cultures everywhere forced out of existence by the overwhelming drive of European techniques; the feeling that these 'simpler' folk must inevitably accept the sanctions of their more efficient rulers as they do some of the outward modes of Life of those under whose control they live; all these reflect a type of ethnocentrism that should be absent from the scientific studies of an anthropologist" (1938:32).

Second, this issue needs revisiting because Herskovits's critique of applied anthropology remains very relevant, given the continuing expansion of such forms of ethnographic practice stimulated in large part by governmental and nongovernmental organization (NGO) enthusiasm for "empowering the local" as an appropriately liberal and humane development strategy. Our ethnocentric values are still reflected in the continuing policies and practices not only of well-intentioned development agencies but also in military counterinsurgency programs that overtly seek to "weaponize culture" (González 2007).

In short, layered over the perennial issues of the ethical basis of ethnographic research as part of a still persistent colonial epistemology are the highly topical issues of the ethics of deploying anthropological methods in support of military programs of "civil reconstruction," as in Iraq and Afghanistan, as well as similar nonmilitary programs connected to health and human rights concerns globally. In light of recent work by, for example, Roberto González (2009) and David Price (2008a)—who very thoroughly document a wide range of involvement by anthropologists in military and counterintelligence programs throughout the twentieth century up to the present day—these issues and concerns need constant reevaluation.

However, rather than question the ethics of those who do or do not cooperate with such programs, the purpose of this chapter is to ask how and why certain forms of knowledge are inherently connected to the exercise of power and to suggest how ethnography is no exception to that. Without appreciating, and constantly revisiting, how ethnographic inquiry can also function as a form of domination over others, we risk an unwitting cooptation into research programs that may have little benefit for their subjects. For this reason, the subject position of the ethnographer, no less than the stated purposes of research and data collection, are central to rethinking anthropology's colonial legacies and developing ethical practices that are relevant to current events.

In the field of applied anthropology, many practitioners are seeking to come to terms with the potentially neocolonial nature of economic aid, social development, human rights, or medical intervention, even in the absence of an overt military component to such "foreign aid." All of these programs are usually perceived as having those "benefits" that go along with liberal capitalist economics and political culture, such as personal freedom, economic autonomy, and gender rights. Nonetheless, powerful aid agencies, such as the United Nations, clearly view some forms of cultural tradition as harmful and in need of eradication (Winter, Thompson, and Jeffreys 2002). The presence of "traditional harmful practices" as they are called within the United Nations bureaucracy, thus illustrates the continuing urge, as noted by Herskovits (quoted above) to use the opportunity of close ethnographic understanding to promote values and behaviors more in accord with our notions of humane and civilized values. For example, the Associated Press reported on August 1, 2009, that an ancient Muslim ritual, practiced in New Delhi, of dropping babies from a mosque roof into a bed sheet to ensure health and prosperity, was the target of "outrage" on the part of child rights activists. Perhaps that is understandable in the light of our own values as to "childhood," but at the same time, as Karen Valentin and Lotte Meinert (2009) argue: "The civilization of the children of the 'savages' in the colonial world was seen as a crucial issue from early on and was an inherent part of the colonization project in Africa, America and Oceania in the 19th century. The idea of civilizing 'the savages,' today's South, through children has continued in the post-colonial era with the development of mass-schooling systems and various child-focused development projects."[1] As a result, anthropology always risks being unthinkingly coopted into such processes, and recent works call for the need to again reevaluate the complex relationship between cultural knowledge and cultural domination (Bricmont 2006; Cowan, Dembour, and Wilson 2001; Sanford and Angel-Anjana 2006). In such contexts ethnography is central to the cultural and political interface with other cultures and a key reason that the results of anthropological fieldwork are often very welcome to other disciplines, as well as nonacademic agencies, all too aware of their lack of cross-cultural perspective. Although lawyers, politicians, and economists may not spend much time reading ethnography, the influence of anthropology is forcefully, if diffusely, present through the way in which its ideas and representations feed into broader cultural attitudes toward non-Western peoples or those who are internally marginal to Western civil society.[2]

By providing intimate knowledge of other cultures, anthropology makes plausible the possibility that the members of those cultures can be influenced, reformed, developed, or converted into appropriately obedient neoliberal subjects. Although, as with racism, "culturalism" (an insistence on the ontological and experiential autonomy of differing cultural worlds) avoids reifying cultural difference, this paradoxically makes it more difficult to perceive those cultures as historically and dynamically changing systems. Instead, a "culture" appears as an aggregation of universalized human subjects ready to interact with other such individuals through the medium of a particular and individualized, rather than a collective and intertwined, cultural heritage. Embracing Western liberal modernity then becomes a mere matter of free choice. So cross-disciplinary or extra-academic collaborations may entail untheorized risks and drawbacks just as ethical dilemmas quickly emerge from fieldwork. This is particularly true as performed under the current political conditions of war in Iraq and Afghanistan, but in many ways no less so than with other forms of "engaged" anthropological work, such as with NGOs, study abroad programs, or international aid agencies.[3]

An urgent and important context in which these issues currently come together for anthropologists are the continuing efforts by military and security agencies to recruit anthropologists to assist as "cultural specialists" in the war on terror and even combat field operations in Iraq and Afghanistan.[4] Although there was a change in administration in 2009, there has not been the hoped-for end to these wars. In any case, the fundamental ethical and epistemological issues provoked by deploying ethnography as a military strategy are, as I hope to make clear, perennial and inevitable; they will remain so unless we more adequately theorize the historical and disciplinary legacies within which anthropology arose and from which it has yet to detach itself.

ETHNOGRAPHY, TORTURE, AND EPISTEMOLOGIES OF CONQUEST

Among the many questions provoked by the way ethnography's potential for "weaponization" is revealed in security and military overtures to the discipline is the need for a critical examination of the practice of ethnography by anthropologists in other contexts of collaboration with government agencies. The refusal of marginal populations to become legible to the state or its institutions of government is globally evident in the ways such agencies may be resisted at a local level. This resistance is made apparent through the way in which popular support is often given to those branded as criminal, rebel, or insurgent (Hobsbawm 2000); through the global phenomenon of the physical retreat and avoidance of government by indigenous peoples (Bodley 2008); or even through the mundane practices of daily life (Nash 1993; Scott 1985). Social conformity is calculated, not unthinking, and beneath the surface of symbolic and ritual compliance there is often an undercurrent of resistance or effacement of actual intentions. In such circumstances, deploying ethnographic information for purposes of colonial occupation or the enforcement of state power need not be a self-conscious or politically overt aspect of state agency because ways of knowing, as much as the knowledge they produce, are culturally shared among the agents of state power. The professionalization of anthropology in the early twentieth century therefore detached ethnographic information gathering from this kind of governmental project and reinvented it as a systematic and scientific technique. The unsystematized knowledge and interpretation of the agents of the government apparatus was downgraded by a newly scientific anthropology to the status of travelogue or memoir or as simply lacking credible insight.[5]

Certainly these were valid criticisms, but the genealogy of ethnographic knowledge is relevant for consideration here, as well as the way the newly "scientific" voice of ethnography might be reattached, recruited, to the purposes of government, as in the case of the Human Terrain System (HTS) program (see also Ferguson, González, Price, in this volume) or other of the current projects for using social science knowledge, such as the Minerva Initiative (Glenn 2008). Whether or not anthropology has critically engaged this legacy to a sufficient degree is therefore tested in considering the difficult and perhaps unwelcome questions as to why we pursue the knowledge goals we do, the nature of the methods we use to fulfill those goals, and whether those goals are the appropriate ones for a postcolonial anthropology that is not to become unwittingly entailed in the projection and inscription of state power (Gordon 2007; Smith 1999).[6] An unwitting or undesired cooptation of existing ethnographic research data into military planning or as a backdrop to interrogation is therefore an alarming prospect for most anthropologists, but is also a reflection of the epistemological character of ethnography itself.[7]

Certainly the prevalent professional assumption would be that the progressive, advocacy, or human justice goals of most ethnographic representation would insulate and inoculate ethnography against being used in this way. Of course not all ethnography is informed by the same values, but the extent to which an ethnography has this rhetorical character does not obviate the epistemological origins and topics of the anthropological research agenda that historically inform our practice.[8]

My own ethnographic work in Guyana has dealt with violence and killing motivated by long-standing cultural beliefs (Whitehead 2002), so I discuss aspects of that research here precisely because it bears directly on issues as to how anthropology might react to "traditional harmful practices." Moreover, as I came to write about my period of fieldwork and ethnography on this subject (which took place during the 1990s), I became more and more uneasy as to the cost that informants were paying in terms of the dangers they invited by speaking to me about killing and those who were the likely perpetrators, as well as the painful nature of memories and their recall, which surrounded my questioning about the details of specific killings and how victims and their families had felt about *kanaimà*.

The term *kanaimà* refers to a particular mode of assault sorcery that involves ritual mutilation and killing of its victims. The word also can allude to a more diffuse idea of active spiritual malignancy that possesses the assassins and has existed from the beginning of time. Thus, kanaimà as an ethnographic issue is complex to research, both ethically and intellectually, because it is a discourse that operates at a number of levels, referring simultaneously to the dynamics of the spirit world, physical aggression by individuals, the tensions and jealousies between villagers and family members, and the suspicions of more distant enemies, as well as outsiders. Because Patamuna people are well aware of many features of the global order, such outsiders are not thought of simply as being missionaries, anthropologists, or Guyanese government functionaries but also representatives of global NGOs, such as Survival International, as well as the shadowy possibility of foreign police or military agents from Brazil, Venezuela, or the United States.[9] For these reasons, kanaimà sorcery is able to engage with any and all of these discursive levels and their differing ontological appearances. The NGO worker, the Central Intelligence Agency (CIA) operative, or the revenant spirit of a long-dead warrior thus mingle and shape-shift in the practices of magical engagement displayed by kanaimàs (Whitehead 2002:174–201). Consequently one is simultaneously dealing with convincing case histories, wild rumors, considered attributions of blame, false accusations, ungrounded gossip, and justified suspicion. Certainly "rumor" and "gossip" are critical social vectors for the construction of violence and its meanings, but to the extent that my own questioning and interrogation of subjects was itself stimulating the circulation of rumors and the invention of new gossip, I was, unwittingly at the time, deeply implicated in the very phenomenon I was supposed to study with scientific detachment. Such detachment in these circumstances could at best be an indifference to the painful consequences of my desire to know more and to transmit that understanding to a wider audience.

However, the pervasive and profound discourse of kanaimà is a central ethnographic fact of the lives of the people of the Guyana highlands. It both dramatizes the human condition and indicates its futility. It is a daily matter of conversation and closely influences the decisions people make through the vision it supplies of a cosmos filled with predatory gods and spirits whose violent hungers are sated on humans. The decisions to go to the farm, to go with another or not, to carry a gun or not, to pass by the spirit abode of a famed killer or to walk by a longer route are thus woven into the texture of everyday life. For those who participate in this discourse, there are also the distant but steady rumors of killings that are the discursive proof of the malign nature of the cosmos and the enmity of others. If, then, my intellectual duty was to record such key ethnographic facts, this nonetheless placed me in what I would now say was a very problematic ethical position. My need to know was no less connected to issues of professional advancement than to a more acceptable, if vague purpose of improving the "human condition" through better models of the cultural bases of violence.

Undoubtedly the practice of kanaimà involves criminal activity, and informants included the families of victims, as well as avowed killers and practitioners. However, a constant theme to commentaries on such killings was the indifference and inattention of the Guyanese national government and police. In this context, my ethnographic forms of witnessing and reporting were felt to be relevant to Patamuna attempts to gain development resources and government infrastructure. At the same time this risked provoking a campaign of law and order being unleashed on the people of the region, and such exercises in justice are themselves apt to become indiscriminately lethal. Given this situation, kanaimà is accepted and endured as a sign of Amerindian autonomy and is often avidly projected to an external audience as part of continuing traditions. In this way it can easily be appreciated how the politics of the ethnographic representation of violence and sorcery in Amazonia, as elsewhere, are ethically fraught,[10] and such concerns factored heavily into my subsequent publications about kanaimà. In short, the issue of how representations of assault sorcery might be used beyond the anthropological community needs careful assessment, including a consideration of how anthropological representations might be used in service of the state. This is not just a matter of "writing culture" in the alert and critical ways suggested by James Clifford and George Marcus (1985) but also a matter of making decisions about the need for and consequences of knowledge of certain kinds for both the ethnographer and those who are the subjects of research.

Therefore, Western ideas about kanaimà sorcery, as with that other notorious category of South American ethnography, "cannibalism" (Arens 1980; Whitehead and Harbsmeier 2008), cannot be taken as simply reflecting the results of an encounter with some objectively present form of native savagery or exoticism. Rather, our interest in the savagery of others—in particular when it supposedly takes the form of sorcery or cannibalism—clearly has served an ideological purpose in both politically justifying and morally enabling violent conquest and occupation of native South America, as it has elsewhere in the colonial world. Nonetheless, this cultural proclivity on our part does not rule out forms of cultural practice by others that are truly challenging to interpret, in the sense that others do apparently give meaning and value to acts that we might abhor or simply deny to be real. However, this lack of "reality" is more often a lack of understanding on our part; what we actually mean is that the act is incomprehensible. Kanaimà perfectly instantiates such a category because the term invokes truly strange and troubling acts. In both the colonial literature and native oral testimony, it refers to the killing of individuals through a violent mutilation of the mouth and anus in particular, into which are inserted various objects. The killers are then enjoined to return to the dead body of the victim to drink the juices of putrefaction.

A moment's reflection on this ritual act should indicate that witnessing physical violence is extremely dangerous and necessarily entails complex ethical judgments as to how (and whether) such events can be described and need to be published. Yet it is equally clear that the only difference between my position and that of missionaries, journalists, or tourists would be a willingness to take seriously—in both an intellectual and an ethical sense—what was so evident: that kanaimà are real people, who do real killing of specific and identifiable individuals, and this is a meaningful and significant part of local autonomy and perceived cultural heritage.

Any observer is necessarily implicated, even as an unwilling or unwitting participant, in the violence they observe because the meanings and thus motivations to such violence are linked in turn to how such acts are interpreted not just locally but also within the wider national society and to the global community of consumers of anthropological text. If acts of violence are partly established as culturally meaningful (in either a positive or negative sense) through acts of witnessing, then the representations of such violence are not just about violence but are actually part of its meaning and motivation. This need not imply that such violence demands ethnographic witness, as if it were otherwise unnoticed; rather, it implies that such witnessing itself is never neutral.

In this context ethnographic witnessing has a wider cultural role not just for ourselves in the construction of our discourses of savagery and sorcery, but also for others as an aspect of their interest in securing a recognized slot in the savage ethnoscape of global victims and perpetrators. Violent acts may embody complex aspects of symbolism that relate to both order and disorder in a given social context, and these symbolic aspects give violence its many potential meanings in the formation of the cultural imaginary. Atrocities and murders feed into the world of the iconic imagination. Imagination transcends reality and its rational articulation, but in doing so it can bring further violent realities into being.

Nonetheless, a critical engagement with this colonial archive of representation is possible and needed, and as a result it becomes possible to envisage new forms of ethnographic engagement that are more strongly driven by local needs and interests, rather than the unexamined agendas of the institutionalized profession of anthropology. It is quite clear that these difficulties and the need to search for alternatives are well understood by many anthropologists, but what is less clear is whether we have fully appreciated the depth of the problem we face.

FROM INTERVIEW TO "ENHANCED" INTERROGATION

"The only reason you are here is to better your understanding of us and our language. The more you understand us, the easier it is for you to kill us," a man told one of my students doing fieldwork in India. The work of many anthropologists engaged with issues of the military and warfare is exemplary in this search for new ethnographic strategies, because they identify new objects of ethnographic interest and new forms of ethnographic engagement with military and security worlds that do not confine us to a simple binary of researching for the military or taking military institutions and practices as our only ethnographic context.[11] They demonstrate that the character of our participation, not just of our observation, in other cultural worlds needs to be examined. With a greater emphasis on thinking about how we participate in other cultural situations, as well as what our knowledge goals are in such situations, many of the dilemmas of research presented by the historical legacies of ethnographic practice can be resolved. In particular the "ethical" issues as to participation in an HTS team or other such military or security programs becomes less of an abstract issue of commitment to the idea of democratic government or academic scholarship and more of an intersubjective issue as to how one conducts oneself as a person in the world, in whatever social roles we perform.

As with other disciplines that interact with people, anthropology is only publicly comfortable with certain kinds of inquiry—broadly those that do not entail deception and physical or mental harm—and for which, in the United States, the federally mandated Human Subjects Review Panels and Institutional Review Boards function as a form of licensing for such research activity.[12] But as the public debate in the United States over torture showed us, we can easily revise those preferred parameters if the urgency and need is thought to be sufficiently pressing. As with the cases of the Tuskegee syphilis experiment or the CIA's MK-Ultra program, we do not need the excuse of active war to countenance all kinds of special or extraordinary governmental actions. This debate also challenged many received understandings of what might constitute "torture" as opposed to "enhanced interrogation technique," but as Marnia Lazreg (2008:6) writes, "discussions of what degree of physical punishment rises to the level of torture . . . generally constitute preliminaries to defending torture as a legitimate form of interrogation." What is unsettling for anthropologists is that, as with torture, the purpose of ethnography is also the gathering of information, data, and knowledge of others, who might be either enemies or allies of the government apparatus in the ethnographer's homeland. How, then, is ethnographic interrogation different from "enhanced interrogation," or is there a hidden epistemological convergence between torture and ethnography? This analogy, although very difficult to countenance given the ways ethnography has been used to produce so many key insights into many forms of oppression and exploitation worldwide, cannot be lightly dismissed. At stake is our "right to know" things, even where such things are kept hidden purposefully (kinship), are only talked about with pain (memories of war, killings, witchcraft), or where there is a cultural silence and "knowledge" that is as yet unarticulated (personal motives, life histories, collective purposes): "This was what made the Atchei savages: their savagery was formed of silence; it was a distressing sign of their last freedom, and I too wanted to deprive them of it. I had to bargain with death; with patience and cunning, using a little bribery . . . I had to break through the . . . passive resistance, interfere with their freedom, and make them talk" (Clastres 1998:97).

In *Chronicle of the Guayaki Indians*, Pierre Clastres stresses the profound significance of Atchei-Guayaki silence in the face of ethnographic inquiry, seeing it as the foundation of their continuing autonomy, "health," and "freedom": "The society of the Atchei . . . was so healthy that it could not enter into a dialogue with me, with another world. And for this reason the Atchei accepted gifts that they had not asked for and rejected my attempts at conversation because they were strong enough not to need it; we would begin to talk only when they got sick" (1998:97). Clastres further engages this threatening isomorphism of torture and ethnography and the "breaking" of savage silence in his essay "Of Torture in Primitive Societies," in which he argues that the tortured body is meaningful only when silent suffering comes to express courage and assent to the torture itself, as in initiation (1989:184–85). Indeed, we do have a terror of the silence of the "savage other," which the torture of "terrorists," if not ethnography of tribal subjects, must rupture. Silence, the absence of explanation or rationality, is part of what is terrifying about both terrorists and savages.

In Western cultural tradition, our desire to speak and be heard stems from the Enlightenment understanding of the cultural and historical foundations of our Cartesian notions about individual existence—to think (i.e., to speak) is to be human. As a result, the absence of speech or its failure to become intelligible (a literal "barbarism") means that silence potentially operates as a form of terror and resistance. Silence threatens our ideas about the humanity of being and may even suggest nonbeing, or "inhumanity." Silence is also a sign of death, but perhaps also the prelude to rebirth. The monk's vow of silence leads to spiritual rebirth, a rehabilitatory silence is enforced on prisoners, and the anthropologist becomes silent culturally through removal to other places with a return marked by an almost excessive narration. The establishment of professional ethnographic credentials therefore takes place through the unsilencing of the now "researched" other (Mentore 2004). Like ethnographic interviews, then, "enhanced interrogation" overcomes the silence of the resistant other; like torture, the results of ethnography are epistemologically problematic, notwithstanding the undergirding justifications of professional academic research and scientific knowledge. As Derek Freeman (1999) revealed of himself no less than Margaret Mead in reevaluating her breaking of the Samoan silence, or with Napoleon Chagnon's (1974) avowedly deceptive tactics for learning Yanomamö kinship relations, the broader significance of the ethnographic question as a token of power relations means the agonistic process of inquiry, in both torture and ethnography, can never produce the kinds of knowledge we culturally desire.

The Greek term for torture was *basanos*, literally meaning an assay or testing of metals for their purity. This agonistic view of how knowledge is produced was part of the Enlightenment revival of Classical thought. The ancient Greeks routinely tortured slaves to extract evidence for legal trials. They considered truth obtained from slaves by torture to be more reliable than the freely given testimony of free men. One may question whether recollection of this fact is merely a curiosity that allows us to marvel at our progress, or whether our very idea of truth, the truth of the philosophical tradition founded by the ancient Greeks, is caught up in the logic of torture, in which truth is conceived of as residing elsewhere, requiring violence and suffering as necessary for its production (DuBois 1991).

The early modern "discoverie" of witchcraft (Scot 1584) throughout Europe was an ethnographic exercise partly serviced by the information gathered through systematic torture.[13] Likewise the dissection of executed criminals, and the auto-dissections by the surgeons themselves, culturally sustained this linking of knowledge and physical torment into the eighteenth century. In the nineteenth century, the scene of torture and torment as a fount of truth was relocated to the agonies of creative and intellectual production, as in the emotional intensity and even self-destruction of the Romantics. The figure of the tormented and tortured genius, like Edgar Allan Poe, was a staple of the nineteenth- and twentieth-century imagination, just as human or animal suffering in scientific experimentation can also be pictured as the (acceptable) price of progress. These examples signal the continuing cultural importance of founding truth in agonistic performance (Guyer 2007), just as the cultural centrality of the crucified Christ sustains yet another linkage to the association of torment with spiritual truth, as well as with ethnographic truth. This is also the import and "truth" of the human qualities revealed in other cultural practices, such as the Hellenistically inspired Olympic Games, which themselves originated as an explicit proxy for war.[14] The massive cultural and economic presence of "sport" worldwide replays this ideology weekly if not nightly in the sports sections of every news outlet, to say nothing of the global industries that service consumption and participation in sport and physical recreation. No pain, no gain in these cultural realms, or in the torture room.[15]

It is quite correct to point out that as a device for collecting particular and accurate information, the theater of torment we know from such contexts as Algeria, Guatemala, or Chile does not work. These violent performances are a form of a ritual meant to dramatize and empower the state or its agents, while marking and ontologically possessing the victims, as Elaine Scarry (1987) has pointed out. In this way our displacement of bodily torment into other cultural realms appears as a progressive and enlightened cultural development, or at least it did until Abu Ghraib and Guantánamo. However, the eruption of support in the United States for the need to torture or use enhanced interrogation techniques suggests that the ritual of torture might also validate and discover truth in a different way. Not the truth to the torturers' question (Alleg 1958) but the truth of the ideas and institutions for which the victim is tortured. Debates as to the effectiveness of interrogation techniques must take account of not only this performative element but also the relation between agony and truth, or else risk becoming akin to those debates as to what degree of mental or physical suffering rises to the level of torture. Expressed through a "lexicon of terror" (Feitlowitz 1998), these ghoulish debates are the direct intellectual descendant of the manuals of ethnography and torture through which earlier imaginaries of covert and unreasoning social opposition and physical threat were discovered and interdicted. As Jean-Paul Sartre (1958) observed of French torture in Algeria, it is a means for the creation of an Other. In the case of contexts like Abu Ghraib or Guantánamo, the creation of an insurgent, terrorist Other, whose coming into existence through torture then validates the "truth" of a "mission accomplished" for American democracy in its "war on terror."

As Franz Kafka's (1977) famous story "In the Penal Colony" makes graphically evident, there is also a relationship between social legibility and bodily inscription. There are two central characters in Kafka's story—the Traveler (as ethnographer) and the Officer (as exotic Other). The execution of prisoners transported to the Penal Colony is carried out by them being laid out on the bed of a machine that then inscribes, through cutting their flesh and dismembering their bodies, the nature of the prisoner's crime. Foreshadowing the tattoos of the Nazi extermination camps but recalling the relation between tattooing, torture, and writing in the Hellenistic world (DuBois 1991:69–74), the torture victim is marked bodily as a means of rendering rebellious subjects visible as servile and broken both to themselves and to others. As with the risk of mere prurience masquerading as "scientific" or "humanistic" interest in observing and representing the sexuality and violence of others (Whitehead 2004a:11), so the passionate but passive witnessing of the testimonies of the tortured and suffering may nonetheless be an ethnographic "finger in the wound" (Nelson 1999). The ethnographic production of narratives of victimhood and the possibility of inscribing others into such ethnographically constructed identities may "only" provoke a psychological mimesis of the original moment of violence, but it is a source of suffering nonetheless (Kleinman, Das, and Lock 1997).

Professionally the response of anthropologists has often been to seek collaborative and overtly dialogical forms of ethnographic engagement. However, even with such a dialogical relationship in place, there is a contradiction for those who wish to practice emancipatory change and who therefore are interested in contesting relations of domination via ethnography because uncritically applying "ethnographic method" simply reproduces the type of relations of knowledge (as power) that they might otherwise overtly and perhaps more effectively oppose as citizens in the political or social sphere. In this case, the interest and attitudes of those studied, as much as the questions that drive doctorates and advanced research programs, need to come into play. Whether the "knowledge" so generated is worth anything on the academic market is a different question, because the fundability of particular kinds of research obviously influences professional choices and career success. So the critical question for the issue of anthropology's potential military and governmental involvement becomes about whether these kind of collaborative methodological practices are ethically sufficient to avoid the practice of torture as ethnography. As Clastres (1998:96) reflected on the historical silence of the Atchei: "I remembered what Alfred Métraux had said to me not long before: 'For us to be able to study a primitive society, it must already be starting to disintegrate.'" It is also then necessary to ask if such methodological practices disable the kind of colonial purposes that anthropology and society have long shared. In both cases, the answer can be "yes"— because collaboration and dialogue allow space for the mutual agreement of "knowledge goals," and at the same time this methodological practice breaks with the idea of "knowledge" as philosophically restricted to Western forms of understanding and interpretation. The notion of the "human" has been central to such an epistemology so that the unraveling of the colonial epistemological project also suggests the simultaneous unraveling of its central subject-object, and this has been precisely the investigation of the *logos* of *anthropos* around which the discipline formed.

WE ARE NOT ALONE

Anthropology is not unique in being faced with issues of ethical practice. Informant confidentiality, patient confidentiality, witness protection programs, priestly confessions, psychiatric counseling, and journalistic interviews are all precedents for thinking about anthropology's preferred practices. Nonetheless, all these professions and codes of conduct have been complicit at some point in time with government information gathering or programs of military research and interrogation. Likewise, chemists, physicists, and engineers may not experiment on people or invade their privacy in the ways that social scientists do, but they can just as surely contribute to killing them through weapons and security research. For guidance as to the ethical choices we must make as anthropologists, we can learn valuable lessons from our colleagues in other disciplines. This does not inoculate us against military collaboration (nor should it), but it does mean we will be thinking more clearly about what such collaboration entails.

"Few would debate that any anthropologist who works with or for an organization engaged in US national security is enabling a flawed system. This is a circumstance that requires constant navigation and vigilance, but is not unique to those engaged with the security sector. Just scratch the surface of traditional academia. Anyone teaching in a traditional academic environment enables the replication of flawed and unjust systems that affect not only their students, but also the communities in which anthropologists traditionally study" (Kerry Fosher, AAA News,

October 27, 2007, p. 3). So let the military/government pay for their own "human intelligence," since that used to be the responsibility of the State Department. In other words, the recent drive to recruit anthropologists and other academics to the cause of war can also be understood as a way of outsourcing government. The loss of autonomy for the universities as institutions and faculty as independent and inventive thinkers is inevitably created by such a constrained vision of the relationship between academia and the military or government—war or no war. The advent of a new administration with different military and security approaches may certainly mean the end of HTS programs or the Minerva Initiative, but that is not clear as yet. In any case, the more or less liberal or conservative character of government does not alter the historical legacies of ethnography and still requires careful thought as to the range and limits of academic and government collaboration.

The trouble is that culturally we also have become enmeshed in perpetual violence and war in pursuit of a global campaign against terror, which prompts Carolyn Nordstrom's (2004b) pertinent question: "when is war?" Seemingly now it is forever and everywhere. It may be that the idiom of "wartime" is now ending, but these fundamental issues of how we see our role, not just as anthropologists but also as faculty, administrators, students, and citizens, are forever with us. Moreover, the military itself, in many places and under different regimes, is ever more present as it assumes roles in "peacekeeping," "emergency," "humanitarian," or "police" operations (Matlary and Østerud 2007). As Sverker Finnström pointed out to me, this nonetheless may still be understood as part of the "magic of the state" (after Taussig) or its persistent exceptionalism (after Agamben) occurring as much in pursuit of a new world order of peace and security as with that alternative cultural hegemony of war and terror. For these reasons, the topical concern as to anthropology and the wars in Iraq or Afghanistan certainly allows us to raise a number of important questions about the practice of ethnography and our efforts to improve it. This, in turn, can become a positive opportunity for anthropology, once again, to reflect on and reform its practice of ethnography not just by seeking different forms of writing or presentation but also by more clearly acknowledging the ethnographer's subject position—no longer just the observer but also necessarily participant. But, as with those wars, it is unlikely we will be declaring "mission accomplished" any time soon.

1. They also point out that this has led to an export of internationally defined standards for a "good childhood" through various foreign-funded development programs in the Global South. While many NGOs, legitimating their work on the basis of the Convention on the Rights of the Child (CRC), are genuinely working for an improvement of children's conditions, they have also taken on the role as a second guardian to cultivate "proper" children and parents who can live up to the supposedly universal ideals of a good childhood. The article adopts a critical view on the child rights movement by shedding light on the crucial role that NGOs play as civilizing institutions in the South. The article specifically draws attention to the double-sided patronization of children and parents and "infantilization" of nations in South, which implicitly lies beneath the CRC and the child rights movement.

2. In many popular and even academic presentations of indigenous "tribal" and "traditional" life ways, the stereotypical message is to the effect that the lives being witnessed are subject to the kinds of arbitrary violence or deprivation that Western liberal democracy has otherwise banished from our everyday existence. Of course other kinds of tropes are used that may suggest a more positive aspect to the lives of others—their harmony with nature, the beauty and satisfaction derived from tradition and custom—but even here the implicit meaning of the representation is that it is an anachronistic route to human happiness and contentment.

3. While revising this article, I received the following email from a former student: "I thought about our course on a number of occasions in India this summer. One moment really stood out. I was spending a bit of time in a predominantly Muslim slum in New Delhi, trying to get to know the various leaders of the different Muslim 'caste' groups that live in the community. One day during a meeting with one of these leaders, a man burst into the room screaming at me in Urdu. He went on about how he sympathizes with and supports the Taliban, and how Americans are far more destructive than they could ever be. More powerfully, he asked me why I was in India and why I wanted to know so much about their community. I told him about my little research grant and what I was doing there, and tried to convince him that I was just a student and had nothing to do with the American government. His response was, 'Whether or not you directly work for the American government, the only reason you are here is to better your understanding of us and our language. The more you understand us, the easier it is for you to kill us.' It really threw off my sense of being an impartial researcher swooping down into these communities to objectively examine their politics and culture. Ethnography, colonialism, and war really aren't so different, huh."

4. In the summer of 2008, I was contacted by a military contractor working for the U.S. Army. I was told that in view of my qualifications I would be offered a remuneration of $480,000 for a fourteen-month deployment to Afghanistan. In

the summer of 2010, I was approached again by a lieutenant colonel in the army and a member of the HTS, this time trying to get the anthropology department (of which I was chair) to stage a campus debate with HTS operatives (see also note 9).

5. Nonetheless, scientific taxonomies shaped both nonfictional and fictional narratives. Thus novels invoked the language of science to lend authority to the project of literary realism (McBratney 2005) and travel writing and memoirs usually offered scientific observation as a token of the travelers' authenticity.

6. Linda Tuhiwai Smith's (1999) important discussion of "decolonizing methodologies" and Lewis Gordon's (2007) analysis of "disciplinary decadence" both point to the need to rethink inherited methodologies and disciplinary categories by examining the openness of ideas and purposes from which their disciplines were born.

7. Exactly these concerns are evident in the debates and discussions of the possible use of a particular ethnography in the torturing of prisoners in Iraq. In a series of articles in the *New Yorker* magazine, the journalist Seymour Hersh suggested that the anthropologist Raphael Patai's *The Arab Mind* (1976, 2007) had been used by interrogators. In fact, this seems doubtful and in discussion of the Patai/Hersh materials nearly all commentators, whatever they think as to the factual issue of whether Patai's work was known and employed by torturers, express outrage and shock at the idea that ethnography might be used in this way. The issue here is not the truth of Hersh's claims but that such claims appeared plausible in the first place.

8. See Robert Edgerton's *Sick Societies* (1992), for example, Napoleon Chagnon's (1968) famous ethnography of the Yanomamö, or Christopher Hallpike's (1977) account of the Tauade in Papua New Guinea, reviewed by Andrew Vayda (1979).

9. This region borders Brazil, and there is a lively smuggling trade involving guns, ganja, gold, and diamonds. In geopolitical terms the U.S. government was seen as having persistent interests in such resources as well as the "traditional knowledge" of the Patamuna. This traditional knowledge was threatened on one hand by biopiracy on the part of representatives from international drug companies, and on the other hand by military interest in the sorcery techniques of kanaimà. As I relate in my ethnographic account (Whitehead 2002:32), this led to me being openly accused of being a CIA agent seeking knowledge of kanaimà so that it could be deployed by the U.S. military, a strangely prophetic suspicion (see note 4) and not without foundation.

10. This was demonstrated by the controversies around Patrick Tierney's *Darkness in Eldorado* (2002), which supposedly revealed the cynical and even criminal basis of the behavior of some ethnographers of the Yanomamö in Venezuela. The charges were so serious that a special task force was convened by the American Anthropological Association to evaluate the claims and counterclaims.

11. A range of ethically complex forms of ethnographic engagement directly with the military inform developing anthropological debates on military cultural expression in the form of "grunt lit" (Brown and Lutz 2007) or YouTube videos, as well as the phenomenon of a culturally expansive militarism itself (Enloe 2007; Finn-

ström 2008; Nordstrom 2004a) and the media and virtual worlds of disembodied war and its production as mass spectacle (Robben 2010b; Stein 2008).

12. Reaffirmed in 2010 in the wake of revelations that U.S. doctors and researchers had used Guatemalan subjects for nonconsensual experiments concerning the sexual transmission of disease; see "Presidential Memorandum—Review of Human Subjects Protection," November 24, 2010, http://www.whitehouse.gov /the-press-office/2010/11/24/presidential-memorandum-review-human-subjects -protection (accessed January 21, 2011), for President Barack Obama's announcement.

13. The most influential manuals on witch-finding, like Scot's *Discoverie*, the *Malleus Maleficarum* (Hammer of the Witches) of Heinrich Institoris (1588), or the *Praxis Criminalis* by Prospero Farinacci (1676), offered protocols for early modern courts in investigating cases of *maleficium* (sorcery, witchcraft). Such manuals laid out the role and function of torture within the system of constructing and justifying truth in court with a resulting impact on patterns of evidence production and interpretation. The *Praxis* is most noteworthy as the definitive work on the jurisprudence of torture, and Scot's *Discoverie* was highly ethnographic, being a compendium of local and folk beliefs and practices that were designed to allow better discrimination between the harmless and the evil, a form of "spiritual terrain system."

14. The International Olympic Committee was founded in 1894 by a French nobleman, Pierre Frédy, Baron de Coubertin. Despite what Coubertin had hoped for, three Olympic Games (in 1916, 1940, and 1944) were canceled because of world wars.

15. The agonistic qualities of the cultural notion of "truth" are but part of the wider "regime of truth" to which Michel Foucault refers as being "produced only by virtue of multiple forms of constraint" (1972:131).

THE ROLE OF CULTURE IN WARS WAGED BY ROBOTS

Connecting Drones, Anthropology, and
Human Terrain System's Prehistory

Virtual dreams of harnessing cultural knowledge in ways that
allow military experts to manipulate other cultures have become
recurrent fantasies of American warfare since World War II.
America's postwar counterinsurgency gurus, such as Edward
Lansdale, liked to mix demonstrations of military might with
targeted forms of soft power in ways that used force to press
compliance and used cultural knowledge to further press insurgents and would-be insurgents to comply with demonstrated
military might. Today, a new generation of counterinsurgency
proponents argue that culturally informed counterinsurgency
campaigns can be used not only to enact less violent occupations or as back-up support for military might, but to somehow
achieve military victories.

A core feature of the Bush and Obama administrations' plans
for victories in Iraq and Afghanistan has been an enhanced reliance on counterinsurgency, and today the U.S. military struggles
with the contradictions of trying to win the hearts and minds
of peoples caught beneath the armed presence of their occupation. Some of these themes have deep roots in American liberal
approaches to foreign policy, and there are similarities between
Kennedy's and Obama's presidential attractions to counterin-

surgency as a tool imagined to have the power to conquer peoples who have historically been difficult (if not impossible) for outside colonial powers to dominate. These are remarkable claims. Even counterinsurgency's staunchest supporters admit that historical instances of successfully using counterinsurgency for military victories have been extremely rare in the past half century, with the British campaign in Malaya being the rare paradigm of claimed success (though this case had more military support than is sometimes claimed), and failure being the general rule (Nagl 2005). But Washington's loyal counterinsurgency believers and a cadre of academic social scientists share a certain vanity that they are clever enough to overcome this daunting record of historical failure and design forms of counterinsurgency that will bring Americans what they hope will be a gentle victory.

Political science was the academic discipline on which the wars of the twentieth century drew; whereas the asymmetrical wars of the twenty-first century now look toward anthropology with hopes of finding models of culture, or data on specific cultures to be conquered, to be used in counterinsurgency operations (Kilcullen 2000; McFate 2005a; Packer 2006, 2008). But anthropology is not political science, and anthropologists have different commitments to those who share their lives and vulnerabilities with them. Anthropologists' ethical commitments to those they study precludes many of the Machiavellian approaches to social science to which military and intelligence agencies have grown accustomed.

The counterinsurgency program generating the greatest friction among anthropologists is the Human Terrain System (HTS)—a program with over four hundred employees, originally operating through private contractors and now taken over by the U.S. Army. The program embeds anthropologists with military units to ease the occupation and conquest of Iraqis and Afghanis—with the expansion of these operations in Africa through expanding units with U.S. African Command (Besteman 2009). Some HTS social scientists are armed; others choose not to carry weapons, instead relying on the firepower of the soldiers with whom they embed. During the first three years of operations, three HTS social scientists were killed in the course of their work, and HTS member Don Ayala pled guilty in U.S. District Court to killing the Afghani who had brutally set on fire HTS social scientist Paula Loyd, an attack leading to Loyd's death (Ayala shot the man in the head execution-style while he was detained with his hands zip-cuffed behind him) (Forte 2011; Stanton 2009).

HTS and other counterinsurgency projects raise serious political, ethical, and practical problems for participating anthropologists (Albro et al. 2009). Central to anthropologists' criticisms of the HTS program are concerns that the reports of these social scientists can be used by military and intelligence agencies in ways that can make studied populations vulnerable because safeguards protecting gathered data for use by military or intelligence agencies are absent. The leaked HTS handbook clarifies the program's utter insouciance for the normal ethical precautions to protect studied populations (Finney 2008; Price 2008b). In November 2007, a little more than a year after the HTS program became public knowledge, the executive board of the American Anthropological Association denounced the program for its failure to ensure that fundamental principles of anthropological ethics were being followed to ensure the safety and protection of people being studied by HTS in the theaters of battle and occupation where it operates. HTS is not some neutral humanitarian project; it is an arm of the U.S. military. It is part of the military's mission to occupy and destroy opposition to U.S. goals and objectives. HTS cannot claim the sort of neutrality claimed by groups like Doctors Without Borders or the International Committee of the Red Cross; its goal is a gentler form of domination—claims of "armed humanitarianism" notwithstanding (see Hodge 2011; Price 2010a).

The current counterinsurgency movement's most philosophical advocate, David Kilcullen, has been honest about the slim prospects of engaging in "humanitarian" projects in counterinsurgency war zones, admitting that "there is no such thing as impartial humanitarian assistance or civil affairs in counterinsurgency. Every time you help someone, you hurt someone else—not least the insurgents. So civil and humanitarian assistance personnel will be targeted. Protecting them is a matter not only of close-in defense but also of creating a permissive operating environment by co-opting the beneficiaries of aid—local communities and leaders—to help you help them" (Kilcullen 2009a:44). He further clarifies how all development and aid projects have natural similarities and differences to counterinsurgency programs, writing:

> For aid officers and other development professionals in a counterinsurgency environment, it is important to note that there is a real qualitative difference between operating in a field environment outside a war zone and operating in a counterinsurgency environment. In "nor-

mal" development work, there are spoilers and local opponents to consider, but the real "enemy" is poverty, disease, and lack of capacity. In a counterinsurgency, all these things remain important, but there is also an enemy aid officer out there, running programs in direct competition with ours. The Taliban run agricultural teams to help farmers get the most out of the poppy crop, for example, along the local law courts and taxation programs and business advice for start-up firms in the drug cultivation, gem smuggling, and timber smuggling businesses that the Taliban exploit. (Kilcullen 2009a:44, author's note)

This is the environment of warfare in which HTS teams seek to dominate, drawing on anthropological knowledge of local conditions to help occupiers maintain dominant relevance against more local counterforces bidding for local loyalties.

Anthropologist Montgomery McFate became the first public spokesperson for the HTS program. Although the broad stream of public criticism of her inability to address fundamental ethical flaws in the program led her to increasingly pull back from public discussions of its workings and implications, McFate's early writings on British counterinsurgency operations against the Irish Republican Army (IRA) provide an important if not bluntly unguarded model of how she (and, it appears, her military sponsors) view the potential of anthropology working as a tool for military conquest.

McFate and other supporters of HTS claim the program uses embedded social scientists to help reduce "kinetic engagements," or unnecessary violent contacts with the populations they encounter by using social scientists to interact with members of the community. Kilcullen envisions HTS social scientists as social engineers monitoring and tinkering with the flow of "cultural evolution" in war zones; he writes that HTS-like social science teams are needed "because of the processes of cultural evolution and adaptation . . . cultural capability must be maintained in an up-to-date fashion, taking into account current developments in a given theatre" (Kilcullen 2009a:224). These human terrain social scientists are claimed to created liaison relationships between occupiers and occupied; the program also claims that HTS social scientists possess adequate local cultural knowledge to reduce misunderstandings that can lead to unnecessarily violent interactions (Kamps 2008; Stannard 2007). These claims led HTS supporters to claim the program's social scientists are "armed social workers," whereas critics of the program have drawn attention to the inherent contradictions that notions of armed social work bring to roles whose success or failure depend on voluntary associations and willing compliance, not on forcing compliance to external wills.[1]

In McFate's rendering, HTS is often presented as a key tool for less lethal counterinsurgency efforts that seek to secure, dominate, and conquer populations by using measured military responses that do not undercut existing social formations, formations that might be drawn up and supported by occupying military forces. The HTS program sells itself to the public though remarkably well-organized domestic propaganda campaigns that have seen dozens of uncritical articles on HTS and personality profiles on the program's personnel appearing in U.S. newspapers, the *New Yorker, Harper's, Elle, More,* and so on. The surprisingly narrow media narrative that emerged in the press during the first three years of HTS depicted the program as a "peaceful" means of achieving victory, with the media's HTS pitchmen arguing that reduced violence (rather than reduced occupation) is a humane response to a bad situation that saves lives (Burleigh 2007; Featherstone 2008; Kamps 2008; Packer 2006).

In contrast to the carefully manicured public narrative maintaining that these HTS counterinsurgency tactics lead to reduced violence, the early, unvarnished, counterinsurgency writings of McFate reveal stark contradictions to the current public claims that anthropologically informed counterinsurgency is primarily a means to achieve victory peacefully. Instead, these early works find her openly arguing that using anthropology for counterinsurgency is also a way for militaries to learn how to kill in more strategic ways, not simply to be kinder and gentler. More significant, McFate's early work also reveals her prescience in foreseeing how programs like HTS would be needed in high-tech-dominated battlefields, where the military's needs for low-tech human ethnographic knowledge grow in proportion to the reliance on futuristic war tools like drones and satellite-based systems.

Back in the early 1990s, McFate realized that as robots come to dominate warfare, humans would increasingly be needed to provide crucial intelligence and interface with occupied human beings. This is a vital unanalyzed element of modern counterinsurgency, and it provides the context for us to understand how HTS fits into a world of postmodern warfare. This is a setting in which anthropologists are sought to serve the machines of warfare, interpreting the world of symbols and meanings in settings dominated by panoptical machines with impeccable vision that are incapable of understanding human meanings. Anthropologists are needed to serve as near-surrogates for machines incapable of understanding the impacts of their actions on the worlds they dominate.

MCFATE'S UNEXAMINED COUNTERINSURGENT PREHISTORY

As the anthropologist critic of HTS Maximilian Forte has pointed out, McFate was not so much the creator of HTS as she was the program's chief spokesperson (Forte 2008). With time, her role as salesperson has obscured some of the credit that should go to Andrea Jackson, former director of research and training at the Lincoln Group, for developing plans for such a field-embedded, ethnographically informed form of cultural education. McFate's interest in conjoining anthropology and counter-insurgency predated (by over a decade) her involvement with what became HTS.

While earning her doctorate in anthropology at Yale University in the early 1990s, McFate undertook fieldwork and library research focusing on the resistance of the Provisional Irish Republican Army (PIRA) and British military counterinsurgency campaigns in Northern Ireland. She focused on British shifts away from strictly tactical military responses to more culturally nuanced counterinsurgency campaigns between 1969 and 1982. McFate's research was supported by an impressive mix of fellowships ranging from the National Science Foundation, the Mellon Foundation, and several Yale-based fellowships directed toward "international security" issues.

In 2008, McFate explained to reporter Louisa Kamps that her dissertation research examined "how cultural narratives, handed down from generation to generation, contributed to war," and "how people legitimate their use of violence" (Kamps 2008:310), an explanation that might lead one to justifiably assume her research was balanced between the positions of the Irish insurgents and British counterinsurgents, but such an impression would be false. Her dissertation instead reads as a guide for militaries wanting to stop indigenous insurgent movements.

McFate's dissertation (written under her maiden name, Montgomery Carlough) was an exercise in sympathetically understanding the internal meaning of IRA resistance, but only so far as this led to models that assisted those wanting to quash such resistance. This was not a cultural study designed to give voice to the concerns of an oppressed people so that others might come to see their internal narrative as valid; it was designed to make those she studied vulnerable to cooptation and defeat (Carlough 1994).

For her dissertation fieldwork, McFate made multiple trips to Ireland and met with members of the occupying British military and of the IRA, but when she wrote up her dissertation she made a conscious decision to not identify whom she had spoken with and also not directly quote from these interactions (Carlough 1994:iii). This second protective step showed an unusual level of precaution, one she based on anthropology's ethical mandate to protect research subjects. In her dissertation, McFate acknowledged that her decision to not quote from these fieldwork experiences was done for disciplinary ethical reasons, writing:

> Ethical considerations and on-going friendships prevent full disclosure of sources. Although I conversed with numerous soldiers, politicians, and theorists on both sides of the ideological and military divide, I have made a conscious effort to use publicly available sources, published elsewhere, in preference to direct informant statements. *Although anthropologists writing about security issues sincerely claim to have concealed the identity of informants, insider knowledge often allows accurate guessing.* When informant statements are used, either in quotations or as evidence to support a point, I do not attribute them, except in two cases where permission was explicitly given. (Carlough 1994:iii; emphasis added)

McFate's interviews and interactions with members of the IRA or British armed forces served as background for her larger contextual understanding of these communities. Her concern in 1994 over the ethical protection of research participants is admirable and stands in stark contrast to HTS's later disregard of such ethical protections. It remains unknown what happened to her notes and other records from interviews with PIRA members, but given McFate's current work in environments requiring security clearances, such past contacts and records would have raised many questions when she applied for her security clearance. It would be standard operating procedure during a background investigation to ask about the identity of her 1990s contacts with the IRA and other groups, as it would be to ask such an applicant for field notes and other such material. McFate's early counterinsurgency years provide a significantly less guarded glimpse at her understanding of the promise of anthropology's role in counterinsurgency than can be found in her later writings. This younger, less cautious McFate avoided the sort of Orwellian softening language of what is now called "independent military subcontractor," preferring the more direct "mercenary" (Carlough 1994:iv). Although she now avoids linking militarized anthropology with killing, in her dissertation days she more openly asked whether "one could conclude that ethnocentrism— bad anthropology—interferes with the conduct of war. But does good anthropology contribute to better killing?" (Carlough 1994:13–14). Though an affirmative answer to this rhetorical question is implied, McFate left this question unanswered. Today she categorically rejects claims that HTS teams use anthropology for what she used to refer to as "better killing," but HTS anthropologist Audrey Roberts told the *Dallas Morning News* that she does not worry that her data may be used by the military when "looking for bad guys to kill" (Landers 2009).

Today, McFate despises postmodern trends in anthropology, blaming postmodernism for everything from disciplinary concerns with research ethics to muddled thinking and writing (McFate 2005a). But back in the 1990s, she was much friendlier to postmodern anthropological approaches, dreaming of the military utility of harvesting thick descriptions for counterinsurgent applications, writing that "counterinsurgency . . . depends on accurate cultural knowledge. [Counterinsurgency] utilizes local knowledge and 'on-the-ground' operations—terms which have crept into the jargon of anthropology—to infiltrate the 'hearts and minds' of the opponent" (Carlough 1994:14).

McFate's dissertation identified two counterinsurgency elements requiring anthropological skill sets. The first involved psychological warfare operations, in which cultural readings could be used for defining perceptions of one's enemy because "creating a mask for the enemy to wear is essential for psychological warfare" (Carlough 1994:86). The second argued that "knowledge of the enemy leads to a refinement in knowledge of how best to kill the enemy" (Carlough 1994:110).

McFate understood the blowback problems created when militaries dehumanize their enemy, processes that create problems for counterinsurgency operations striving to make enemies who have been labeled irrational or less than human as being rational actors who must be understood as such if they are to be *controlled*. The desire to understand and rehumanize an enemy and the rationalizations of its motivations is at the heart of counterinsurgency operations, and McFate argued these goals hold vital roles for anthropology, writing, "The fundamental contradiction between 'knowing' your enemy in order to develop effective strategy, and de-humanizing him in order to kill efficiently is a theme to which we will return. Suffice to say, that *the dogs of war do have a pedigree, which is often 'anthropological' and that counter-insurgency strategy depends, not just on practical experience on the battlefield, but on historically derived analogical models of prior conflict. Paraphrasing Levi-Strauss, enemies are not only good to kill, enemies are good to think*" (Carlough 1994:114; emphasis added). McFate expressed clear desires for psychological operations to use anthropological conceptions of cultural relativism to understand how enemies view the world and use this information to better understand how one's own actions or use of symbols will be interpreted by enemies. She advocated studying ethnographies of enemies to outthink them, because "understanding the possible intentions of the enemy entails being able to think like the enemy; in other words, successful preemptive counter moves depend on simulating the strategy of the opponents" (Carlough 1994).

McFate wanted military forces to understand how their actions have undesired consequences that they cannot understand unless they learn to see things from within the enemy's mindset. She and her supporters often spin this approach as being a desire to use anthropology so that less force will be used by the U.S. military. But McFate and HTS supporters desire minimal force because they believe it leads to a more efficient occupation, cooptation, and conquest of enemies, not because they object to occupation, cooptation, and conquest. This presents serious political problems for most anthropologists, and given anthropology's problematic role as a handmaiden to colonialism in the past, these issues easily move from the realm of individual politics to disciplinary politics and properly raise the attentions of disciplinary professional associations.

When I asked anthropologist Roberto González how he viewed HTS's efforts to maintain efficient occupations, he wrote me that he is less sure that HTS cares all that much about efficient occupations. Instead, he wrote,

> [the more I learn] about HTS and the new forms of counterinsurgency, the more I think that they are convinced that "stability operations" or "Phase 4" is qualitatively different than occupation, conquest, or im-

perialism. Somewhere there is an ideological disconnect. Perhaps it is a view of American exceptionalism, that we are the "shining city on the hill"—that we are not occupiers, we're stabilizers. But no matter how this is rationalized, counterinsurgency programs always include "kinetic engagements"—that is, deadly encounters—with civilians. This was the history of failed American counterinsurgency operations in the Philippines, Haiti, Guatemala, el Salvador, and Vietnam. (Roberto González, personal communication, August 14, 2009)

Whatever the self-justifications for using anthropology for these neocolonial occupations, like many of her more openly colonial British anthropologist predecessors, McFate's dissertation embraced functionalist theoretical approaches linked to British colonialism as a suitable means for analyzing and attempting to manage the cultures encountered in warfare. Her dissertation relied on what she refers to as a "neo-functionalist" perspective to analyze the "systemic equilibrium of military cultures [that] is not disturbed, but maintained through the death of soldiers during combat, as long as they do not exceed the limits of the system but remain within acceptable levels. Anything that maintains war at an acceptable level sustains conflict" (Carlough 1994:188).

Although human terrain has historical roots stretching back to colonial ventures in Africa and elsewhere, it is a new generation of remote, robotic warfare technologies that hold the key to understanding why the military now so strongly desires such forms of cultural interactions with occupied populations.

WORKING FOR ROBOTS

Today, the increased reliance on military robotics and drones in Iraq and Afghanistan progresses at a startling rate. Consider how within the span of the past decade the robotic presence in these theaters has increased from a state when there were no military robotic units to today's total of more than twelve thousand robotic devices in use—with more than five thousand flying drones as of this writing. Unmanned aerial vehicles (UAVs) like the Predator (with a flight range of over two thousand miles, an ability to remain airborne at high elevations for more than twenty-four hours at a time, incredible optical surveillance capabilities with the remote pilots linked by satellite half a world away) can track and kill humans on the ground. Other earthbound robots like the PackBot and TALON detonate landmines or roadside bombs, and some like Special Weapons Observation Reconnaissance Detection System (SWORDS) have options of being armed with functioning M-16s and other weapons (Singer 2009).

Today, UAV pilots command drones operating in Iraq, Afghanistan, and Pakistan from bases located thousands of miles away. Outside Las Vegas, Nevada, drone pilots at Nellis Air Force Base guide Predator drones on reconnaissance and targeting missions from nearly halfway around the world. The abstractions of performing these distant missions from upgraded game consoles, then returning home each night to the mundane joys of suburban family life creates its own states of unreality, and these game system "soldiers" are having increasing difficulties rationalizing and mentally processing these remote killing sessions. The physical distance and remote invocations of death from afar have their own qualities of magical death. The demands of killing distant humans take a mental toll. These are social worlds in which drone pilots take the lives of distant others with the simple movement of a joystick, and then drive home through commuter traffic to waiting spouses, children, soccer games, and PTA meetings. Such relations of production place demands on these killing commuters, who must cope with their own roles in these kills, as processes of distancing take on metaphors of magical death as these soldiers rationalize their direct roles as remote video killers.

While increases in the military's reliance on drones and UAVs have mostly escaped the American public's attention, the impact of this tactical shift has radically changed the U.S. military's ability to track and control occupied and enemy populations. To some degree, many of the changes credited with "the surge" can be attributed to concurrent increases in high-tech monitoring and targeting in Iraq. As P. W. Singer shows in *Wired for War: The Robotics Revolution and Conflict in the 21st Century*, the battlefield and occupations are being revolutionized in ways that are quickly progressing beyond strategists' ability to understand how these increases in remote tracking, controlling, and killing are impacting the cultures they are physically dominating. But increases in robotic-panoptical monitoring and control appear to paradoxically be damaging some facets of the U.S. military strategy, as mechanical manipulation reveals deep divisions between the worlds of machines and humans (Singer 2009). To her credit, a decade and a half ago, McFate understood how such dynamics would play out, though her "practical" solution to such dilemmas is mired in irresolvable political and ethical problems for the anthropologists that she would have become the sensors for the machines dominating these battlefields.

McFate's most insightful early statements concerning military needs for anthropological knowledge focus on high-tech warfare's inability to decipher or address the human reactions and problems created by warfare. As early as 1994, she clearly understood the future importance of high-tech developments in waging nonconventional warfare, but she also sensed the shortcomings these nonhuman developments would bring because technological accomplishments would mean increasing panoptical intelligence, but such monitoring and tracking would not necessarily mean increases in *understanding*. McFate understood that "global positioning systems and cruise missiles won't pay for your ammunition in Kurdistan. Low-intensity conflict requires human generated intelligence, local knowledge, and mission-oriented tactics. Atavistic modes of intelligence collection—espionage, infiltration—take precedence over more sophisticated techniques in these conditions. Thus, an interesting inversion occurs: as the technological sophistication of the enemy declines, reliance on intelligence derived from human sources (HUMINT) increases" (Carlough 1994:216). McFate's prescience was brilliant. What was lacking in her analysis is any discussion of the political and ethical implications of using anthropology to fill these real military needs. Specifically, her analysis (both here and in her later publications) avoids political analysis of the neocolonial uses to which such ethnographic knowledge will inevitably be used, just as she avoids explaining how the sort of anthropological ethical issues raised by such work will be addressed. As warfare becomes increasingly tied to satellites and robotics, local, on-the-ground ethnographic knowledge grows in expediential importance; this realization shows both McFate's intellect and the roots and latent importance of the HTS program.

Anticipating how increased reliance on remote monitoring and killing technologies such as drones or other high-tech war systems would paradoxically simultaneously dominate and undermine war efforts, McFate observed that "When low-intensity conflict reverts to prior forms, most cybertech systems go blind. War in the post-modern era is not necessarily post-modern war: the war of the space age resembles, in fact, the war of antiquity. The methods of the guerrillas are almost impervious to the technical intelligence apparatus of the state, and as a result, the less sophisticated the army, the better equipped it is to defeat 'insurgency'"

(Carlough 1994:217). She bolstered these claims with references to British counterinsurgency campaigns that went native, using Dyak headhunters to guide Malayan patrols, and T. E. Lawrence's immersion in and reliance on Bedouin culture.

McFate's early insistence that successful counterinsurgency operations must work close to local populations takes on a new importance in the current campaigns being waged in Iraq and Afghanistan. But with today's high-tech means, such as the use of the Predator and other UAVs to target so successfully, one might wonder why the military even needs anything like HTS for such an automated "distant" battlefront. McFate answered this question back in 1994 when she observed that "the war-machine cannot produce a military meta-theory to cope with low-intensity conflicts: hearts and minds and bellies don't respond to firepower" (Carlough 1994:218). Presumably, such a meta-theory would need a rich understanding of local culture, and McFate would have anthropologists provide the data and analysis for a meta-theory that understands how human enemies respond to the machines dominating them.

These war machines need human input. The machines need not so much anthropologists' eyes and ears (they see and hear better than we ever will), but they need our *spirits*—our ability to symbolically and humanly process the human environments these machines dominate. The war machines are technically efficient but humanly stupid. They can track and control the movement of human bodies, but they cannot understand the webs of cultural meanings of those they physically dominate. They cannot sense their own effectiveness on the lives they control: this is one of the reasons something like human terrain teams are needed to function as nerves, feeling and reporting the cultural-emotional responses of occupied peoples so that the machines of war can more exactly manipulate and dominate them. It is useful to metaphorically consider themes of *The Matrix* when considering the ways that humans (anthropologists) are needed to be the interface with and serve the machines of high-tech warfare.

While battlefields become increasingly dominated by high-tech gadgetry and panoptical drones, iris scanners and computer tracking software, something like the currently attempted human terrain teams will be needed to gather human knowledge on the ground. McFate's early writings clarify why those designing counterinsurgency campaigns crave anthropological knowledge. Given the economic collapse's impact on the anthropology job market, I would not preclude the likelihood of some measure of success, especially as these calls for anthropological assistance are increasingly framed under false flags of "humanitarian assistance" or as reducing lethal engagements (Price 2010a). But the ethical and political problems of using anthropology for cultural domination will not easily be resolved—never mind the very real practical problem that culture-hacking counterinsurgency can never work in the ways that McFate, Kilcullen, and others are selling it to the military.

ANTHROPOLOGY'S MCFATE

Vladimir Nabokov riddled his novel *Lolita* with references to a form of destiny referred to as "McFate," which are cruel turns of apparent coincidence that set characters on paths linking their destinies with larger themes. In Nabokov's world, the "synchronizing phantom" of McFate arranges what might have been chance events into patterns revealing if not providence then at least a recurrence of trajectories (Nabokov 1955:103). In only a partial Nabokovian sense, anthropology's McFate merges old anthropological and military themes together in ways that reveal new uses for anthropology, which the discipline will be increasingly unable to control regardless of how offensive these uses are to core anthropological values.

It is not that anthropology and warfare haven't merged before; they have fatefully merged in all sorts of ways that have been historically documented in detail elsewhere. One stark difference is that today's counterinsurgent abuses of anthropological knowledge occur after the discipline of anthropology has clearly identified these specific activities as betraying basic ethical standards for protecting the interests and well-being of studied populations. Anthropologists' contributions to World War II occurred without the existence of professional ethical codes of conduct; it was a direct result of anthropological misconduct during the Vietnam War that the American Anthropological Association formalized its first Code of Ethics in 1971—with its insistence on anthropologists' primary loyalties being to those studied, research not leading to events harming research participants, no secret research, and mandates for voluntary informed consent. That HTS throws up weak sophistic arguments claiming that their involvement in warfare reduces harm changes nothing. The program's confused mixture of anthropological methods and inquiry with the needs of warfare while addressing basic anthropological ethical concerns betrays anthropology's most fundamental commitments to those who share their lives with us.

Anthropology's past is interwoven with state needs of warfare, colonialism, and neocolonialism, but institutionally, today the bulk of the discipline of anthropology knows better—and I was surprised to learn, when reading about McFate's dissertation, that she once insisted on taking serious steps to protect her research participants. Her reasons for betraying her past commitment to ethically protecting those she studied remains obscure.

In a *New York Times* op-ed piece from 2009, David Kilcullen and Andrew Exum question the military's use of drones for lethal attacks in Pakistan (Kilcullen and Exum 2009). They criticize the military's increasing reliance on drones for lethal attacks, arguing that U.S. military reliance on these remote machines presents dangers to American interests because they reinforce cultural images among Pakistanis of a reckless American siege mentality that flippantly considers the robotic killing of innocent civilians as "collateral damage." Kilcullen and Exum call for a reduced reliance on drones arguing that "expanding or even just continuing the drone war is a mistake. In fact, it would be in our best interests, and those of the Pakistani people, to declare a moratorium on drone strikes into Pakistan" (Kilcullen and Exum 2009). At the heart of this critique is a concern over how these drone attacks culturally play out on the ground. They argue that the increased reliance on drones is undermining U.S. military interests, asking readers to "imagine, for example, that burglars move into a neighborhood. If the police were to start blowing up people's houses from the air, would this convince homeowners to rise up against the burglars? Wouldn't it be more likely to turn the whole population against the police? And if their neighbors wanted to turn the burglars in, how would they do that, exactly? Yet this is the same basic logic underlying the drone war" (Kilcullen and Exum 2009).

McFate's, Kilcullen's, and other anthropologically informed counterinsurgency planners' recognition that increases in technological means to dominate battlefields and regions of occupation creates important gaps in understanding that need human beings with cultural knowledge to fill these gaps is tactically logical. But all that is logical is neither necessarily ethical nor politically wise. Notions of using anthropologists and other social scientists to gather information, probe, and soothe the feelings of those living in environments increasingly monitored and controlled by machines strikes me as an anthropological abomination. In addition, given what we anthropologically know about the complexities of *how* culture works, it seems doomed to be a failed project.

The military is being sold notions that culture is a commodity or a set of easily identifiable and controllable variables, and this is part of a larger problem with the way that culture is being represented by many of the anthropologists now working for the military (Price 2009a). Simple notions of mechanical disarticulated representations of culture can be found in the army's *Counterinsurgency Field Manual*, in which particular forms of anthropological theory were selected not because they "work" or are intellectually cohesive: they were selected because they offer an engineering-friendly promise of "managing" the complexities of culture as if increased sensitivities, greater knowledge, and panoptical legibility could be used in a linear fashion to engineer domination. Such notions of culture fit the military's structural view of the world. The false promise of "culture" as a controllable, linear product drives today's counterinsurgency sales team's particular construction of "culture" (Price 2009a). Within the military, the counterinsurgency believers are not alone in this folly. In 2009 I read a leaked Special Forces Advisor Guide (TC-31-73) and found dated 1950s anthropological notions of culture and personality theories selected and used to produce simplistic reductions of entire continents as having a limited set of uniform cultural traits—a feat that finds the military embracing a form of anthropology that quantitatively tells it the world is a lot like it already understood it to be (Price 2010b).

Ethnographers' sympathies commonly, even naturally, ebb toward those they study; yet the complexities of employment can shift such delicate alignments in ways that leave ethnographers conceiving of themselves as aligned with populations they simultaneously render vulnerable to employers. Anthropologists' alignments with power transform their work, and anthropologists working for militaries in war zones frequently convince themselves that the cultural knowledge they collect and process reduces, rather than creates, vulnerabilities.

Neil Whitehead argued that ethnography can share features of interrogation. In similar ways, counterinsurgently aligned anthropology's root commitment to social engineering links it to a range of corporate applied anthropological projects that seek not to represent and advocate for the "research subjects"[2] in ways historically associated with Sol Tax's "action anthropology" approach, but instead strives to make these research subjects legible or align them with the desires of power (Tax 1950).

Although many applied anthropological projects align ethnographers with those they study, increasing numbers of corporate sector applied projects position anthropologists as allies with employers. In this sense, counterinsurgent anthropological projects can be viewed as a subset of applied anthropological projects striving to make research subjects vulnerable to employers. In the context of drone wars, or militarized environments where anthropological knowledge is used to inform military actions in human or robotic-dominated environments, anthropologists increasingly take on roles of cultural engineers.

McFate's early vision of the coming linkage between on the ground ethnographic engagements and technological dominance from above assumed that anthropological knowledge could be used for forms of social engineering that would allow military anthropologists to manipulate those they studied. What her writings and those of fellow counterinsurgency supporters do not address is just how difficult it is for anthropologists, or anyone else, to successfully pull off the sort of massive cultural engineering project needed for a counterinsurgency-based victory in Iraq or Afghanistan. Those advocating anthropologically informed counterinsurgency are remarkably silent concerning just how difficult it is to bring about engineered culture change. There is no mention of applied anthropologists' failures to get people to do simple things (like recycling, losing weight, reducing behaviors associated with the spread of disease, etc.) that are arguably in their own self-interest. These writings do not address the fact that no amount of cultural shinola can hide from occupied people the brutal facts of their situation—yet this is just what complex counterinsurgency seeks to do. As Roberto González observed, "The fact that some social scientists have warmly embraced HTS reveals historical amnesia, opportunism, and a profound lack of imagination" (personal communication, August 16, 2009).

Whereas counterinsurgency techniques can assist military operations, reducing casualties, and smoothing over interactions in particular operations, historically they have rarely been used to achieve military victories by foreign military forces. Counterinsurgency operations can be used to great advantage by domestic political and military powers (because domestic powers do not have to struggle for *legitimacy*), but foreign powers lack such forms of local legitimacy, and thus the efforts by foreign military and political forces to successfully use counterinsurgency to achieve military victory have been rare (see Price 2009a).

Today's counterinsurgency advocates think they can leverage social structure and hegemonic narratives so that the occupied will internalize their own captivity as "freedom." The metaphor of "leveraging" culture is an enduring one with great currency in military-counterinsurgency circles; Kilcullen values it so highly that he considers "the highest level of cultural capability is the ability to use culture to generate leverage within an insurgent system" (Kilcullen 2009a:224; see also Price 2010a).

Beyond HTS, the military and U.S. State Department can come up with other counterinsurgent uses for anthropologists—many of which will not alarm anthropologists in the ways that HTS does, with its armed presence. But given the manipulative forms of cultural engineering goals behind these projects, many of the same ethical and political issues are raised by anthropologists' participation in this work. Anthropologists and others being recruited to try and enact these counterinsurgency dreams risk confusing assisting in the occupation and subjugation in the wake of military decimation with engaging in humanitarian work. Soft power's reliance on the sweetness of building hospitals, building schools, microloans, and other agents of apparently gentle persuasions will help bring many liberals into the counterinsurgency fold, but it does not resolve the problems of the larger project even if the machines seeking our help are armed not with bombs and bullets but with the needed loans, food, water, health, and infrastructure (see Price 2010a).

NOTES

This chapter benefited from the comments and critiques of Jeff Birkenstein, Alexander Cockburn, Sverker Finnström, Maximilian Forte, Roberto González, Hugh Gusterson, Cathy Lutz, Steve Niva, Marshall Sahlins, Jeffery St. Clair, and Neil Whitehead. An earlier version appeared in *CounterPunch* (Price 2009b).

1. It should be noted that David Kilcullen rejects notions that HTS social scientists are engaged in "armed social work," writing: "Some critics of the application of social science to counterinsurgency have decried [the statement that 'counterinsurgency is armed social work'] as a perversion of the independence and 'impartiality' of disciplines like anthropology and sociology. While I firmly believe that these disciplines do indeed have a valid and valuable role in counterinsurgency—efforts to improve U.S. troops' cultural understanding of local societies have saved hun-

dreds of Iraqi and Afghan lives through the Human Terrain System program, for example—I would emphasize that this article is talking about something else: not 'armed social science' but social work—community organizing, welfare, mediation, domestic assistance, economic support—under conditions of extreme threat requiring armed support" (Kilcullen 2009a:43, note). Yet it remains odd that he does not include the discipline of social work in the group of fields who have decried his perversion of claiming counterinsurgency is "armed social work." If there are any social workers who welcome such notions, I do not know who they are.

2. In this instance I abandon contemporary respectful terms of "research participants" in favor of "research subjects" because their lack of acquired meaningful voluntary informed consent means they have become objectified "subjects."

CYBERNETIC CRYSTAL BALL

"Forecasting" Insurgency in Iraq and Afghanistan

Imagine a humanoid robot that calculates which neighborhoods in a distant city—Baghdad, Kabul, or Islamabad—are most dangerous. The android's computerized voice informs users whether these neighborhoods are prone to riots, gun violence, sniper attacks, or bombings. It forecasts when these events are likely to occur. With all the speed and imagery of a video game, the robot's glowing display screen also identifies the names of people who are likely participants in the violence, as well as their addresses, fingerprints, photos, and names of relatives, friends, and associates.

Such a machine might appear to be beyond the realm of possibility, but the U.S. Department of Defense (DOD) is spending hundreds of millions of dollars to create a cybernetic crystal ball that predicts hot spots, ranging from organized protest marches to full-blown insurgent attacks, in occupied Iraq and Afghanistan. Many of these efforts have been funded through a series of social "forecasting" initiatives officially called Human Social Culture and Behavior Modeling (HSCB). According to the DOD (U.S. Department of Defense 2009a:1), the overarching goal "is to enable DOD and the US Government to understand and effectively operate in the human terrain during non-conventional warfare and other missions." Pentagon planners, weapons manufacturers, military contract corporations, and university researchers who have been awarded DOD grants hope that some of the raw data for HSCB programs will come from teams collecting demographic and ethnographic information—what military personnel refer to as "human terrain" data—from the Middle East and central Asia. They are deriving data sets from the work of medical researchers, economists, political scientists, psychologists, and others as well.

A newsletter published by the Office of the Secretary of Defense titled *Human Social Culture Behavior Modeling Newsletter* gives some insight into the extraordinarily ambitious range of projects under way in this burgeoning field. The first issue features an article about a Target Audience Simulation Kit for Influence Operations (TASK-10), a product developed by a Michigan-based company called Soar Technology. TASK-10 simulates how a "virtual target audience" will react to "influence operations," such as "a simple presence patrol in an Iraqi neighborhood" or "the strategic use of 'shock and awe' to guide an invasion" (Taylor 2009:3). The program "implements facets of Cultural Schema Theory, specifically to capture the mental representations and processes used by members of a culture in understanding and behaving in their environments," as well as "Appraisal Theory to capture how perceived events and situations are evaluated with respect to an actor's needs, goals, and expectations." These social science theories originate primarily from the fields of communication studies and psychology, but a Soar Technology researcher, Glenn Taylor, has also been influenced by the work of the cognitive anthropologist Roy D'Andrade.

In the same issue of the newsletter, a piece titled "HSCB: How We Got Here and the Next Steps" notes that "in fairly short order we progressed from modeling largely quantitative logistics interactions and movements onward to war-games with multi-variate interactions between quantitative and qualitative data and player units in more dynamic 'free play' exercises, and now to building the means to model true the 'soft factors' that are so essential to HSCB programs. . . . [They involve] a combination of detailed research, increased computing power, and a joining of social sciences and computing approaches" (Schwark 2009:9).

A subsequent issue features reviews of programs like AutoMap, "a text-mining system for extracting semantic networks from texts and then cross-classifying the information using an organizational ontology into the underlying social, knowledge, belief, resource, and task networks. . . .

[It] has been used to extract information on the North Korean political elite, Hamas, al-Qaeda, and activities in the Sudan from open source texts" (U.S. DOD 2009b:13). The program was developed by a computer science research group at Carnegie Mellon University with support from the National Science Foundation and the U.S. Army.

The *Human Social Culture Behavior Modeling Newsletter* also highlights HSCB communications research and notes that an ongoing project is focused on improving "strategic communication" by countering the "narratives" of insurgents and extremists. The project "is developing a pragmatic model of narrative, consisting of archetypes, story forms, stories, and narratives." According to the article, the West Point–based project "will lead to a relational database of these elements, stocked from extremist rhetoric using linguistic analysis of explicit stories plus humanistic study of narrative fragments" (Holladay 2009:16).

I inadvertently stumbled across this technological world while researching the origins of the human terrain concept, an idea rooted in domestic counterinsurgency efforts in the late 1960s, when U.S. spy agencies hoped to neutralize the Black Panthers and other militant groups. After a long hiatus, human terrain resurfaced and expanded quickly across many domains—including technological ones. Now it is among the main concepts being deployed in the virtual worlds of behavioral modeling and simulation.

HSCB modeling and simulation programs offer a glimpse into the future of twenty-first-century warfare and military occupation. In some ways, "forecasting" insurgency represents the merging of two streams: technical engineering approaches to war (commonly associated with unmanned drones, "precision-guided" munitions, laser weapons, night vision goggles, cyber-warfare, etc.) and social engineering approaches to war (commonly associated with mass behavior modification, psychological warfare and operations, "strategic hamlet" and other forced relocation programs, military checkpoints, rural development schemes, etc.). Though some observers have claimed that in recent years, there has been a struggle between these approaches—sometimes described as the Rumsfeld way of war versus the Gates way of war (or "hard" versus "soft" power)—it is clear that both share many basic assumptions: a belief in the necessity of U.S.-led military occupation and its absolute benevolence, a faith in hyperreductive positivism, and a deep underlying ethnocentrism rooted in the idea of American exceptionalism (the idea that our society is fundamentally different from and superior to other societies). Significantly, corporations often sell the tools for employing both "hard" products and "soft" services. BAE Systems produces high-tech Bradley tanks and trains Human Terrain System (HTS) employees; L-3 Communications manufactures surveillance equipment and military-grade lasers and also provides "knowledge management" services; Science Applications International Corporation creates components for the Mine Resistant Ambush Protected vehicle and delivers support services for biometric data collection, intelligence services, and linguistic expertise; Lockheed Martin builds the F-35 Lightning II fighter jet and offers "counterterrorism analysis" courses focused on "terrorist threat profiling" and "the Jihadi mindset" at its Center for Security Analysis; and Textron designs and constructs the Bell UH-1Y "Huey" combat helicopter and is developing a version of the Mapping the Human Terrain (MAP-HT) computer program. Clearly, a driving force behind the growth of cybernetic software and modeling and simulation programs is the power and influence of "Pentagon capitalism" (Melman 1970). As the editors of this volume have suggested (see the introduction), "war is increasingly becoming a never-ending social routine among other open-ended social routines."

This is not the first time that the Pentagon has created an initiative integrating hard and soft power. In the late 1960s, Pentagon officials famously used IBM mainframe computers to compile ethnographic and demographic information collected by U.S. civil affairs officers to eventually create a database of suspected Viet Cong supporters. U.S. advisors, mercenaries, and South Vietnamese soldiers then used the database—called the Viet Cong Infrastructure Information System (VCIIS)—to methodically assassinate more than 25,000 people, mostly civilians. According to Douglas Valentine (1990:259), "VCIIS became the first of a series of computer programs designed to absolve the war effort of human error and war managers of individual responsibility." For its users, the program magically transformed what would otherwise appear to be a subjective, arbitrary, and messy assassination campaign into a rational, objective, and antiseptic process of controlling the human "infrastructure." Such episodes stand as a warning to those who uncritically accept the notion that high-tech or cybernetic tools offer a more enlightened means of fighting wars or occupying foreign lands.

Emergent modeling and simulation programs also challenge the popular nineteenth-century idea (still current among many today) that only "primitive" societies practice magic. According to this notion, science all but replaced magic in "civilized" societies with a few odd exceptions: the lucky rabbit's foot, persistent taboos involving black cats, and other quirky beliefs were simply remnants of the premodern, prescientific past. But in many ways, the new computer-based modeling and simulation programs appear as a form of twenty-first-century magic—a way of helping anxious Pentagon planners, military commanders, and combat soldiers cope with unpredictable and uncertain situations. The programs also have the potential of creating a kind of dark magic (perhaps *witchcraft* is a better term) that introduces a sense of terror and even paranoia among people in the United States who fear they might become targets of domestic surveillance or who might begin to believe that Iraqi and Afghan "Others" are irremediable members of an alien, enemy culture—not fellow humans worthy of cross-cultural understanding. What is more, Pentagon modeling and simulation initiatives reveal a peculiar cybernetic version of "culture" itself—that is, culture as a discrete set of codifiable (and even programmable) behaviors, phobias, attitudes, gestures, and symbols. Under such circumstances, culture appears as a heuristic device, a form of virtuality engineered to effectively leverage "kinetic" actions by military units.

BUILDING A "WORLD IN A BOTTLE"

Recent Pentagon budget documents reveal a clear commitment to "cultural knowledge" acquisition, and today a small but growing group of engineers, mathematicians, and computer scientists are tapping into DOD funding and access to ethnographic data for modeling and simulation programs.

Among them is Barry Silverman (2007), a University of Pennsylvania engineering professor who bluntly asked in the title of a research report: "Human Terrain Data: What Should We Do with It?" Silverman and his team of graduate students developed computerized behavior modeling programs designed to uncover the hidden motivations of terrorists and their networks, and they hope to integrate information collected by HTS teams into these programs. Their simulations, funded by the Pentagon's Defense Modeling and Simulation Office, integrate "more than 100 models and theories from anthropology, psychology, and political science, combined with empirical data taken from medical and social science field research, surveys, and experiments." The goal is to predict how terrorists, soldiers, or ordinary citizens might react to "a gun pointed in the face, a piece of chocolate offered by a soldier. . . . [Silverman] is now simulating a small society of about 15,000 leader and follower agents organized into tribes, which squabble over resources" (Goldstein 2006).

Silverman's simulations incorporate "physical stressors such as ambient temperature, hunger, and drug use; resources such as time, money, and skills; attitudes such as moral outlook, religious feelings, and political affiliations; and personality dispositions such as response to time pressure, workload, and anxiety" (Goldstein 2006). Silverman (2007) notes that "the HT [human terrain] datasets are an invaluable resource that will permit us in the human behavior M&S [modeling and simulation] field to more realistically profile factions, and their leaders and followers." Ironically, he has not yet obtained data from the U.S. Army's HTS program.

Gary Ackerman, director of the Center for Terrorism and Intelligence Studies (a division of Akribis Group, a security company based in San Jose, California), provides a vivid description of the way modeling and simulation programs work. "There are tools where they build a world in a bottle. They put down every single mosque, river, camel, and school in, say, Saudi Arabia. Then they have millions of software agents who each have desires, grievances, all these different variables. They go about their little lives and then you ask a question: What if we build a McDonald's in Mecca? Does this lead to more people joining terrorist groups or not?" (Goldstein 2006). Ackerman's comments reveal an extraordinarily reductionistic perspective that dismisses context and complexity. It treats the virtual "little lives" of Saudi avatars as mere stimuli receptors that react in knowable, predictable ways to the arrival of Big Macs, Happy Meals, and Ronald McDonald to the most sacred Islamic site.

Dartmouth researchers have created the Laboratory for Human Terrain, "focused on the foundational science and technology for modeling, representing, inferring, and analyzing individual and organizational behaviors" (Dartmouth Laboratory for Human Terrain 2009). It includes an engineer, a mathematician, and a computer scientist who specialize in "adversarial intent modeling, simulation, and prediction," "dynamic social network analysis," and "discovery of hidden relationships and organizations." The Pentagon awarded a $250,000 grant for one member to develop an algorithm for "predicting how individuals or groups . . . react to social, cultural, political, and economic interactions. . . . [It] can evaluate how rhetoric from religious leaders combined with recent allied killing of radical military leaders, and perceptions of potential economic growth

3.1 A researcher at the Naval Postgraduate School in Monterey, California, demonstrates the computerized Modeling, Virtual Environments, and Simulation (MOVES) program using an urban warfare training exercise, July 2009. Photo courtesy of the U.S. Navy.

can cause shifts in support from moderate or radical leadership" (Dartmouth Laboratory for Human Terrain 2009).

Another wartime simulation project includes Purdue University's Synthetic Environment for Analysis and Simulation (SEAS) which "gobble[s] up breaking news, census data, economic indicators, and climactic events in the real world, along with proprietary information such as military intelligence." Purdue's Iraq and Afghanistan computer models each have "about five million individual nodes that represent entities such as hospitals, mosques, pipelines, and people" (Erwin 2007).

Other researchers are orienting their work toward the creation of three-dimensional computerized avatars designed to improve the cultural competency of U.S. soldiers. Glenn Taylor and Ed Sims have tried to create believable interactive characters that model the physical and cognitive behaviors of people from different societies. Their efforts focus on modeling the behavior of Arabs; to this end Taylor and a colleague have identified more than two hundred physical gestures from interviews with Baghdad residents. Their goal is the creation of a training tool that relies on humanoid three-dimensional avatars that can be displayed on computer screens. The researchers note:

There are many subtleties of communication that are not immediately apparent to someone unfamiliar with that culture: gestures, eye contact behaviors, and the like. The focus of our physical 3D models is in the generation of these subtleties. . . . [Our software system] has developed a library of culture-specific avatars, gestures and expressions that can be invoked on demand. These libraries consist of over 60 culturally diverse virtual human models as well as 40 facial expressions and 500 gestures, and can automatically lip-sync to over 22 mouth shapes that map to over 100 speech sounds of the International Phonetic Alphabet. (Taylor and Sims 2009:4)

This research, funded by the DOD, also attempts to integrate "cultural cognitive architecture" that uses "knowledge learned by living in that culture: knowledge about the correct ways to interact (e.g., norms), about what is important in the culture (e.g., values), etc." (Taylor and Sims 2009:4). By creating virtual Iraqis, the researchers hope to provide a low-cost alternative to "immersion in a target culture."

Another research group from the Art and Technology Program of the University of Texas at Dallas has designed the First Person Cultural Trainer, an interactive computer game designed to teach military personnel about Iraqi and Afghan ideas and values. According to the lead investigator, Marjorie Zielke, "Much of the cultural data is being developed in real time by the military. . . . We can generate culture in certain aspects of the game on the fly. . . . We could change it overnight if we needed to." In this game, the player views an Iraqi or Afghan village or neighborhood from a "first-person" point of view, and the goal is "to understand the social structures and issues, then address those issues and work with the community to affect [military] missions." Virtual villagers form opinions based on how the player interacts with them, while the player gathers data about characters from his or her observation of "verbal and non-verbal cues" (University of Texas at Dallas 2010).

This video game—sponsored by the U.S. Army's Training and Doctrine Command and G-2 Intelligence Support Activity—reveals several remarkable things. The notion that culture can be generated "on the fly" or even "overnight" implies that programmers have the ability to shape and reshape human values, norms, thoughts, and behaviors at will. Furthermore, the creators of the game appear to believe that "cultural data" collected by U.S. soldiers on the battlefield can be used to generate an increasingly accurate model of Iraqi or Afghan culture—as if there is a simple, predictable means of accomplishing this aim. The problem is that such efforts pursue an outdated model of a reified, neatly bounded, homogeneous culture that doesn't really exist. Finally, throughout this process it appears that the programmers (and those playing the game) are viewing Iraqis and Afghanis not as people but as nonpersons, virtual persons. This kind of dehumanization process in many ways resembles the workings of witchcraft, as Sverker Finnström notes in this volume (see chapter 5).

At Carnegie Mellon University, sociologist Kathleen Carley heads the Center for Computational Analysis of Social and Organizational Systems, which includes a team of thirty researchers, that works with the Central Intelligence Agency, the Army Research Laboratory, and the Office of Naval Research, among others. The engineering journal *IEEE Spectrum* reports that Carley's group has developed a "counterterrorism software package" made up of three components: "a program that constructs social networks from text files such as newspaper stories and intelligence reports; one that statistically profiles networks in terms of subgroups, individuals, resources, and communications; and a multi-agency simulator that shows how social networks evolve over time" (Goldstein 2006).

MODEL TERRORISTS AND VIRTUAL "TRIBES"

The research projects under way at the University of Pennsylvania, Dartmouth, Purdue, University of Texas at Dallas, and Carnegie Mellon are only five examples in a growing field in which "culture," "tribes," "moral outlook," and other constructs appear as independent variables in equations that do not recognize the ambiguity, creativity, or characteristic unpredictability of *Homo sapiens*. It is as if the programmers and researchers are helping military personnel view human beings as dehumanized nonpersons.

The Pentagon has budgeted nearly $200 million to funding similar research under the auspices of HSCB between 2008 and 2013 (see table 3.1). Since "current military operations need and future operations will demand the capability to understand the social and cultural terrain and the various dimensions of human behavior within those terrains," the research program "will develop technologies for human terrain understanding and forecasting" for "intelligence analysis," "database infrastructure," "human behavior based theory for DOD models," and "visualization infrastructure" (U.S. Secretary of Defense 2009:1). The program is

TABLE 3.1

U.S. Department of Defense Budget for Human Social Culture Behavioral Modeling

FISCAL YEAR	AMOUNT (IN MILLIONS OF DOLLARS)
2008	10.21
2009	23.06
2010	28.44
2011 (projected)	29.80
2012 (projected)	48.62
2013 (projected)	57.40
Total	197.52

Source: Office of the U.S. Secretary of Defense (2008), *RDT&E Budget Item Justification (R2 Exhibit)*; http://www.dtic.mil/descriptivesum/Y2009/OSD/0602670D8Z.pdf.

geared toward "development of the methods and tools to allow remote and 'boots on the ground' collection of pedigreed social and cultural information relating to a population (local, regional, global), including the print, voice, and video media, social networks, and cultural, religious, and tribal alliances" (U.S. Secretary of Defense 2009:1).

A prime goal of HSCB is forecasting human behavior. According to the program description, "work will focus on computational/analytical anthropological data collection, theory development, and application methodologies and tools" for creating software "to allow decision makers (intelligence analysts, operations analysts, operations planners, wargamers) to have available forecasting tools for socio-cultural (human terrain) responses at the strategic, operational, and tactical levels" (U.S. Secretary of Defense 2009:3).

Another crucial goal of HSCB is predicting the effects of U.S. military actions on people living under occupation. In more euphemistic terms, the "creation of validated, human terrain forecasting models that enable examination of 2nd, 3rd, and higher order effects of kinetic and non-kinetic actions within a theater in support of Effects Based Operations." (In military parlance, the phrase "kinetic action" is a euphemism for bombings, shootings, or other lethal attacks.) According to the HSCB description, such "work will provide DOD capability to model intended or unintended political, military, economic, societal, infrastructure, and information effects of military actions" (U.S. Secretary of Defense 2009:4).

VISUALIZING THE FUTURE WITH HUMAN TERRAIN MAPPING

Apart from HSCB, another project designed to help predict human behavior is under way. MAP-HT, Mapping the Human Terrain, was initially conceived in 2006 as an integral part of the U.S. Army's HTS. According to early documents describing HTS, team members would record ethnographic data on computers equipped with MAP-HT, which would in turn transmit it to a centralized database accessible by other U.S. government agencies—and eventually by Iraqi and Afghan governments.

In an unclassified document dated August 2006, Pentagon staff reported:

> Operations depend on the military's ability to operate effectively in a foreign society. . . . One of the most important intelligence objectives is to ensure that operators in the field have knowledge of host populations: social structure (ethnic groups, tribes, elite networks, institutions, organizations and the relationships between them), culture (roles/statuses, social norms and sanctions, beliefs, values, and belief systems), cultural forms (myths, narratives, rituals, symbols), and power and authority relationships. This information must be appropriately linked to geospatial coordinates and provide a basic map of the human terrain that will improve the operational effectiveness of US forces. (U.S. DOD 2006:14)

By February 2007, the Office of the Secretary of Defense's budget draft provided a more explicit description:

> The outcome of MAP-HT is to develop an integrated, open source, spatially/relationally/temporally referenced human terrain data collection and visualization toolkit to support BCT/RCTs [brigade combat teams/regimental combat teams] in understanding human terrain. The objective is to deploy MAP-HT toolkit to Joint, Interagency, Intergovernmental, and Multinational (JIMM) elements (e.g. USAID, DEA, Coalition Partners). . . . MAP-HT will provide a joint common relevant picture of the human terrain for use by tactical elements, operational commanders, theater planners, interagency organizations, and coalition partners. . . . A capability (people, process, and tools) must be

further developed to provide a means for commanders and their supporting operations sections to collect data on human terrain, create, store, and disseminate information from this data, and use the resulting understanding as an element of combat power. (U.S. Secretary of Defense 2007:18)

Ultimately, the Pentagon chose a company called Overwatch Systems—a subsidiary of weapons giant Textron—to develop MAP-HT following several failed attempts to implement the toolkit. According to one former HTS member I interviewed, early versions of MAP-HT were useless; another told me that the program was so poorly designed that it was "sitting on a shelf." Overwatch System's website states (as of this writing) that MAP-HT is a part of the Army's Joint Capability Technology Demonstration program and will move "beyond the JCTD to fielding and deployment in multiple Areas of Operation" (Overwatch Systems 2011). However, MAP-HT has reportedly "failed to materialize in any form" according to investigative journalist John Stanton (2010).

For more than a century, colonial administrators and imperial police forces have recognized the importance of "human terrain" mapping. Joseph Gallieni (1849–1916), a French commander and colonial administrator who was stationed in Indochina, French Sudan, and Madagascar during the late 1800s, described how ethnographic intelligence was essential for social control: "An officer who succeeds in drawing a sufficiently exact ethnographic map of the territory he commands has almost reached its complete pacification. . . . If there are customs and habits to respect, there are also rivalries which we have to untangle and utilize to our profit, by opposing the ones to the others, and by basing ourselves on the ones in order to defeat the others" (Salemink 1999:282–83). Under these conditions, social science can easily become a martial art—a tool or a technique to be sold to the highest bidder.

ROLE PLAYING AND VIDEO GAMING

The possibility of forecasting insurgent attacks has led Pentagon officials to prepare and plan for countermeasures. Computerized role-playing exercises and video games are already used for this purpose. For example, the U.S. Army's National Training Center (NTC) in Fort Irwin, California, has developed software called Reactive Information Propagation Planning for Lifelike Exercises (RIPPLE) to improve battlefield intelligence:

3.2 A U.S. Army National Guardsman detains a role player in a mock Iraqi village located at the National Training Center in Fort Irwin, California, March 2009. Photo courtesy of the U.S. Air Force.

"RIPPLE is network-modeling and artificial intelligence software that tracks all role players, roles, and relationships among the 1600 Iraqi role players. It maps all social, familial, and business relationships in the scenario as well as each role player's personal history and motivation. Based on this mapping the NTC can dynamically assess and model the effects of [U.S.] unit interaction with Iraqi role players" (Cone 2006).

The NTC handles much more than just software development. At this site, in the middle of the Mojave Desert, the U.S. Army has constructed several mock villages from scratch and has employed resident Iraqi Americans for twenty-eight-day stints in which they play assigned roles of insurgents, allies, and neutral Iraqis while U.S. combat units practice counterinsurgency techniques in a virtual battlefield that resembles an eerie kind of parallel universe (see figure 3.2). The NTC employs film industry producers, directors, actors, and special effects technicians who have helped develop scripts and scenarios, train role players, and create explosive special effects—all to replicate the sights, sounds, and smells of occupied Iraq (Cone 2006). This surreal, magical theater blurs the lines between fantasy and reality.

The Air Force Research Lab has requested new proposals for modeling programs and suggests that "researchers should investigate cultural, motivational, historical, political, and economic data to determine if there are mathematical and statistical models that can be used to predict the formation of terrorist activities." According to the request, the "goal is to determine sets of actions that can influence the root cause behaviors and cultivate a culture that does not support the development of criminal activity," an objective that effectively puts the air force in the business of social engineering (Schachtman 2007a).

The Office of Naval Research has requested proposals for a simulation tool resembling a video game: "We are looking for innovative ideas that explore and harness the power of 'advanced' interactive multimedia computer games (e.g. 'sim games') . . . [incorporating] the best-practices of the videogame industry, including intuitive controls, story-telling, user-feedback . . . scenario editing, and high quality graphics & sound" (Schachtman 2007b). The navy also issued a separate request for "rapid ethnographic assessment," which illustrates how human terrain data might fit into ongoing projects:

> The aim is to better understand the socio-cultural context in which these military missions operate. . . . [Rapid Ethnographic Assessment] will ensure that military analysts will not just collect data, but also be able to know what data matters, in order to make sense of tribal, ethnic, and social class relationships, understand environmental factors (for example, the control of water in arid climates), land rights, disputes, the role of religion in everyday life, and the structure of the elites. . . . Candidate methodologies include: cognitive anthropology, social network analysis, other methodologies with a structuralist focus, linguistics, applied anthropology, development anthropology. (Schachtman 2007b)

This proposal and others like it reveal a deeper point—that ethnographic research conducted under such rigid rules and restrictions is flawed because it involves acquiring data that conforms to predetermined theories for consumption by computer scientists, modelers, simulators, programmers, or engineers. This takes ethnography far from the methodological prescriptions of anthropologists like E. E. Evans-Pritchard (1937:242), who eloquently and convincingly argued that the reality of informants must direct research: "The anthropologist must follow what he finds in the society he has selected for study. . . . I had no interest in witchcraft when I went to Zandeland, but the Azande had; so I had to let myself be guided by them. I had no particular interest in cows when I went to Nuerland, but the Nuer had, so willy-nilly I had to become cattle-minded too." More recently, anthropologist Don Handelman (2009:220) stated: "There is little point, little incentive to doing longer-term intensive fieldwork if the problematic to be studied is established ideologically before the student goes to the field. And when the purpose of fieldwork itself becomes more anecdotal, of fragments that will be used in order to illustrate the theoretical presuppositions established prior to coming to the field." The blatantly ideological form of ethnography employed by the Office of Naval Research, the U.S. Army, BAE Systems, and other parts of the military-industrial complex in many ways resembles the ethnography used in certain kinds of applied anthropology (for example, development anthropology and marketing anthropology)—which have become a growth industry. As Neil Whitehead and Sverker Finnström note in the introduction to this volume, "The deeper question [is] to what extent the apparent facility of such information sharing represents a hidden history of the epistemology of ethnography itself, making it uncomfortably similar to the agonistic processes of torture, which then appears as a shortcut rather than a negation of ethnographic inquiry."

It is not difficult to imagine scenarios in the near future in which agents use cultural profiles, social network analyses, and "visualization of the human terrain" for preemptive targeting of statistically probable (rather than actual) insurgents or extremists in Iraq, Afghanistan, Pakistan, or other countries deemed to be havens for terrorists. Perhaps we are not so far away from the dystopian visions of science fiction writer Philip K. Dick. In his 1956 story *The Minority Report*, he describes a society in which three babbling mutants are supposedly able to foresee crimes days before they occur. The data they produce is channeled into powerful computers designed to help police prevent crimes, but the protagonist of the story learns that mutants and computers are all too capable of misjudging future events.

SOCIAL ENGINEERING AND THE SOCIAL SCIENCES

DOD forecasting raises at least three sets of questions. First, there are basic questions of utility: Does the Pentagon really need to model the political, economic, and societal effects of U.S. actions like aerial assaults—for example, the destructive attack on the village of Granai, Afghanistan, in May 2009 that killed 143 civilians? Will HSCB, SEAS, MAP-HT, or other programs lead to startling new insights regarding what Iraqis or Afghanis think about living under military occupation, or about government corruption, or about neoliberal shock therapy? (Neoliberal policies such as those analyzed in Naomi Klein's book *The Shock Doctrine* [2007] have created such misery and desperation that they might be considered a form of global economic warfare—though at times those being attacked reside within the borders of the so-called first world.) Although the answers would be relatively straightforward for many anthropologists, and indeed, for many ordinary citizens, there appear to be some within the military and intelligence establishments unable to comprehend why others would be angry or resentful about military occupation. As David Price (2009a) has noted, counterinsurgency advocates apparently think "they can leverage social structure and hegemonic narratives so that the occupied will internalize their own captivity as freedom," a kind of twenty-first-century magical spirit possession that would allow U.S. officers to transform the very substance of Iraqi and Afghani souls.[1]

A second set of questions has to do with what Hugh Gusterson (2009) calls the "epistemology of confidence" underlying the efforts of counterinsurgency's proponents, a confidence that treats societies "like machines whose behavior can be diagrammed and predicted." What are we to make of hyperpositivist statements like those made by Steve Fondacaro (director of the HTS), who argues that "when you have a fundamental knowledge of how tribes work, you can non-kinetically neutralize enemies using those relationships" (quoted in Beyerstein 2007)? What are we to make of U.S. Army Lieutenant Colonel John Nagl's extraordinary statement: "The soldiers who win these [counterinsurgency] wars require an ability not just to dominate land operations, *but to change entire societies*" (quoted in Bacevich 2007; emphasis added)? Fondacaro and Nagl are influential members of what some refer to as a "cult of counterinsurgency"—a group whose members portray themselves as revolutionaries railing against the Pentagon's old guard, but who in fact are thoroughly entrenched in both the civilian and military hierarchies of the DOD. As their words make clear, counterinsurgency involves much more than rooting out "insurgents"—the goal is nothing less than "to change entire societies," which is social engineering on a sweeping scale. For this reason, the Pentagon, its subcontractors, and other components of the military-industrial complex have become increasingly attracted to the work of social scientists.

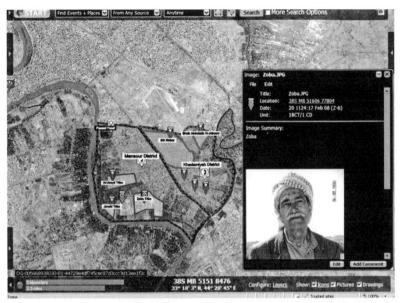

3.3 Many proponents of the Pentagon's "new" counterinsurgency methods appear to be supremely confident in the ability to predict and control the behavior of people living under military occupation in Iraq and Afghanistan. Photo courtesy of the U.S. Army.

More than a few scholars have responded to the call, which raises a third set of questions: By what processes are social scientists—ostensibly trained to reflect critically on their work—able easily to transform a landscape of homes reduced to rubble, of refugee camps, of charred flesh and mass graves into a grid of color-coded tribal maps, flow charts, Venn diagrams, and bar graphs, ready to be inserted into a PowerPoint slide show? The magical transformation of war's violence is perhaps the inevitable product of "security-speak elites with an interest in perpetuating war rather than finding solutions" to it (Robben 2009:3).

At the height of the cold war, C. Wright Mills (1961:114) cautioned social scientists about the "bureaucratic ethos." He was concerned about the rapid transformation of scientists into mere technicians of power, lacking any sense of social responsibility. Mills's criticism of social engineers advocating "prediction and control" was devastating: "To talk so glibly as many do about prediction and control is to assume the perspective of the bureaucrat to whom, as Marx once remarked, the world is an object to be manipulated. . . . But we, as social scientists, may not assume that we are dealing with objects that are so highly manipulable, and we may

not assume that among men we are enlightened despots. . . . No historical society is constructed within a frame as rigid as that enclosing my
hypothetical army division. Nor are social scientists—let us be grateful—
generals of history."[2]

Perhaps there are more valuable contributions for critically minded
social scientists to make—for instance, a more detailed exposition of
twenty-first-century positivism, a modern-day Machiavellian mentality
encompassing technical and social engineering approaches applied in
zones of neocolonial occupation. A more critical social science field might
ask how these technical and sociocultural engineering approaches—what
might be called the Donald Rumsfeld and Robert Gates / Leon Panetta
ends of an American counterinsurgency continuum—effectively reflect
today's "conservative" and "liberal" approaches to empire. Those who
hoped for a different approach from President Barack Obama have been
disappointed: the defense budget for 2012 authorized $707.5 billion for
the Pentagon's base budget and contingency operations in Afghanistan,
Pakistan, and other countries.

Assumptions underpinning the work of counterinsurgency technicians include a fundamental acceptance of modern warfare in general
and the ongoing U.S.-led occupations in particular. They subscribe to the
false notion that counterinsurgency is more antiseptic, more humane,
and less damaging than conventional warfare, and they adhere strictly
to Machiavellian principles: do not question the prince or his war, but
use the most efficient means to achieve his aims. Within this schema,
the new Machiavellians calmly discuss the relative merits of divide-and-
conquer strategies versus support of puppet governments, bribing stub-
born "tribals" versus threatening them with force, and "ethnic cleansing"
versus the construction of apartheid-style "separation barriers." It is hard
to know whether to be more shocked by the reckless proposals offered by
these planners in the name of "stability operations" (read: "pacification")
or by the cool equanimity with which they discuss these suggestions.

Under such circumstances, anthropologists clearly have an opportunity to support the new Machiavellians as they pursue a dream that is
both magical and technological: a cybernetic crystal ball that can forecast
insurgency and facilitate control. The human sciences might be used as a
means of prolonging the deadly self-delusions of social engineers.

But social scientists also have another opportunity: to hold up a mirror for critical self-reflection. Stepping back for a moment from the utilitarian, uncritically "applied" uses of our discipline, it is worth considering how anthropological insights might lead to a deeper understanding of what is occurring. In a trenchant analysis in *Magic, Science, and Religion*, the British anthropologist Bronislaw Malinowski (1948) suggested that *all* societies make use of these three forms of knowledge. Malinowski's research among fishermen in the Trobriand Islands revealed that the Trobrianders employed science—knowledge about the predictable, mundane world (tidal and lunar patterns, seasonal changes, and boat construction)—and also employed magic when undertaking relatively dangerous fishing trips on the open ocean. Magic, from Malinowski's perspective, thrives in any society whose members face unpredictable, hazardous situations.

Given such insights, a more critical and relevant social science might help us better understand why HSCB modeling and simulation and other forecasting programs are unfolding so rapidly. The boundaries between the techno-modern and the magico-primitive are largely irrelevant for understanding these computer programs. The "modern" cannot be separated from the "premodern": seen through an anthropological lens, the twenty-first-century technologies appear not so much as scientifically based tools for confronting knowable, predictable phenomena, but as amulets or talismans for dealing with dangerous, unknowable events by means of sacred formulae (or algorithms). At the very least, our discipline might suggest that computer programs, modeling and simulation software, and other cybernetic counterinsurgency tools are forms of magic (in the Malinowskian sense) that Pentagon planners and their corporate contractors employ in unpredictable, dangerous situations—popular uprisings, armed rebellions, peaceful revolutions, and demands for radical democratic change—over which they really have very little control.

NOTES

1. The interest in narratives is taking an increasingly important role in modeling and simulation. The Pentagon's Defense Advanced Research Projects Agency recently invited literary theorists, anthropologists, psychologists, and other social scientists to a meeting for a workshop on Stories, Neuroscience, and Experimental Technologies—with the goal "to establish fertile ground for connecting our understanding of the neuropsychology of stories with models, simulations, and sensors salient to security concerns" (Vanasco 2011).

2. Now, in the Petraeus era, some might argue that some social scientists have indeed become "generals of history": General David Petraeus holds a Ph.D. in international relations from Princeton University; Secretary of Defense Robert Gates holds a Ph.D. in history from Georgetown University; Lieutenant Colonel John Nagl holds a Ph.D. in political science from St. Antony's College, Oxford; and Lieutenant Colonel David Kilcullen holds a Ph.D. in politics from the University of New South Wales.

FULL SPECTRUM

The Military Invasion of Anthropology

THE DEPARTMENT OF DEFENSE'S CULTURAL REVOLUTION
Counterinsurgency Reborn

Military thinking was manifestly inadequate for the conquest of Iraq (Melillo 2006; West 2009). By mid-2004, that was obvious. According to one commander, "I had perfect situational awareness. What I lacked was cultural awareness. Great technical intelligence . . . wrong enemy" (Scales 2004:1). Major General Robert Scales (2004:3) called for a new form of "culture centric warfare," although his concept of culture was very limited, and his idea about implementation correspondingly undeveloped (2004:9; and see McFarland 2005:66).

Into this vacuum of military need stepped an anthropological entrepreneur, Montgomery McFate, who wrote of anthropologists' past participation in colonial, war-fighting projects as an advertisement for their potential utility today. She and others proposed a wide-ranging engagement of anthropology and military needs (McFate 2005a, 2005b; McFate and Jackson 2005). The proposals found enthusiastic backing from a circle of military intellectuals—"warrior-scholars"—who came out of West Point's Department of Social Sciences, or "Sosh" (Axe 2010:62–63). Number one was David Petraeus. In his vision, the military had to retool for a future of long wars—for population-centric counterinsurgency (COIN). Another major visionary from Sosh was John Nagl (Center for a New American Security n.d.), author of a history of counterinsurgencies (Nagl 2005).

Petraeus, Nagl, and those around them reanimated COIN theory, directed at "winning the hearts and minds" of the population in the counterinsurgency area of operations (Kilcullen 2006). To do that, cultural awareness and detailed ethnographic information are needed. As the debacle of Iraq became more glaringly apparent, higher powers in the Bush administration threw their weight behind this vision (Bacevich 2008). The new doctrine went public with FM 3-24, *Counterinsurgency* (Department of the Army [DOA] 2006; and see González 2009:8–12; Nagl n.d.).

Within two years of Scales's call for culture-centric warfare, culture-oriented programs were widespread. In September 2006, Mitre Corporation, which manages federally funded research and development centers, conducted a one-day conference called Socio-Cultural Perspectives: A New Intelligence Paradigm at the Center for National Security Programs in McLean, Virginia. Its premise was "that cultural intelligence is important for a wide range of national security endeavors and that this fact is increasingly recognized in many government quarters." Representatives of "more than 50 different government organizations attended the conference" (Friedland et al. 2007:iii, 9).[1]

The field has grown rapidly since that time. The Defense Science Board Task Force on Understanding Human Dynamics (DSB 2009) was tasked to compile information about every Department of Defense (DOD) "effort or group" dealing with "human dynamics/human terrain/culture" (2009:98–99). Their final table contains 111 entries, which does not include "the extensive network of expert cultural consultants" maintained by the Army, Air Force, and combat commands (DSB 2009:xiv). Even with this proliferation, the task force calls for "direct increases in the 'cultural bench' by factors of three to five" (2009:xiv–xv). That includes expanding curriculums in military education, improving career paths for human dynamics advisers, providing advanced degree education, and developing innovative processes for recruiting and rewarding outside expertise.

What is "culture" for the DOD? Military authors recognize, with distress, that there is no single definition of culture within anthropology or within culture-oriented sectors of the military. It is ruefully amusing to read that on the question of "what culture is and why it is important . . . at symposia and other technical workshops, once the subject of definitions is broached, whatever the purpose for the meeting, participants often become mired in a turf war" (Alrich 2008:37). Anthropologists are long accustomed to cacophony about culture, but for the DOD, this is a real problem. "Without a shared definition and ontology, the ability to link formal and computational models of culture to the wealth of cultural data collected in the field can be haphazard and some models will not be interoperable." Nevertheless, "it is unlikely that a single definition of culture will emerge, given that there is no common view as to why a single definition is needed." Different elements of the military see different applications of "culture" in their own tasks, so "the DOD may be better served by asking 'what it is about culture that the soldier needs to know to improve performance at the tactical, operational, and/or strategic level?' At each level, different aspects of culture are mission critical" (DSB 2009:70).

This diversity of needs within the DOD stems from the breadth of cultural applications. The military is fond of the phrase "full spectrum." In its application of culture, there are at least three spectrums. One is the spectrum from the raw recruit up through all the higher echelons and all the organizational divisions relating to field operations. All must be culturized. Another is the spectrum of deployments, from stability missions during "Phase 0," before armed conflict begins, through foreign security force assistance, to COIN and full-scale war. A third spectrum is the range of operations, from "kinetic" lethal attacks to nonlethal cooperation aimed at winning hearts and minds. Through all these spectrums, the unwavering objective is to fight smarter to win. The following is a typical statement: "The Army's operations concept is *full spectrum operations*: Army forces combine offensive, defensive, and stability or civil support operations simultaneously as part of an independent joint force to seize, retain, and exploit the initiative, accepting prudent risk to create opportunities to achieve decisive results. They employ synchronized action—lethal and nonlethal—proportional to the mission and informed by a thorough understanding of all variables of the operational environment" (DOA 2008:3-1).

Applying Culture in Areas of Operations

Most discussion of anthropological engagement focuses on actual war zones, as with human terrain teams. As discussed elsewhere (Ferguson 2011), claims by Human Terrain System (HTS) advocates that their actions support only nonlethal actions are belied by consistent statements by military writers that cultural awareness and ethnographic information are to be fully integrated into *all* of a commander's options. Information gathered by social scientists may be combined with other information and used in lethal targeting. This usage for killing is one reason anthropologists should not participate.

It is important to study the human terrain issue, in part because the topic is sufficiently discrete to throw stark light on broader ethical concerns. But human terrain teams are just a small piece of culture-oriented efforts in the field. Sociocultural approaches permeate the battle space. One critique of HTS from within military circles is that troops on multiple rotations long ago learned fundamentals of local cultural organization and interactions (Connable 2009:62; Ephron and Spring 2008:2; Sepp 2007:218). A journalist in Afghanistan found soldiers who had hardly heard of the HTS were diligently "mapping the human terrain" themselves and trying to assimilate culturally appropriate ways of interacting with the locals. Within military field operations, civil affairs and provincial reconstruction teams are already known for their special "linguistic and cultural skills," and the DOD is seeking ways to integrate them with HTS teams (QDR 2010:24–25).

To achieve decisive success in future missions, military writers call for two things: "cultural competence and situational awareness" (DOA 2009a:18). This requires turning members of the armed forces into conscious agents capable of intercultural actions. They must internalize the concept of culture and its role in shaping human life, and then use that competence to immerse themselves into and assimilate the particulars of local situations. "Such skills make a better warfighter AND a more dynamic civilian as the soldier moves back into a very competitive and global workforce" (Masellis 2009:14).

A few years ago this was just an idea being put in motion (McFate and Jackson 2005). The army created a new Training and Doctrine Culture Center, seeking ways "to leverage cultural knowledge to enhance military operation . . . from instruction for baseline Soldiers at the lowest level to key military decision makers at the highest" (Hajjar 2006:89). Soon, the need for cultural competence ascended to doctrine (DOA 2009a:1–24).

Culture-specific knowledge comes from compiling thorough knowledge of local society, which is imagined as a table of discrete variables, all of which can be operationally specified (DOA 2009a:1–7). A chart of "typical civil considerations" contains 115 cells, including such entries as ethnicity, social gathering places, security, gangs, parks, power grids, jails, religion, illicit organizations, visual (graffiti, signs), and religious gatherings (DOA 2009a:1–9). All are to be distilled into easy-to-understand map overlays (DOA 2009a:10) and, of course, PowerPoint slides (see Bumiller 2010).

These overall characteristics are to be made concrete and personal by being combined with network and event analysis of specific individuals, identified by name with notes, as emphasized in *Counterinsurgency* (DOA 2006, appendix B). The *Human Terrain Team Handbook* also details information to be collected for other kinds of mapping, including social networks, association matrixes, and event coordination registers (Finney 2008:36–37).

Being culturally attuned is expected to give U.S. forces almost a sixth sense in dealing with local populations, granting them the power to "anticipate the population actions, and detect subtle changes within the population. Actions inconsistent with the population's behavioral norms could be indicators of guerrilla activity, internal conflict, or the confirmation or denial of intelligence" (DOA 2009a:1–23). Put it all together, and what do you get? "A leader or Soldier has begun to achieve culturally influenced situational awareness when he/she can ask and answer such questions accurately: What is my adversary thinking and why? What are my Host Nation security forces thinking and why? What are groups of people thinking and why? What will my adversaries, groups of people, adjacent units, and coalition partners, and Host Nation security forces do if I take action w, and why? How are cultural factors influencing my operations? How can I make groups of people and Host Nation security forces do what I want them to do?" (DOA 2009a:1–26). As the DSB (2009:5) puts it, "Knowledge of the value system of an actual or potential competitor helps in deterring undesirable behaviors and compelling desirable behaviors."

ABOVE AND BEYOND

Discussion so far has been confined to a fairly delimited use of culture in military operations. But the DOD sees culture as one aspect of much wider knowledge integration, involving other sorts of data, other social science perspectives, higher levels of aggregation, and broader purposes of use. This larger vision is unknown to most anthropologists, even though it may transform the discipline. The following discussions tour these broader applications of culture.

To begin, cultural competency and ethnographic intelligence are required in organizational layers above soldiers in the field, beginning with commanders of larger units. They are enjoined: "Know the people, the topography, economy, history, religion, and culture. Know every village, road, field, population group, tribal leader, and ancient grievance. Your task is to become the world expert on your district" (DOA 2009a:C-2; Kilcullen 2006).

For strategic assessment and planning, this detailed knowledge must be made available in usable form at levels above individual areas of operations. Major General Michael Flynn, the head of military intelligence in Afghanistan, is behind a big push for theater-level comprehensive knowledge. Flynn, Matt Pottinger, and Paul Batchelor (2010) are scathing about the failure of traditional intelligence operations, which focus on covert information leading to killing enemies and the problem of improvised explosive devices. They note that established intelligence operations provide little information that is useful for leveraging the population against the insurgents, and this opacity gets worse the higher up you go: "The tendency to overemphasize detailed information about the enemy at the expense of the political, economic, and cultural environment that support it becomes even more pronounced at the brigade and regional command levels" (Flynn et al. 2010:7–8). "We need to build a process from the sensor all the way to the political decision makers" (2010:4).

Flynn, Pottinger, and Batchelor (2010:4–15) are not calling for intelligence analysts to become anthropologists. Open-source publications by anthropologists or field observations by human terrain teams are just information sources in the bigger mix. Their model for intelligence gatherers and analysts is an aggressive reporter, extroverted, hungry, who will roam everywhere to extract all relevant information and bring it back to "teams of 'information brokers' at the regional command level who will organize and disseminate proactively and on request—all the reports and data gathered at the grassroots level." It is these go-getters who would debrief the social scientists.

Stability Operations Information Centers are envisioned as functioning much as the current Intelligence and Security Command's Information Dominance Center, which currently integrates multidisciplinary information for U.S. major commands (Altendorf n.d.; FAS 2002), but the new units would make such knowledge much more accessible. Virtually anyone with a reason the military deems legitimate, including local security forces, "should be able to walk in and obtain mission-related information with ease"—comprehensive, succinct, and current (Flynn et al. 2010:19–20).

This accumulated mass of data will not remain in overseas areas of combat. The broader goal is to archive all cultural information from the DOD, the Department of State, and the U.S. Agency for International Development in permanent, searchable, interoperational data bases. Currently, the Defense Intelligence Agency's Socio-Cultural Dynamics Working Group is the key node for managing work by the "federation of defense intelligence organizations performing socio-cultural dynamics analysis" (DSB 2009:73). In the future, the Distributed Common Ground Station may be given the charge to "organize, store, and distribute 'human terrain information,' provide tools to keep that data current, and continuously provide cultural insights from competent social scientists to analysts and operators alike"—right along with its current task of integrating satellite, aircraft, CIA, and signal intelligence (2009:xix, 44). On top of that, there is a call for a new Center for Global Engagement, "as a collaborative hub for U.S. government innovation in cultural understanding, communication technology, resource identification, and creative program development," directed to "engage experts, thought leaders and creative talent from the private sector and civil society" (2009:30). Supporters of the HTS often claim they do not produce information that can be used in lethal targeting. When local cultural information is processed at these higher levels, it all goes into unified systems, available for any military or intelligence purpose.

Transforming Societies

This operational omniscience will be employed to reach goals beyond combat or stability operations. Its application goes far beyond old-style counterinsurgency. DOD doctrine aims to get to the roots of the problem and eliminate those discontents that fuel insurgencies. The avowed goal is to find out what the local population wants and needs and then make that happen. This is clear in General Stanley McChrystal's preliminary report on Afghanistan (2009:2/12–18). His COIN orientation involves basics such as providing clean water and electricity, collecting garbage, and building roads, but that is only the beginning. New businesses are to be conceived and started, jobs created, schools built, and crop substitutions guided. Local and transparent systems of civil administration, finance, and criminal justice are to be developed in place or purged of corruption, or both. Local communities will be empowered. In Afghanistan, all of this is to be done in the face of a government that, where it exists at all, is seen as incompetent and venal. In this vision, U.S. boots on the ground would help build new societies from the ground up. Nagl sees the U.S. military as tasked "not just to dominate land operations, but to change entire societies" (quoted in Bacevich 2008:2).

Tactics in Counterinsurgency (DOA 2009a:7-5–7-28) details the required stability tasks to be implemented by U.S. armed forces, many requiring local cultural understanding (presented here as listed headings and subheads):

- *establish civil control*: establish public order and safety, establish interim criminal justice system, support law enforcement and police reform, support judicial reform, support property dispute resolution, support corrections reform, support public outreach and community-rebuilding programs;
- *support governance*: support transitional administrations, support anticorruption initiatives, support elections;
- *restore essential services*: provide essential civil services, tasks related to civilian dislocation, support famine prevention and emergency food relief programs, support public health programs, support education programs; and
- *support economic and infrastructure development*: support economic generation and enterprise creation, support public sector investment programs, support private sector development, protect natural resources and the environment, support agricultural development programs, restore transportation infrastructure, restore telecommunications infrastructure, support general infrastructural reconstruction programs, use money as a weapon.

One important goal in Afghanistan (Batson 2008) and elsewhere around the world (e.g., Mexico—Herlihy et al. 2008; Mychalejko and Ryan 2009; Sedillo 2009) is to effect the transfer of communal landholdings to clear, transferable individual titles—showing, if there was any doubt, that Pentagon world restructuring is neoliberal world restructuring.

This is a controversial vision. One friendly critic applauded McChrystal but believed that the close circle of advisers around him had turned this doctrine into a "theology," for "armed social engineering" (Corn 2009:11)—though it is fully in line with the doctrine of the warrior-scholars around Petraeus. A more blistering assessment came from DOD analyst Kalev Sepp (2007:222): "Call it militant Wilsonianism, call it expeditionary democracy, call it counterinsurgency, but this is . . . decidedly not stabilizing. It is an overturning of nations. It is, at its core, a revolution. American soldiers are the instruments of this revolution. . . . The army would have to lead revolutions on a scale so vast as to completely eclipse what the USA experienced in breaking from Great Britain's imperial rule, or in reconstructing the defeated slave states of the South following the American Civil War." Or in the restructuring of colonial societies in earlier ages of imperialism.

Besides the overweening ambition and imperial hubris of this vision, one has to consider that this social transformation is to be implemented by the U.S. Army. The only local evaluation I know of U.S. development effort comes from a human terrain team observation in Iraq. A sheik who seemed very friendly to U.S. forces was quite different when addressing other tribal leaders. He loudly complained, "things are never done right, never completed, and how things are never improved." The human terrain experts explained that this was due to intercultural confusion, because local culture could not entertain the idea that invaders actually wanted to help rebuild their society (Schaner 2008:59). A more straightforward interpretation is that U.S. development efforts are seen as incompetent failures, the United States is still seen as an occupying army, and local power brokers manipulate the conquerors by telling them what they want to hear (Ferguson 2011:110–11).

This imagined ability to penetrate "the locals'" hearts and minds and then make their wishes come true may well be self-deluding, but it is the essence of COIN doctrine. We bring them over to "our side," thus isolating the really "bad guys" and setting them up for targeting and defeat. This is a fantasy, but as U.S. armed forces and its fellow travelers carry out actions around the world, the consequences will be very real.

Employing Culture to Build Local Security Forces

Another major category of cultural application in current or prospective battle zones has largely escaped notice by anthropologists: using cultural understanding to enhance communication and cooperation between U.S.

and local security forces. Raising the performance of these agencies is seen as key to all counterinsurgency and stability operations, as detailed in *FM 3-07.1 Security Force Assistance*, invoking the National Defense Strategy from 2008: "Our strategy emphasizes building the capacities of a broad spectrum of partners as the basis for long-term security. . . . By helping others to police themselves and their regions, we will collectively address threats to the broader international system" (DOA 2009b:1-2).

FM 3-07.1 has a chapter on society, culture, and cross-cultural communication and a separate one on "cross-cultural influencing and negotiating." This knowledge and ability is seen as essential for building up forces "including but not limited to military, paramilitary, police and intelligence forces; border police, coast guard, and customs officials; and prison guards and correctional personnel" (DOA 2009b:1-1). Anthropologists might see a problem with that, because that array of forces has often brutalized the people we study.

Culturally attuned security force assistance is cost-effective and has the benefit of bringing our partners' local knowledge into joint operations. Currently, culturally attuned security force assistance is helping "seek out and dismantle terrorist and insurgent networks while providing security to populations" in the Philippines, the Horn of Africa, the Sahel, Colombia, and elsewhere. "As U.S. forces draw down in Iraq and make progress toward building stability in Afghanistan, more capacity will be available for training, advising, and assisting foreign security forces in other parts of the globe" (QDR 2010:27–28).

An example offered of successful security force assistance is the training and supervision of Salvadoran armed forces in the 1980s. For instance, there is Gabe Acosta, a U.S. military intelligence officer in El Salvador. "During his first tour in 1983–1984 he established a set of friendships and relationships that were very helpful . . . [but] the real pay off came on his second tour in 1990–91. Between tours in El Salvador, as part of his stateside professional military education, Acosta attended the School of the Americas, where he made the acquaintance of thirteen more Salvadoran officers. As a result, those officers were completely comfortable in sharing information with him during his second tour in country" (Renzi 2006a:18). Lesley Gill (2004) should be consulted on the horrible human rights record of the School of the Americas.

Throughout all the discussions on the future of cultural awareness and human terrain intelligence in war, the premise is that this is a *global* necessity. Andy Marshall, the secretive director of the super-secretive Office of Net Assessment—they call him Yoda (McGray 2003)—has called for "anthropology-level knowledge of a wide range of cultures" (quoted in McFate 2005b:46).[2] Today the focus is on Iraq and Afghanistan, but plans are in process for Africa, the Pacific, and Latin America (Axe 2010:68; Hodge 2009).

DOD savants see a need to develop deep cultural knowledge and connections all over the world *now*, to begin gathering cultural information for possible future deployments. This was recognized from the first statements of the DOD's new cultural needs:

> At the heart of a cultural-centric approach to future war would be a cadre of global scouts, well educated, with a penchant for languages and a comfort with strange and distant places. These soldiers should be given time to immerse themselves in a single culture and to establish trust with those willing to trust them. . . . Global scouts must be supported and reinforced with a body of intellectual fellow travelers within the intelligence community who are formally educated in the deductive and inductive skills necessary to understand and interpret intelligently the information and insights provided by scouts in the field. They should attend graduate schools in the disciplines necessary to understand human behavior and cultural anthropology. (Scales 2004:4–5)

This concept was fleshed out in an article in *Military Review*, "Networks: Terra Incognita and the Case for Ethnographic Intelligence" (Renzi 2006b; and see Renzi 2006a):

> The proliferation of empowered networks makes "ethnographic intelligence" (EI) more important to the United States than ever before. . . . Today, we have little insight into which cultures or networks may soon become threats to our national interests. For this reason, America must seek to understand and develop EI on a global scale, *before* it is surprised by another unknown or dimly understood society or network. . . . .

The United States could develop a corps of personnel dedicated to the task and base them out of a more robust military annex to our embassies. . . . A low-key, constant interest in overt ethnographic matters would show that the United States cares and is indeed watching. Perhaps this constant attention would serve to subtly constrict the amount of safe-haven space available for dark networks. The overt information gathered by military ethnographers could complement the covert work done by the CIA (and vice versa). . . . Ethnographic intelligence can empower the daily fight against dark networks, and it can help formulate contingency plans that are based on a truly accurate portrayal of the most essential terrain—the human mind. . . . The Nation must invest in specialized people who can pay "constant attention" to "indigenous forms of association and mobilization," so that we can see and map the human terrain. (Renzi 2006b:16–17, 20–22)[3]

Integrating, Modeling, and Predicting

In the DOD vision of omniscience, ethnographic information and theory will be joined with higher-tech knowledge to enable behavior prediction. The DSB (2009:54–57) describes efforts to integrate a cultural focus with neuroscience and sensors. Among them, the Defense Advanced Research Projects Agency (DARPA, the people who gave us the M-16, drone aircraft, and the Internet [Lal 2006:7]), is "exploring the potential of neuroscience research and development and its applications to understanding human dynamics. Advances in using neuroscience to understand the basis for human cognition, including non-invasive sensor technologies, may be applicable for understanding perception, the neurological origins of trust and compliance, and the neuroscience of persuasion—all relevant to the topic addressed in this report. The broad concept is to develop quantitative neuroscience tools and techniques to predict the effects of 'ideas' within diverse populations." Because DARPA is also implanting sensors into drivable insect cyborgs (DARPA 2006), the possibilities seem endless.

Cultural knowledge will be brought into high-tech targeting systems. In 2007, Assistant Deputy Under Secretary of Defense John Wilcox (2007) gave a presentation to a meeting of the Precision Strike Winter Roundtable, in which the focus was on futuristic weapons systems to eliminate any target anywhere in the world within sixty minutes (called Prompt Global Strike). His first bullet point was "Need to 'Map the Human Terrain' across the Kill Chain—*Enables* the entire Kill Chain for GWOT" (global war on terrorism). (The Kill Chain is a linked sequence of operations: plan, find, fix, track, target, engage, assess.) When the engagement critic Roberto González called attention to this, McFate retorted that Wilcox "is in no way connected with HTS" (González 2008:22, 25; McFate 2008:27). That is precisely the point. Cultural information collected by HTS and other DOD cultural programs will be totally integrated within the full spectrum of DOD operations.

In the DOD vision, cultural perspectives will stream into a new, security social science (Jaschik 2008a). Working together over time, diverse disciplinary perspectives are imagined as developing transdisciplinary, *predictive* theory for application to security issues. Hypotheses and data will be run through sophisticated computer models (see González's chapter in this volume). For instance, the *Journal of Defense Modeling and Simulation* recently called for papers for a special issue: "Modeling, simulating and prognosticating the Human Terrain of deployed force's area(s) of operation is recognized as being increasingly important for U.S. and Coalition Forces during counter-insurgency and stability operations. . . . This special issue is therefore interested in contributions that forecast population response to different messaging (e.g. kinetic operations, cordon and search, reconstruction . . .)" (Society for Modeling and Simulation International 2009).

The deputy director of the Information Exploitation Office of DARPA saw this coming years ago (which is typical):

> We believe the way forward is clear. . . . What is needed is a strategy that leads to a greater cultural awareness and thorough social understanding of the threats comprising the new strategic triad [failed states, weapons of mass destruction, terrorism]. . . . The path to understand people, their cultures, motivations, intentions, opinions and perceptions lies in applying interdisciplinary quantitative and computational social science methods from mathematics, statistics, economics, political science, cultural anthropology, sociology, neuroscience, and modeling simulation. . . . These analytical techniques apply to cognition and decision-making. They make forecasts about conflict and cooperation and do so at all levels of data aggregation from the individual to groups, tribes, societies, nation states, and the globe. . . . Victory in the 21st century strategic threat environment no longer belongs to the side that owns the best and most sophisticated ISR [intelligence, sur-

veillance, and reconnaissance] or weapon systems. It belongs to the side that can combine these cutting-edge technological marvels, which emerged from the physical sciences, with methods from the quantitative and computational social sciences. (Popp 2005)

The fighting arm of the United States will know all, everywhere that matters—what makes locals tick, how to make them move. Their projects will integrate everything from social science hypotheses to neuroscience findings to HTS data to signals intelligence into a seamless, constantly updated, computer-modeled, and continually evaluated system of intelligence, prediction, and prescription. The DOD (and associates) will have its thumb on the local pulse wherever U.S. power centers see "U.S. security interests" at stake—monitoring, predicting, channeling, even transforming societies from the ground up to neutralize even potential threats.

INTERMEZZO: VIRTUAL WAR AND MAGICAL DEATH

What I have described thus far is how cultural awareness and ethnographic intelligence are being built into the virtual war simulacrum. The overarching goal of this full-tilt press is to create a computer copy of the real world, the ultimate divination machine. Actual or *potential* areas of operations include much of the planet, but it is mostly directed at peoples of color, in areas where modernism has not extirpated "traditional" identities and loyalties. In theory, wherever imagined "threats to American security" are seen, security practitioners at any echelon would just have to ask the right question. What if x happens, or if we do y? The answers will roll out: who is involved, what do they want, how do they think, what can they do? What will happen? How can we control events to serve our interests? The all-knowing system of systems will be able to predict the future, and might be dubbed the "crystal ball"—if that name was not already in use by DARPA (2007) (for a battle system that will virtually read commanders' minds from statements and sketches, then produce battle options and probable outcomes).

Some time ago I compared national intelligence agencies to sorcerers, divining the hidden and disrupting our adversaries (Ferguson 1999:428). Current DOD plans take this magical aspiration to whole new levels, beyond the imagination of any warlock. This is not merely a fantasy of omniscience, but one of omnipotence. Through tightening up the Kill Chain, Prompt Global Strike should be capable of destroying any target anywhere in the world in under an hour. Impressive, but not compared to trans-forming whole societies, to make them like us and *be* like us. That ambition is positively alchemical. The universal solvent of modernity would gradually dissolve the traditional ties that impede neoliberal integration, be a panacea for the disruptive infections that ail our global ambitions, and metamorphose the enemy into friend, ally, or client.

For all the talk of "war without blood," blood will gush in abundance, and the intensifying grip of the American empire will lead to incalculable violence spread through the lives of those people anthropologists traditionally study, an expectable consequence of building up local security forces of all stripes. Will the dead be killed by magic? Usually, bullets, rockets, and jails do the job. But the thinking behind this global is magical. Many parallels can be drawn. Picking among the classicists, others in this volume discuss E. E. Evans-Pritchard's ideas. But consider Bronislaw Malinowski (1979). Humans often confront situations that "put them in harm's way"—drought, storms at sea, war—in which practical knowledge is no help. Humans want to believe they have control over these existential threats, or they find it difficult to go forward. In giving the illusion of control, magic is practical. It prescribes concrete measures to alleviate the anxiety of plunging into the unknowable and uncontrollable. If it fails, there are always reasons to explain the failure without questioning the premises.

This bears comparison to current security ambitions. The cultural turn of the DOD creates the *illusion* of control. The HTS, as a critical test of concept, does provide useful information to combat commanders, but there is no evidence that it is making any headway toward its announced goal of transforming areas of operations into more secure, friendly spaces (see Ferguson 2011). The simulacrum is a glamour, a false construction that deceives those under its spell. The savants of security, the magicians of DARPA, who envision a world of secure predictability, are captured by a naive faith that is justified neither by advances in social sciences nor those in hard sciences such as molecular biology, where greater knowledge means recognition of expanding dimensions of ignorance.

I research and teach on issues of "human nature." The advent of the genomic era was once foreseen as unlocking the secrets of what we are and why. There was heady talk of genetic interventions and finding specific genes for specific predispositions. What the great research progress of recent years has actually produced is realization of just how rudimentary our understanding is. The developmental, systemic interactions of functional genes, noncoding regulatory DNA, epigenetics, multiplying classes of RNA, and proteomics—all of which are open and influenced by non-predictable environmental factors—are far beyond our ability to comprehend. "It's all in the genes," it was once thought, and genomics would show us how. Now we have to recognize that cellular systems may be irreducibly complex and in important ways nondeterministic. We should expect nothing less from whole human beings.

The prophets of intelligence seem incapable of drawing the conclusion that the ability to know and predict the world is inherently limited, despite such glaring "intelligence failures" as the fall of the Soviet Union and the democratic uprisings across the Middle East. The lesson always drawn is that more and better intelligence is needed. The first half of this chapter has described how the DOD is pushing relentlessly to develop an all-encompassing virtual world of threat detection and neutralization. There is no call here for an "anthropological perspective"—that could be critical of U.S. military expansion around the world. But an essential ingredient is anthropological *product*—what anthropologists know about culture that can be absorbed and used for more effective military control. And the DOD is doing everything it can to get it.

It is impossible to imagine how this boundless program will penetrate and affect the lives and cultures of peoples around the world. Certainly there are many precedents in previous efforts of "insurgency prophylaxis"—as Project Camelot was called—yet never before has such money, technology, and intense focus of the U.S. military been directed at monitoring and controlling "indigenous networks." It brings empire up to a whole new level, and without question the impact will be great. But the permanent war has and will transform life not only in foreign lands but also right here at home. The second part of this chapter takes on one small part of the ongoing militarization of U.S. society, what the Pentagon's quest for culture means for anthropology, social science, and U.S. universities.

MILITARIZING ANTHROPOLOGY

How will the security demand for culture be manifested for the discipline of anthropology? To borrow a phrase, the impact will be *full spectrum*, changing conditions in education, employment, and research.

Military Education

A very large impact is expectable in education—in teaching possibilities within the DOD, in a militarization of campuses in general, and strains on anthropology programs specifically. Inside the military, a vast archipelago of educational programs demand cultural perspectives. That means a lot of anthropology teachers and instructional products.

The Institute for Defense Analysis was charged with surveying in-house military cultural education programs. It was surprised by how much already existed. "In addition to the vastness of the landscape with respect to the programs and initiatives, the variety of emphases and missions cannot be overstated" (Alrich 2008:2). Instruction comes in many forms. There are one-off lectures for predeployment forces and short courses on military bases, such as an introduction to anthropology or Islam (Capuzzo 2007). A major growth area is online training and education resources, beginning with a Warfighter Cultural Awareness curriculum, and including specialized instructions about particular areas for soldiers in the field (Masellis 2009:14).

There are higher level collegiate and postgraduate venues for anthropological instruction within the military, beginning with the service academies of West Point, Annapolis, and the Air Force Academy, and extending through command and staff colleges, most of which have military think-tanks or research groups (Roxborough 2008:2–3). Across levels, however staffed or structured, a great surge in military education in foreign languages and cultures is assuredly on the way. The Quadrennial Defense Review in 2010 sees this expansion as one of the DOD's most important investments (QDR 2010:25–26).

Militarizing Campuses

Moving outside the Camo Tower to consider our universities, Secretary of Defense Robert Gates, former president of Texas A&M, called ringingly for greatly increased cooperation between the DOD and research universities. Campuses as a whole are targeted for a major increase in military/security engagement: opening them for more Reserve Officers' Training Corps programs, "actively promoting the military as a career option, or giving full support to military recruiters on campus . . . [and] wide-ranging initiatives to recognize veterans for the knowledge they have." Online courses should be offered for military personnel that are "immediately relevant—the history of the Middle East, anthropology classes on tribal culture, and so on." To encourage participation, universities could offer degree credit for these courses—"the Department could offer logistical advice" (Gates 2008:3). Beyond individual universities, Gates envisions "a consortia of universities that will promote research in specific areas" (2008:2), encouraged by Minerva Initiative funding. After a closed-door meeting with Gates, presidents of major universities were reportedly enthusiastic, even "extraordinarily excited" by the proposal of greater collaboration between the Pentagon and U.S. universities (Jaschik 2008a:2).

The intelligence community (IC) is already farther along than that. Two current programs bring intelligence agencies onto campuses. The Pat Roberts Intelligence Scholars Program (PRISP) was the first manifestation of security engagement to attract attention within anthropology (see Price 2005a). PRISP is a scholarship program for individual students, who receive substantial funding to study languages and topics, cultural and otherwise, that are of direct interest to the CIA and other intelligence agencies. Applicants go through a security investigation, polygraph, and drug screening. Recipients must have an internship with an approved agency. After graduation, they are required to spend one and a half the duration of their funded studies in the employ of an intelligence agency, or pay back the scholarship at punitive rates of interest (DIA n.d.; Price 2005b). Faculty members have no way of knowing whether one of these intelligence trainees is in their class.

Only recently coming to broad attention (Price 2010c) is the IC Centers of Academic Excellence (CAE) Program. Presently offered are renewable grants for adjusting universities to long-term intelligence needs. CAE will "create a new diverse talent pool from which the intelligence community can recruit" (CAE n.d.). All participating universities are required to enhance curricula needed by the IC, hold colloquia with other consortia universities on IC issues and careers, send IC scholars abroad for education and immersion, and reach out to local high schools about intelligence careers. By 2010, twenty-two universities had signed up, including the University of Maryland, College Park; the Universities of New Mexico and Nebraska; Pennsylvania State; and Virginia Polytechnic (CAE n.d.). Of course, a major intelligence presence on U.S. campuses is hardly something new (Price 2004, 2008a).

Anthropology Programs

My guess is that most who teach in colleges and universities already have servicemen and -women in their classrooms. At Rutgers University, Newark, I get many, and they and their interests are welcome. I also get the standard office hours question, "What can you do with an anthropology degree, even a bachelor's?" I include the military and intelligence possibilities, and we talk about it. At graduate levels, a professor should be prepared for a surge of enrollments in anthropology master's degree and certificate programs. For anyone charting a military career today, or someone from another social science wanting to retool in an ethnographic direction, a master's or certificate would be a solid investment, especially if tuition is somehow subsidized by the DOD. University administrations love master's degree and certificate programs.

Then there are doctorates, military persons who obtain the highest degree from research universities. It is frequently emphasized that training senior officers "should extend to the world's best graduate schools" (Joint Forces Command 2008:49). This is a challenge facing diverse disciplines, and it is especially pointed for anthropology programs. If they enroll a military person for a Ph.D. in anthropology, will they do fieldwork under departmental auspices, like any other fledgling anthropologist? How would institutional review boards handle this dual orientation? How would a department even categorize someone as a military person? Many would come in after leaving active duty, intending to use their anthropological training in future security contexts. If graduate anthropology departments have not considered this, they should.

> As more *military anthropologists* achieve higher degrees, they will expand the possibility of the "grow our own" alternative, in which higher-level anthropology training takes place within military post-graduate institutes, thus bypassing AAA professional concerns. (Connable 2009:64)

Regrettably, the anthropological community in academia has tremendous reservations about working with the military. . . . A specialized group of ethnographers is urgently needed. The solution is for the Department of Defense to grow its own cultural experts—hybrids between soldier and anthropologists, who may not have to be uniformed, but do have to look at cultural matters from a security standpoint. (Renzi 2006a:12–13)

According to John Allison, a cultural anthropologist who joined and then resigned in protest from the HTS program, this is happening already. "The military is beginning to do an end run by producing its own anthropologist/social scientist PhDs at West Point, the Air Force Academy, the Naval Academy and other cooperating institutions; thus marginalizing the criticism" (quoted in Price 2010d:4).

Funded and Promoted Research

Another broad front of the military invasion will be in anthropological research. In April 2008, Secretary Gates announced the Minerva Initiative (Asher 2008; Gates 2008; Jaschick 2008a, 2008b). Building on a series of private meetings with leaders of the Association of American Universities, Minerva aims to engage disciplines such as history, anthropology, sociology, and evolutionary psychology on topics of "strategic importance to U.S. National Policy." Between the directly administered grants and a parallel program outsourced to the National Science Foundation (NSF), upward of $74 million over five years is dedicated to new research.

In the first twenty-four grants announced for both programs, the largest number (six) concern terrorism or insurgency, with additional clusters on group behavioral psychology and dynamics (four), environmental security (two), conflict in weak or authoritarian states (three), postconflict recovery (two), plus several that cannot be lumped with others (Minerva Initiative n.d.a). One cannot tell the value of a proposal from its title, but by the titles, most of these seem like worthwhile projects. Notably absent is any title that hints at a critical perspective on U.S. military or other security projects. The Social Science Research Council posted a panel of thoughtful commentaries on the Minerva Initiative and its prospective effect on social sciences. Hugh Gusterson (2008) and Catherine Lutz (2008) notably worry that expanded engagement through Minerva/NSF funding will bend the priorities and practices of anthropology into the military orbit. Researchers may gravitate toward studying what the DOD wants studied. No doubt additional sources of security-related funding will come.

Both research funding programs are explicitly intended to cross disciplines, to build a new community of security science researchers, "to foster a new generation of engaged scholarship in the social sciences" (Minerva Initiative n.d.b). Besides creating a network of civilian security researchers, the DOD also intends to connect multidisciplinary scholars directly to the military establishment. The HTS calls for development of a network of area specialists to call on as needed (Kipp et al. 2007:14). The DSB Task Force (DSB 2009: xiv) notes that "both the Army and Air Force reported that each maintained an extensive network of expert cultural consultants. The combatant commands also have their own 'rolodex files' . . . [but the DOD as a whole lacks] procedures, funding lines, and automated expert finder/locator for effectively engaging and leveraging expertise in industry and academia"—and needs to develop them. "Recognizing the importance of such cross-disciplinary interactions, Secretary Gates is actively working to reassure those who may be reluctant to collaborate with the Department of Defense." As anthropologists and other social scientists are drawn into security studies, regular interaction with security professionals will become normal.

Security Appropriation of Normal Anthropological Research

Perhaps the broadest connection of the military and anthropology is already at hand, not through funding new work but through the diligent mining and absorption of normal, published research and dissertations. The most important fount of anthropological data will not be from HTS social scientists but from what security people call "open sources." The head of military intelligence in Afghanistan concludes open-source information makes up 90 percent of the intelligence future, clandestine work merely being more dramatic (Flynn et al. 2010:23). The standard operating procedure now for human terrain teams is to pose a problem for the Reachback cells Stateside to investigate through open-source materials. As the anthropologist John Allison wrote to David Price (2010d:3), before he quit the HTS: "One interesting fact that was revealed today is that *the time that an anthropologist or social scientist has to finish an interview before the probability of a sniper attack becomes drastically high, is about 7 minutes.* How deep an understanding, rapport or trust develops in 7 minutes? It seems that the 'data' sought is very limited to operationally tactically useful stuff. For anything deeper, they 'reach back' to the research centers for work from anthropologists that they will use without permission and without attribution" (emphasis in original). A similar evaluation was made by another HTS team member in the field: "Without the ability to truly immerse yourself in the population, existing knowl-edge of the culture . . . is critical. Lacking that, we were basically an open-source research cell" (Ephron and Spring 2008:2).

HTS Reachback specialists, and "deskbound analysts" in other pro-grams and institutions, constitute another major source of employment for anyone with any anthropology degree (see Kipp et al. 2007). These analysts will be part of the process of streaming together anthropologi-cal data with other sources of intelligence. For instance, BAE Systems, the former contractor of the HTS (see Feinstein 2011), advertised for a "Senior Human Terrain Analyst" to use new toolkits to "address specific, often time sensitive topics that normally include the fusion of SIGINT data, tribal/cultural patterns, message traffic, imagery, open source and advanced geospatial technologies" (BAE 2009).

Given the overarching emphasis on standardizing information and integrating it within interoperational data sets, it can safely be assumed that these textual sources are being analyzed and coded for recovery and modeling. High aspirations are plain in a DARPA (2008) call for propos-als for a Universal Reading Machine, capable of reading everything, cate-gorizing information, processing it through programs for analyzing be-havior, and passing it along to whomever or whatever can use it. This proposed system would apply to academic publications, print media, and Web postings, going beyond what may be accomplished by human reader/processors. "Manually encoding such knowledge can become pro-hibitively expensive . . . the goal of the MRP [Machine Reading Program] is to create an automated Reading System that serves as a bridge between knowledge contained in natural texts and the formal reasoning systems that need such knowledge" (2008:6). All anthropologists working in any area of potential interest to U.S. security agencies—and that is much of the world—should understand that any ethnographic information they publish, any sort of explanation of why those people do what they do, will be assimilated into the great network of security data bases and modeling systems, and through them made available to military, intelligence, and other security practitioners.

Price (2008a) describes how U.S. military needs around World War II contributed to the development of basic anthropological research projects and tools, such as area handbooks and the Human Relations Area Files (HRAF). Thus he notes the irony in that the leaked *Human Terrain Team Handbook* calls for contributing human terrain data to the HRAF database: "This practice will also allow us to tie into the HRAF database and compare the existence of one social practice, symbolic system, or historical process in our area of operations with others elsewhere in the world. Such cross-cultural analysis enables us to get closer to explaining causation and make weak assertions of what will likely happen in the population in the near future" (Finney 2008, quoted in Price 2008b:3). Given the plans for data integration and modeling described in this chapter, the new DOD efforts will make HRAF correlational studies seem like the horse and buggy. Given high level pledges of research openness (Gates 2008), anthropologists probably will be invited to use these tools—or some of them anyway—although these tools may have a built-in bias toward topics of security interest. The scholarly possibilities will be bedazzling.

CONCLUSION

The DOD cultural revolution will have a profound impact on anthropology and its intellectual environment. People with degrees from bachelor's to doctorate will find work with the military as teachers and analysts. (What may be distasteful for a tenured professor may seem quite different for a young person trying to set up a job, life, and family.) Campuses and social sciences will reorient to security needs. Militarily oriented culture seekers will filter into anthropology teaching programs. Militarily useful anthropology will be trained into soldier-anthropologist hybrids, who then can reproduce their own. Academic research will be funded and otherwise channeled into security-relevant topics. All "open-source" work with possible security relevance will be assimilated into the great security networks and nodes of synthesis, analysis, and prediction.

Of course, all this assumes that the DOD emphasis on culture will continue in the years to come. Although details and outcomes are debated, can anyone claim that the DOD's turn to culture has turned the tide in Afghanistan? Some in power have questioned the new counterinsurgency, Vice President Joe Biden among them. Yet it is very unlikely that a lack of success will lead to a turn away from culture-centric counterinsurgency. As with the CORDS/Phoenix counterinsurgency program in Vietnam, blame can go elsewhere—the program got started too late, it was misunderstood, the American public had lost the will to fight, and so on (Andrade and Willbanks 2006). The emphasis on global COIN and counterterrorism (CT)—often put in harness with stability operations (SO)—will not go away. The DOD cultural revolution has gone too far to turn back, permeating its power centers, while a new generation of COIN combat officers is rising within the Pentagon.

COIN/CT will not go away because too much is riding on it. These spotlighted global challenges give the Pentagon something it desperately needs—an unending rationale for massive military spending. As the Quadrennial Defense Review (2010:20) puts it: "Stability operations, large-scale counterinsurgency, and counterterrorism operations are not niche challenges or the responsibility of a single Military Department, but rather require a portfolio of capabilities as well as sufficient capacity from across America's Armed Forces and other departments and agencies. Nor are these types of operations a transitory or anomalous phenomenon in the security landscape. On the contrary, we must expect that for the indefinite future, violent extremist groups, with or without state sponsorship, will continue to foment instability and challenge U.S. and allied interests."

Even if many of the DOD's high-budget items are of little relevance to COIN/CT/SO, terrorist-linked insurgents provide the critical fear factor that supports massive security spending and bleeds the federal government dry for domestic spending. "It's a dangerous world out there," the militarist mantra goes. "We are locked in a life-and-death struggle with deadly fanatics who thrive on disorder. We must spend whatever it takes to give our brave soldiers whatever it takes to prevail, and to protect America."

This volume raises the question "when is war?" For the DOD, war is always, everywhere. Even when there is no realistic threat to U.S. security interests, the potential exists. The envisioned global surveillance system will be vigilant against a threat's emergence, peering into the shadows, sweeping out the corners, turning over rocks. That is how to get ahead of the curve. Actually fighting and winning a war is just one aspect of this project, a cleanup when prior forms of surveillance and control have not done their jobs.

This premise of existential threat underlies political discourse in the United States. Take away terrorism and insurgency, and where is the visceral danger for U.S. voters? (North Korea and Iran work, too, but China?) Why should the federal government channel about *half* of its entire discretionary spending into the military? Why should the United States maintain some 600 to 700 overseas military bases? (It is a telling fact that no one has been able to ascertain the number of bases more precisely than that; Turse 2011.) Say the magic words: "to safeguard American security." Yet look at the man pulling the levers behind the curtain. What is really thriving on perceptions of global "instability and challenge [to] U.S. and allied interests" is the U.S. military-corporate-political complex.

Anthropologists working in war zones (Lubkemann 2008; Richards 1996) have come to understand that war may not be a defined period, separate from ongoing projects of everyday life, but a chronic state of existence, the context for ongoing life projects. So it is for the United States. Catherine Lutz (2002a), other anthropologists (Gusterson and Besteman 2009), and earlier pioneers such as Seymour Melman (1974, 1984) document the myriad ways that U.S. society and culture have been thoroughly reoriented to a permanent war footing. This is always the way of militaristic societies and empires (Ferguson 1999). Questioning military projection is ruled out of bounds within "legitimate" political discourse. Language is bent to the cause. U.S. forces are "put in harm's way," rather than sent to do harm—which is what any army is about.[4] Anthropology is now being pulled into this total war complex.

The DOD is only the biggest dog in the room. The Department of State, think-tanks, and private corporations will all be looking to put culture to use. Civilian surges (Binnendijk and Cronin 2008; DeYoung 2009; Jelinek 2009), stability operations, and the rapidly expanding Department of State Civilian Response Corps (U.S. Department of State n.d.) will all offer increasing opportunities for social scientists to work not for but with the military, complicating choices about individual engagement. But they, too, will bring anthropology closer to the security world.

To be clear, *I am not against all manner of security engagement.* Opportunities should be considered situation by situation. But all those situations are being created by powerful agencies with lots of money, and they are manipulating incentives to increase cooperation. The sum total of individual situations and choices may result in a profound shift for anthropology as a whole.

Any anthropologist considering closer work with the DOD and other security agencies should make themselves aware of the record of past engagements (see Price 2004, 2008a). They should also be thinking about our future. The military invasion of anthropology must be recognized in its scope and ambition. What will it mean for anthropology if our research, expertise, and practitioners are assimilated into the imperial apparatus? One response to this global challenge would be to reorient scholarly efforts in countervailing directions—studying, publishing, and teaching more on U.S. militarism and its consequences, at home and abroad, as this book does.

Resistance is not futile.

NOTES

1. I recently met an engineer from Mitre Corporation, who works with StratCom, the current incarnation of the Strategic Air Command. He told me that anthropological input was essential for their intelligence work. Anthropologists—he told me twice—fill the same function today as Indian Scouts did in the days of the old West.

2. A proposal by the anthropologists Anna Simons and David Tucker, "Improving Human Intelligence in the War on Terrorism: The Need for an Ethnographic Capability," was submitted to the Office of the Secretary of Defense for Net Assessment in 2004. It has not been made public (Renzi 2006b:22).

3. Renzi references the proposal to Net Assessment by Simons and Tucker, and he studied under Simons, so it is not unreasonable to expect this position reflects ideas in that proposal.

4. I recall Johnny Carson commenting on the Reagan administration's renaming a new nuclear missile "the Peacekeeper—which sounds a lot better than World Ender."

TODAY HE IS NO MORE

Magic, Intervention, and Global War in Uganda

The point of my sermon is simply this. However incomprehensible the acts of the terrorists may seem to be, our judges, our policemen, and our politicians must never be allowed to forget that terrorism is an activity of fellow human beings and *not* of dog-headed cannibals.

—Sir Edmund Leach, *Custom, Law, and Terrorist Violence* (1977)

In what follows, I revisit a few months of intensive fieldwork conducted in late 2005. This fieldwork spell was part of a much longer engagement with war-torn Acholiland in northern Uganda starting in 1997 and still ongoing. But back in 2005, I could follow closely the unfolding of local news as the International Criminal Court (ICC) unsealed its arrest warrants for the leaders of the globally infamous Lord's Resistance Army/Movement (LRA).

From this horizon, I discuss the intersection of media reporting, international interventions, and violent insurgency/counterinsurgency warfare in Uganda and beyond. In sketching an ethnography that trails violent death, I will not just focus on any instrumental goal of violent acts but more on what such acts *do*. I thus sketch how perpetrators, victims, and witnesses of violence alike "are directed toward the ever-shifting horizons of their existence" (Kapferer 1997:4), and also how such existential horizons may implode in *vital conjunctures* that are not only highly violent but also magical. I build on David Riches's (1986) triadic model of violence. Besides the performer and the victim of violence, this model integrates into the equation the role of the so-called witness, the supposed outsider, adding depth to the analysis of today's violent political makings. In the violence of the everyday, the LRA's targeting of noncombatants amalgamates with the Ugandan state's counterinsurgency warfare, and also with a massive international interventionist apparatus. Here, to avoid a description of inexhaustible mass violence as inevitably developing into an end in itself, I find further inspiration from Pamela Stewart and Andrew Strathern's suggestion that we never lose sight of expanding cycles of violence as "schemes of coercive reciprocity" that are socially and historically grounded in the "semantics of polarization" (2002:36, 40). Such schemes are manifestations of the global nature of the war in Uganda, even if the battlefields have been locally situated.

So, unfolding in the Ugandan context is a triangulated scheme of coercive reciprocities and of war as fragmented rather than homogeneous, global rather than only local. The violent magic of vital conjunctures is a significant facet of global war, whereby spaces of magical death are produced primarily not *by* the often claimed primitives of Africa but in the placement of global forces *on* the African scene. For example, LRA leaders have always followed national and international news closely. When media outlets present them as primitive and driven by religious fundamentalism or superstition to devalue their resistance to outside interventions, individual rebels might as well understand the magical as an effective and significant way to resist. I even suggest that magic may appear in these very entanglements. It is a circular and cross-fertilizing development that evokes and constitutes the magic of terror, and consequently, as I argue toward the conclusion of this chapter, the violent emplacement of globalization can be likened with witchcraft processes known from the classic anthropological literature. My intention in applying such a parallel is to expose the massive Manichaean master narrative that neatly divides a murky reality of global war into virtual extremes of black and white. In short, this narrative of the human terrain is a story of the secularized and modern Ugandan government and its international partners in development, which together defend the Ugandan citizenry against the primitive barbarians of the LRA.

My critique of such Manichaean narratives draws on two somehow different perspectives: one focusing on sociopolitical history and collective representations, and the other focusing on personal rationalization from the angle of existential psychology. The chapter is intended to illustrate that witchcraft and magic are deeply entailed in violence in these two ways, and their very cross-breeding is a "force multiplier" for untrammeled violence.

THE WAR ON TERROR AT THE GLOBAL PERIPHERIES

Almost since the beginning of the war in northern Uganda in 1986, Joseph Kony and his rebel army, the LRA, have fought the Ugandan army and the Ugandan citizenry. Since the early 1990s, Kony's rebels have operated from bases in south Sudan. In 2005 they shifted base to northeastern Congo, and around 2008, they expanded to the Central African Republic and Darfur (Cakaj 2010; Schomerus 2007). Always pursued by the Ugandan army, the LRA rebels have gone regional, and consequently the war in Uganda has been exported to neighboring countries (Allen and Vlassenroot 2010b; Atkinson 2009, 2010: afterword). The expansive moment was given an important push in the aftermath of the September 11, 2001, attacks on the United States. The United States soon included the LRA on its list of terrorist groups with which no negotiations, as the George W. Bush administration stated, would be initiated under any circumstances (U.S. Department of State 2001).

The Ugandan government welcomed the rhetoric of no dialogue, and as allies in the war on terror, the U.S. military provides equipment and logistical support to the Ugandan army against the LRA. In early 2002, without parliamentary approval, the Ugandan army launched a campaign in Sudan called Operation Iron Fist, later relaunched as Iron Fist II. Operation Lightning Thunder, a massive attack on rebel bases in the Congo in December 2008, again involved direct American support (Atkinson 2010:315–16). Sometimes before this attack, "U.S. military advisers and analysts" surfaced in northern Uganda, and they "could be found in bars boasting that a surgical strike was straightforward" (Allen and Vlassenroot 2010a:1; see also Branch 2011:chapter 7). An executive order from the White House in August the same year prepared the ground, proclaiming Kony a "Specially Designated Global Terrorist" whose international assets and supporting networks were to be blocked. As with previous military operations on foreign territory, the Ugandan parliament was not informed about Operation Lightning Thunder and thus did not have the chance to approve or disapprove it; indeed, it was a flagrant transgression against the Ugandan constitution. Local realities have become deeply entangled with larger regional, even global warscapes.

Ever since these operations, the trail of death continues unabated in Uganda's neighboring countries (e.g., Human Rights Watch 2010). In an escalating development over the years of war, the rebels have been stealing from others what they cannot gain themselves. They have abducted and forced into fighting tens of thousands of minors, and they have committed crimes of extraordinary violence. The ICC eventually issued arrest warrants for the rebel leadership. The warrants were unsealed and immediately published in Ugandan papers during my fieldwork in late 2005. Rebel leader Joseph Kony's warrant listed "thirty-three counts on the basis of his individual criminal responsibility," including both war crimes and crimes against humanity (see, e.g., the *Daily Monitor*, October 17, 2005). Four other leaders were wanted as well. Vincent Otti, deceased in 2007, had thirty-two counts to answer to. Okot Odhiambo's list included ten counts, and Raska Lukwiya, deceased in 2006, had five counts on his head. Dominic Ongwen, abducted into rebel ranks when he was only ten years old, was to answer to seven counts.

Only the rebel side was indicted, and it is unlikely that the ICC has conducted any proper investigations of possible crimes committed by the government side. Tellingly, the Ugandan army—or the Uganda People's Defence Forces (UPDF)—promotes itself as the rational, disciplined, and modern party to the conflict. President Yoweri Museveni has described his enemies as a bunch of peasants and criminals driven by intoxication, witchcraft, backwardness, mysticism, and obscurantism (see, e.g., Museveni 1992; see also Finnström 2010a), thereby recycling the most essentialist colonial stereotypes about primitive savages in darkest Africa. This is a powerful discourse whereby the rebels are reduced to wild men, "encountered at the edges of the civilized world" (Hinton 2010:38). General Carter Ham, when still new as the head of AFRICOM, the U.S. Africa Command, declared Kony and the LRA to be the "real evil in our world" (U.S. Africa Command 2011).

Basically, this rhetoric has been central to an intense and media-wary campaign in the United States that attracted the hearts and minds of young college people in particular (see Branch 2011), and which culminated in October 2011 when President Barack Obama publicly announced that he had ordered 100 U.S. troops to follow those AFRICOM "military advisers" already supporting the Ugandan army on the ground. Hereby the United States, while fiercely rejecting any jurisdiction of the ICC, officially secured yet another physical warfront in its global war on terror on yet another continent. In a development whereby humanitarianism increasingly defines itself through military intervention, military thinking, and even militarism, the lobbyists who paved the way for this move proudly announced that "this is the one of the most exciting developments in the history of our work, and our leaders need to hear about our support" (Poffenberger 2011).

In a parallel and equally dominant discourse, Museveni and his associates' language of denigration took a symbolic dimension understandable to most Ugandans. Periodically, Museveni calls rebel insurgents "hyenas" (quoted, e.g., in *Daily Monitor*, February 16, 2000). To call them hyenas implies that they are wild creatures, which in many African cosmologies means that they have vitality and power, but further, that they represent the uncultured wilderness, danger, depredation, death, and indeed, sorcery and witchcraft. "Hegemonic groups are able to define such a vocabulary, an ability that enables them to identify opposition and protest as witchcraft, banditry, and terrorism," writes Winans (1992:110) with reference to south-central Tanzania on the eve of independence.

The rebels have made themselves coauthors in the process. Kony sometimes claims to be fighting for a new moral order, purified from corruption, sorcery, witchcraft, and past evils—a full break with Uganda's violent postcolonial history. But in a kind of boomerang effect, his moral claim has turned against him. Informants sometimes told me that because of the many unlawful killings of innocent people he has ordered, Kony acts as the very witches he claims to be fighting (Finnström 2008:201–4; Behrend 1991:176). Indeed, the rebels are responsible for some of the worst crimes against humanity we can imagine, often described by outsiders as simply incomprehensible. But violence is always relational and a performative act of communication (Jackson 2002; Whitehead 2004b); however horrendous, it can be understood through contextualization. I will now sketch the violent realpolitik, including its magic, that unfolded on the ground following the unsealing of the ICC warrants.

THE DEATH OF JOSEPH KAPERE

In late December 2005, the Ugandan army airlifted journalists for a press briefing deep in the war-torn bush of Pader district, northern Uganda.

5.1–5.3 *After the human terrain mapping, rural northern Uganda.* Once the finest house in the village, now bullet-ridden and in shambles. Unlawfully occupied by the Ugandan army; used as an intelligence outpost; therefore shot at by the rebels; and finally ransacked, looted, and deserted by the army. Photos by Sverker Finnström, 2007.

This particular area, nicknamed Kandahar in the local parlance, was known for years of fierce fighting between the Ugandan army and the LRA. There, in the scorched grass of the hot dry season, on display for the journalists, was the body of Brigadier Joseph Kapere, at the time one of the most senior rebels operating inside Uganda, while the majority of the high command was in south Sudan or in bases in northeast Congo. The army's ambush had been well planned, with massive deployment in the area where Kapere was supposed to link up with another rebel commander, who escaped.

In an effort to reprise an earlier story claiming the death of Dominic Ongwen, one of the commanders wanted by the ICC, the army's propaganda machinery created a media spectacle of the successful killing of a senior rebel commander. A few months earlier the *New Vision* had reported the story of Ongwen's presumed death: "Ongwen was buried on October 1, after his body was paraded at Soroti Public gardens" (October 6, 2005). A color photo of a body being exhumed for DNA testing illustrated the *New Vision* story. But the army was mistaken, and the body on display for journalists (it turned out months later) was not that of Ongwen. He got away. With the death of Kapere, an analogous color photo appeared on the front page of same state-controlled daily. It depicts Kapere in torn, dirty, and bloody clothes, lying dead on the ground, in the wilderness of the bush, surrounded by the boots of the UPDF dignitaries of the day: "Kapere was killed in an ambush . . . in Atanga sub-county, Aruu county, Pader district. . . . Journalists were taken to view Kapere's body. Present during the press briefing were the jovial UPDF acting 601-brigade commander, Maj. Joseph Balikudembe, flanked by the UPDF 4th division intelligence officer, Maj. Mike Kisame and the 5th division spy chief Maj. Ddamulira Sserunjogi" (*New Vision*, December 27, 2005). The Ugandan army was guided to the secret rebel rendezvous by a defected rebel fighter, and Major Balikudembe described the army's "search and destroy offensive" for the media crowd: "I pitched camp at Goma hills planning with my commanders to make sure that Kapere is killed and we are happy that today he is no more." The *New Vision* journalist writes that Kapere "reportedly cried for mercy, pleading with soldiers to take him alive." Yet the shootout was chaotic, with Kapere's escorts firing back. A group of ex-rebels, now rearmed and commissioned by the Ugandan president himself, "shot Kapere several times on the left arm and leg."

More recently, as U.S. forces have joined with the Ugandan forces, rebel defectors have become essential in the pursuit of still active rebels in the larger region of central Africa. As an American officer describes the tactics of dirty war he is involved in, these ex-rebel "guys don't have many skills, and it's going to be hard for them to reintegrate. But one thing they are very good at, is hunting human beings in the woods" (quoted in *New York Times*, April 10, 2010). Here the U.S. Army's mapping of the human terrain establishes the enemy as the primitive and wild other. Yet the only ones who seem able to track down this otherness in the making, lingering out there in the so-called woods, are seasoned rebels/ex-rebels themselves who have to choose their allies of the day. In contrast to the American officer interviewed by the *New York Times*, these rebels/ex-rebels are coming of age in a world of violence, temporary survival, and unavoidable proxy decisions, coerced by existential crisis and extreme structural constraint. It is a fix they cannot overcome, a "choiceless choice"—many were children when abducted into rebel ranks, and later, when expected to join the hunt for their former comrades in arms, they again "are offered an option that is no option" (Langer 1982:72, 121; see also Finnström 2008:9, 221–22; Cakaj 2011).

A few months before Kapere's spectacular death and just after the un-sealing of the ICC warrants, rumors started to circulate that the rebel leaders were angered with the warrants on their heads and had issued a counterorder: humanitarian aid workers and expatriates should leave northern Uganda, or they would be killed. The rumors certainly made sense, and they made me—a Swede in Uganda—think twice before I left the relative safety of Gulu town where I stayed for the rural surround-ings. From my fieldwork horizon, as I listened to my Ugandan friends, I concluded that through such a rationalization senior rebels tried to make sense of their own situation of increased stigmatization and marginal-ization, which now officially defined their and my inclusion in the wider world order (see also Finnström 2010b). As the rumors continued and the stories persisted, Kapere's name figured frequently in them.

When I investigated the matter, I was met with a complete denial from Ugandan authorities. I recognized the politics of denial from my previ-ous research efforts. Yet an acquaintance of mine eventually provided me with a photocopy of the rebels' written response to the arrest warrants. She attended a United Nations meeting in the Ugandan capital where the document had been discussed. The letter, here a reproduction of the handwritten original, reads in part:

> Make sure that the ICC question is answered and we have been di-rected to kill any white person moving anyhow in this region, they come like NGOs but they are the one talking bad about LRA, so you should also know that white people are like Museveni.
> [Signed]
> Brigadier Kapere
> FOR LORDS RESISTANCE ARMY

The threat was for real. Balam Bongonyinge, a Ugandan, was killed and five of his colleagues injured in a rebel ambush in late October 2005. He was working with the international organization Accord. Another aid worker, this time from the Catholic organization Caritas, was killed in a separate ambush. After these ambushes, most humanitarian organiza-tions suspended their operations (*Sunday Monitor*, October 30, 2005). However, perhaps most widely reported in Uganda and beyond was the killing of a Briton and a former employee of the British High Commis-sion in Uganda, Steve Willis. Interviewed by the state-controlled daily, a Ugandan army commander immediately declared that Willis's death was an "isolated incident" (Brigadier Mugisha in *New Vision*, November 10, 2005). But in all its sadness, it was a typical rebel ambush, straightforward and with no magic to it whatsoever. After more than twenty years of war, with a history of countless rebel ambushes just like this one—and indeed a number of army ambushes on civilians as well—it was anything but an isolated incident. It was part of a systematic pattern of wartime violence. For Ugandans living in the immediate war zone, at times ambushes happened on a daily basis, something that has sustained the experience of war, making it and its multiple forms of violence routine among other routines in everyday life.

DOGS OF WAR?

In an influential article, Ruddy Doom and Koen Vlassenroot describe the LRA as "the dogs of war." They write that "the Acholi people at grassroots level can easily identify the dog that bites, but cannot see its master," while "better informed persons are fully aware" of the international complexities (Doom and Vlassenroot 1999:30). The metaphorical comment suggests that people on the ground do not have a proper idea of the complexities of global war, only that, as is also the official standpoint of the Ugandan government and many outside observers, they find the rebels to be incomprehensible. Yet having in mind the international justice intervention and the rumors of Kapere's letter, in all its brutality, the rebels' targeting of aid workers made complete sense to my Ugandan friends. Again, violence reveals itself as a form of communication.

For many years, international organizations have observed and registered the activities of the rebels, and they have meticulously reported on their pervasive violence and the victims' massive suffering (e.g., Amnesty International 1997, 1999; Human Rights Watch 1997, 2003a, 2005). Yet the rebel leadership never regarded such outside interventions as neutral, and some of the most gruesome attacks have been carried out with the explicit ambition to attract more attention and challenge outside interventions. For example, as an immediate response to Operation Lightning Thunder, the U.S.-supported military operation in 2008, the rebels killed more than 865 people in different central African locations (Human Rights Watch 2009). The "Christmas Day massacre" in the Congolese town of Faradje, with 143 people brutally murdered and globally reported on, was carried out on the rebel leader's explicit orders. Kony chose a Congolese town because the Congolese government, under pressure from U.S. diplomats, had ordered its army to join with the Ugandan army against the LRA. Moreover, Kony chose Faradje because "it was the nearest place where such massacres would have an impact and where they would get international publicity," the rebel commanding the attacks told journalists when he defected a year later (quoted in *New Vision*, November 22, 2009; see also Human Rights Watch 2010). After receiving amnesty, this renegade rebel had to join the Ugandan army.

Here the human terrain mapping is not only about "looking for bad guys to kill," to borrow David Price's quoting of human terrain advocate Audrey Roberts in this volume. Perhaps more notably, Roberts and colleagues assist the military when looking for bad guys to *recruit*. But behind the grotesquely spectacular events in Faradje and subsequent proxy developments of local alliances and global war, is yet another layer of entanglements. As the rebels write in a letter to the public that found its way to my hands during fieldwork in December 1999, well before the intervention of the ICC and the massacres in the Congo:

> Today several UN agencies like UNICEF, other human rights organizations and NGOs like World Vision are masquerading as relief workers during trouble and times of war. But these organizations operate on a set agenda to deplete your natural resources. Those operating among you are actually the shield and spears for Museveni against you. You should know that they are in Gulu, Lira, Kitgum or Apac [districts of northern Uganda] not as relief workers, but to fulfill the agenda of Museveni. Do not be deceived that we [the LRA] have no political agenda. Where were the UN, the human rights agencies and UNICEF at the time you were herded into the camps? (Translated from the Acholi original)

The statement speaks directly to Riches's (1986) model on violence that considers not only perpetrator and victim but also the position of outside observers. Riches furthermore suggests that the meanings of symbolically loaded words such as *war* and *violence* "are established, in the first instance, from their use" (1991:282). Unfolding in front of me right there in Uganda were the makings of war and political violence, the entanglement of the global with the local—a field of contested legitimacies, loaded with potential and emerging meanings. As Maurice Merleau-Ponty (1962:xix) puts it in his investigation of what he calls the existential structures, "Because we are in the world, we are *condemned to meaning*, and we cannot do or say anything without its acquiring a name in history." The intervention of the ICC and human terrain mapping added new dimensions to the theater of war, both cultural and political. The rebels' targeting of humanitarian organizations and expatriates was also something new, and it hit the world news. Outsiders could no longer escape the triangle of violence.

THE DEATH OF STEVE WILLIS

On November 8, 2005, not long after rebel commander Kapere issued his letter, Steve Willis drove through Murchison Falls National Park after assisting some stranded tourists. Despite an increasing number of rebel ambushes targeting foreigners, Ugandan authorities later claimed that Willis had refused armed escorts. Without warning, his four-wheel-drive vehicle was sprayed with bullets. Rebels immediately entered the scene to loot items they usually need—batteries to charge their communication radios, seatbelts to be used as shoulder straps on backpacks, cash, knives, and clothes. Willis's fellow travelers were injured but jumped out through the windows of the vehicle, and some ran into the bush. Willis, behind the wheel, died in the initial shooting. The rebels eventually left the scene without killing the rest of the party. Although the Ugandan army declared that the ambush had been carried out by a few hungry ragtag bandits, later interviews with the survivors in the international press revealed that the rebels were well armed and cold-bloodedly calculating in their attack.

A few days before the ambush of Willis and his friends, on the borderlands between Uganda and Sudan a different rebel unit ambushed and killed another Briton. This time the deceased had been working with International Aid Services, a relief and development organization (*New Vision*, November 7, 2005). Some days before this attack, two mine-clearance experts were killed in yet another rebel ambush in southern Sudan (*Daily Monitor*, November 2, 2005).

New Zealander Cam McLeay, one of the stranded tourists Willis came to assist, soon wrote a survivor's firsthand account for the *New Vision*:

There has been a string of falsehoods, fabrications and speculation printed in the world's media since the tragic death of Steve Willis on November 8, 2005 in Murchison Falls National Park in northern Uganda. It is the purpose of this letter to correct some of the myths surroundings the tragedy. . . . The Uganda Peoples Defence Forces (UPDF) acted in an exemplary manner in responding to the ambush. Within minutes of hearing of the attack, Brig. Nathan Mugisha had ordered a military helicopter to the scene fully equipped for such a tragedy with paramedics on board. The helicopter was supported on the ground by two armoured personnel carriers which arrived swiftly on the scene. Under the command of Lt. Col. Kidega, there can be no other army in the world that could have responded in a more professional or timely manner. The expedition team . . . and myself would like to express our sincere thanks to President Yoweri Museveni, Brig. Mugisha, Lt. Col. Kidega and the entire UPDF 4th Division for responding so swiftly in coming to our rescue. (*New Vision*, November 16, 2005)

For Ugandan authorities, this praise of the Ugandan army as the world's most professional, again published by the state-controlled *New Vision*, was timely. Two years earlier, the Ugandan army had charged several international human rights bodies as propagating the cause of the LRA. Human Rights Watch, for example, had published a report on Uganda that criticized not only the rebels but the conduct of the Ugandan armed forces as well (Human Rights Watch 2003a). An army spokesperson immediately "dismissed the report as the work of those bent on mobilising for the LRA," as reported in the *New Vision* (July 15, 2003). During my fieldwork in 2005, Human Rights Watch (2005) launched a new and equally critical report. In a long *New Vision* article, the Ugandan minister of defense wrote that this report was "unfounded, partisan and politically motivated" and a "deliberate attempt to distort the truth" with "outrageous allegations" (*New Vision*, October 3, 2005). Human Rights Watch had rebuttals published in Ugandan papers, and the issue was debated in the country. Many Ugandan commentators, as well as my informants, found the stand of the Ugandan government ridiculous. Interestingly, a few months earlier, the Ugandan prime minister had stopped human rights activists from filming in the squalid camps for the internally displaced persons in the war-torn north, arguing that a number of documentaries had portrayed a negative image to Uganda's international partners in development (*Daily Monitor*, June 20, 2005).

HUMANITARIAN DEATH

"The death of one man is a tragedy," the infamous quote attributed to Joseph Stalin goes. "The death of millions is a statistic." An increasing number of Ugandan commentators and academics have started to ask why the ICC did not proceed with any investigation of the Ugandan army's arbitrary killings and rape of civilians, torture, forced labor at gunpoint, or the forced displacement, often at gunpoint, of millions of people to squalid camps, all potential crimes against humanity. From the mid-1990s to the Juba talks in 2006, the official Ugandan policy was to forcefully resettle large numbers of the country's citizens in camps, where governance and military control came to function under a harsh but for some army actors economically lucrative displacement regime. As long as the fighting continued, high-ranking army officers wanted the camps to remain as a valid military strategy, as they regard all Acholi people in northern Uganda as potential rebel supporters who must be controlled and monitored. A statement from Major Kakooza Mutale, a friend and longstanding advisor to the Ugandan president, puts this habitual antipathy in historical perspective. "The depopulation of the villages removes the soft targets and logistics for the survival of the rebels," he said in 1996. "They will lack food, information, youth to abduct and people to kill. Desperation will drive them to attack the Army and the camps. That will be their end" (quoted by the *New Vision*, November 13, 1996, see also Branch 2005:19; Finnström 2008:ch. 4). Indeed, the rebels did attack the camps. Contrary to Mutale's claim, however, forced encampment did not mean the end of the rebels but in cynical ways, given the failure of the government to provide adequate protection, essentially concentrated what they needed the most, namely "food, information, youth to abduct and people to kill."

For example, during a period of fieldwork in 2002, war again descended on Purongo camp, located along the important truck route from Kampala to the West Nile region and the Congo, a road that also marks the border to Murchison Falls National Park. The rebels burned some fifty huts and killed a local government official and at least one Ugandan soldier. They also abducted some people to carry their loot. At the time, rebels were operating all over northern Uganda, and deadly attacks were reported daily. When the Ugandan soldiers realized that Purongo was under attack, they withdrew and shelled the camp from a distance. At least one mortar hit a hut, and a married couple and their three children died on the spot. Common as it was throughout the war, displaced people in northern Uganda used to call such random shelling "To whom it may concern." When my research colleague Ladit Anthony and I followed up on the Purongo attack, we found that some fifteen people died in the crossfire, soldiers excluded. But in the Ugandan media, one could read the usual dominant-view conclusion. "Kony kills 18 in game park," read the headline of one of Uganda's newspapers, the *Daily Monitor* (June 30, 2002). There can be little doubt that the Kampala-based editors wanted to add drama to the attack by locating it at the very heart of one of Uganda's most beautiful tourist sites. State authorities, however, were quick to point out that the squalid camp of Purongo and thus the war zone was located just *outside* the game park, not in the park itself. "Uganda is politically stable, peaceful and safe for tourism and investment," the press release from the president's office read (printed in the *Daily Monitor*, July 8, 2002). No correction was given for who was actually responsible for most of the deaths.

In 2002, there was seemingly not much worry for tourists. Yet the events unfolding in Purongo and neighboring camps were a naked illustration of today's global order of unequal populations. Internally displaced persons, herded into camps like cattle into corrals, are seldom recognized in life or death as they try to survive war just a few miles from the luxurious tourist lodges in the game park, where expatriate humanitarian aid workers could afford an illusionary break from their daily work. The Ugandan government's counterinsurgency warfare was in fact conditioned by massive international humanitarian interventions. With humanitarian organizations coming in to provide aid to the camps, an apparatus with a money-spinning tendency of its own, Ugandan military authorities had their hands free. External aid enabled the brutalization of the Ugandan army's violent counterinsurgency campaign, to the extent that humanitarian interventions became "accessories to this crime" (Branch 2008:151; see also Dolan 2009).

With the murder of Steve Willis, the international debate on the Ugandan government's use of its own citizenry as a buffer against the insurgents and the complicit role of the international community evaporated. In shifting focus, any demand for "humanitarian accountability" to replace the many years of "humanitarian impunity" (Branch 2008) was effectively rendered invisible. Instead the international radar of attention again focused on the LRA's "pointless terrorist activities against innocent civilians," whereby the rebel army "cowardly attacks unarmed civilians, retreats animal-like into the bush at the first sign of any engagement," to again quote Cam McLeay's account of Willis's tragic death. Spectacular as it was, with the murder of an innocent Briton, the focus was again on the rebels, portrayed as animals coming from the wild bush only to retreat back into it. Perhaps to the satisfaction of the Ugandan government, the hyenas were back, if not in town then surely in the surrounding bush. Few external observers paid any further attention to the debate on human rights abuses committed by the government forces. With the killing of Kapere, even more so because of the public display of his bullet-ridden body, the Ugandan army retook the propaganda initiative, a ritualized public showing off of power, a virtual spectacide intended for both national and global consumption.

One could even conclude that Kapere's last months of life embodied international intervention translated into the local, which violently and magically boomeranged back into the global, an argument I soon develop. When killing Kapere, the Ugandan army admitted, if only implicitly, that rebel attacks during the months following the unsealing of the ICC arrest warrants had been quite well coordinated. In December 2005, as Kapere's body was displayed to the media crowd, army commanders confessed to the invited reporters that "Kapere had given them hard time," and more, that he was the very rebel who "had written a letter threatening to kill charity workers based in the north" (*New Vision*, December 27, 2005).

WRITING HISTORY, HUMAN TERRAIN, AND THE MEDIA

Only with Kapere's death was the story of his letter officially released. Perhaps this is the very magic of the Manichaean and essentialist vocabulary, defined by dominant groups, "that helps stabilize categories of group identity" and "fixes fear and anxiety" in places located elsewhere, with the non-Western other, caused by the non-Western other (Hinton 2010:38). It is the Janus face of identity, as Alexander Hinton argues, whereby we need the primitive and violent other for "us" to cohere. In describing the LRA rebels as "animal-like" bush creatures, outside witnesses like McLeay can think of themselves and the Ugandan government as civilized and benevolent; of outside interventions in African wars as purely humanitarian and thus neutral; and finally of outside reporting of the state of affairs as objective. Such a black-and-white logic is part of the perpetuation of global war today. Moreover, it is a magical vocabulary that, as Edgar Winans (1992) pointed out, enables those in power to identify opposition and protest as witchcraft, banditry, and terrorism.

The so-called human terrain is hereby mapped, with the hyenas always and only on the enemy side. But if McLeay's claim that the rebels are acting animal-like suggests that they somehow have lost their senses and thus their humanity, there is an additional twist to the Ugandan president's description of them as hyenas. Rather than simply losing humanity, shape-shifting back and forth between human and animal form is regarded as a form of witchcraft in many African tales (see, e.g., Jackson 1989:ch. 7). In East African ethnography, in particular, the hyena is associated with witchcraft. If witchcraft and black magic in the history of anthropological theory have come to represent the reversal of ordinary values—often described by the anthropologists' informants as utterly unpredictable and the image of evil incarnate—then this is, to again follow Riches's triadic model, a potentially violent equation essentially including also the witnessing and writing anthropologist. Indeed, for the ethnography of violent death described here, labeling the rebels as creatures less than human that retreat into the bush is a magical aspect of the very violence itself. In a long and rare firsthand interview in June 2006, rebel leader Joseph Kony told Mareike Schomerus that she was actually the first European journalist to visit him in the bush. "I am now here," Kony tells her. "You have now seen me, I am a human being like you. I have eyes, I have brain. . . . I wear clothes also. But [until now] Museveni has been spoiling our name, [saying] we are animals" (2010b:114).

The rebel leader's statement has some resonance with Edmund Leach's (1977:36) words that open this chapter—the terrorist is also a fellow human being. But the course of history would have it differently. Sam Farmar, a colleague of Schomerus who operated the camera during the interview with Kony, immediately ran off with the rare footage and edited it in ways that made it look like the rebel leader spoke directly to him, and then he had it broadcast on BBC *Newsnight*. In Farmar's editing, we again see the work of magic and shape-shifting tendencies (see Jackson 1989:113). With this TV broadcast, Farmar immediately made it into world fame. Amnesty International wanted to enter the story for their journalism awards, and *Newsnight*'s senior editor wanted to enter it for the Royal Television Society Awards in the United Kingdom (Schomerus 2010a:109, 298 n. 21). To illustrate his point about the ruthless rebels, Farmar used a third journalist's footage of women and children killed by Ugandan helicopter gunships a few years earlier, and the noninformed viewer could easily conclude that these very deaths were caused by the rebels. This is the raw power of the so-called human terrain mapping, a reconstitution of the virtual that ritualizes global war, here magically condensed to Kony and the LRA. "As long as Kony is there in the bush," a friend and longtime informant told me with resignation when I visited northern Uganda in 2010, "he should be prepared to take *all* the blame."

Farmar also sold the scoop to *The Times*. Now his story begins with a standard headline when it comes to international reporting on the LRA. "I will use the Ten Commandments to liberate Uganda," it declared, with the quote attributed to the rebel leader. But Kony never said this in the interview. "The imagination of London-based newsroom staff had outweighed what the person at the centre of the conflict, the interviewee, actually said," Schomerus writes. But her complaints were in vain, and in retrospect she could only note the irony of the whole affair, because "Kony said in the interview that people were using his Christian beliefs as propaganda" (2010a:111; see also Finnström 2010a). The journalist Matthew Green, on the other hand, recounts how an editor at Reuters in London ordered him to restructure his reporting on the LRA to get "the bit about the Ten Commandments up high." Green complied and "dutifully shuffled the paragraphs to emphasize Kony's apparent insanity" (2008:316).

NARRATIVES OF WAR AS WITCHCRAFT

At issue in Uganda's theater of war is not primarily a search for any truth, as we most often think of it, but a magical discourse whereby the course of events is influenced and the future controlled, even altered. In trying to keep track of Farmar's story and its shape-shifting tendencies, I am reminded of Bronislaw Malinowski's old thesis that "magic is to be expected and generally to be found whenever man comes to an unbridgeable gap, a hiatus in his knowledge or in his powers of practical control, and yet has to continue in his pursuit" (1979:43). The dominant narrative on the war in Uganda is largely a cynical discourse of fantasy and denial. Rather than the Malinowskian legacy just alluded to, in a more contemporary understanding magic is what we do not yet understand, a measure of our incomprehension of local explanations. It even involves an active decision not to understand and a refusal to see the assumed terrorist as a fellow human being.

Such a process is structured in ways similar to that of witchcraft accusations among the non-Western other known from classic anthropological literature. I claimed in the beginning of my chapter that spaces of death and magical terror are produced not primarily *by* the assumed primitives of Africa but in the emplacement of global forces *on* the African scene. "In the system of witchcraft belief and anti-witchcraft action,"

Ulf Hannerz (1981:32) notes in an article on the management of danger, "one may discern a gap between the witch as a thought-of being, the unreservedly evil creature of collective fantasy, with nonhuman habits and capabilities, and the witch suspect, a real person of flesh and blood who may have personality quirks but who has been experienced by others in the many dimensions of daily life, and probably often as a quite ordinary human being." The extreme violence of the LRA *and* authoritative Ugandan state propaganda *and* the obsession of the international press with central Africa as exotic and a heart of darkness here collapse in a vital conjuncture comparable with witchcraft processes. "The trick of successful witchcraft accusations," Hannerz (1981:32) continues, "is to close the gap by assimilating the idea of the suspect as a person into the realm of witchcraft ideas, a rather dramatic example of labeling process." Tellingly, the existence of Joseph Kapere as a person with a reason was denied until he was killed and his bullet-ridden body put on display. Only after his death were his actions acknowledged. When fighting resumed in 2008 after two years of arduous peace talks, most inside observers were disappointed but perhaps not surprised. Ugandan Archbishop John Baptist Odama met rebel leader Kony several times during this period. "Not enough of his humanity was touched to make him come out more fully instead of stigmatising and bedevilling him," Odama concluded in an interview with Mike Wooldridge (*BBC News*, January 19, 2011).

At play in these instances is a magical scheme, as Michael Taussig (1987) points out, because magic is not so much an entity out there, elsewhere, true to itself. Nor is it really something that primarily stems from the experiences of perpetrators and victims. Rather, to borrow from Stewart and Strathern (2002), here magic exists as a relation of coercive reciprocity and increased polarization, as an imaginary other to the imagined absoluteness of ourselves as civilized and modern. Those who have the upper hand in defining such a discourse are also those with the most power, on the battlefields as well as in the news rooms. Simply speaking, this is the magic of power—truths are produced and written, and the human terrain outlined. The outside witness is a likely contributor to such a magic. The Ugandan army's initial denial of Kapere's letter as well as the state-controlled *New Vision*'s powerful stories on the deaths of Kapere and Willis, but also Farmar's shape-shift editing of the interview with Kony are all examples of coercive reciprocity and increased polarization.

In revisiting those months of fieldwork in 2005, and in acknowledging the sad deaths of Willis and others, I could observe how a long-standing dominant and highly simplified narrative of black and white again made itself manifest. In Uganda, the government has had the upper hand in defining the discourse on meaning, whereas the LRA, as obvious and violent coauthors in the process of war, has become the moral category of evil. All in all, this is a magical conjuncture that perpetuates global war.

THE LAST FREEDOM?

Now and then I hear my informants say that Kony, after many years of being told that he is a terrorist, something his actions prove him to be, has decided to be one. As one young man said to me in 2002 when he imagined Kony's way of reasoning, "They say that I am a terrorist. Well, let it be so, and let me then give them terrorism" (Finnström 2008:128). By way of concluding this chapter, I want to suggest, perhaps provocatively, that the supposed reasoning of the rebel leader resembles the anthropologist Michael Jackson's painful account of a Sierra Leonean woman who confessed to witchcraft and thus to have caused the death of her brother. After her confession, whereby she turned into a *non*person that in the local context deserved no respect, the woman was buried alive. In retrospect, Jackson interprets the exposed woman's self-confession to witchcraft as her last freedom, when the state of affairs had robbed her of any power to act differently. She was "a victim of a world," which denied her "any legitimate outlet for her frustrations and grievances," and her confession was "a desperate stratagem for reclaiming autonomy in a hopeless situation" (Jackson 1989:100). Jackson builds his interpretation on an autobiographical story from Jean Genet's childhood, famously taken up by Jean-Paul Sartre. As a small boy, Genet's stepmother caught him in the act of stealing. Facing this situation, Genet "suddenly saw himself reduced to an object for others, a projection of their fears, a scapegoat for their anxieties" (Jackson 1989:101). To recapture a feeling of freedom and agency, the boy decided to become the thief the crime had made him to be. Like the internationally indicted LRA leaders on the road of no return, the boy decided "to become his fate, to live it as though he himself had conceived it" (Jackson 1989:101).[1]

More than being anchored only in any allegedly closed local cultural belief system, such a self-confession is born out of the violent intersection of those facets of the world that we often think of as the most isolated, made manifest in the metaphor of central Africa as the heart of darkness, and those facets we think of as locations of global democracy, for example, Western media outlets and international justice interventions (Whitehead 2004b:75; see also Finnström 2009). All this becomes evident when the analysis of rebel violence also incorporates the workings of state-sponsored counterinsurgency, including aspects of enforced domination and massive internment, paradoxically with the international community as complicit and bystanders of a sort.

From this threefold perspective, I note that Kapere's targeting of Westerners and humanitarian aid workers rather than only fellow Ugandans was an effort to resist the apolitical and magical discourse of war as propagated by outside witnesses such as Farmar and his predecessors. Out there in those unknown woods of central Africa, to combine the partly mystic and partly mythic imageries of the two AFRICOM representatives quoted herein, is real evil and thus the essence of the so-called human terrain mapping—a never-ending, multilayered, and most strange hunt for characters who are no longer fellow human beings. In the perspective of Kapere and his subordinates, and in the light of prejudiced media reports and the ICC's one-sided intervention, there are no neutral bystanders in this scheme of things. The so-called international community had long been deeply entangled with the realpolitik of war. This is also what Riches's triadic model of violence suggests. Unfolding in front of me in Uganda during those months of 2005 was yet another historical moment of the magical makings of global war—existential, sociopolitical, and virtual at the same time.

NOTES

This article reports from a research project on global war and transnational (in)justice, funded by the Bank of Sweden Tercentenary Foundation. Fieldwork in 2002 and 2005 was financed by the Department of Research Cooperation of the Swedish International Development Cooperation Agency, and endorsed by the Uganda National Council for Science and Technology. An additional visit to Uganda in 2010 was financed by the Royal Swedish Academy of Sciences. For support and careful feedback, I thank Ron Atkinson, Per Brandström, Michael Jackson, Anthony Odiya Labol, and Neil Whitehead.

1. In Jean Genet's words, quoted by Jackson, "J'ai décidé d'être ce que le crime à fait de moi—un voleur."

THE HOSTILE GAZE

Night Vision and the Immediation of Nocturnal
Combat in Vietnam and Iraq

"In 'Nam it seemed like we were always in the brush. Once in a
while we would have some clearings. It was real difficult to see
very far ahead. You had to keep your eyes moving to see what was
in front, to the side, and most of all where you were walking." So
wrote Vietnam War veteran Ed Smith in April 2006 to his son,
Captain Will Smith, stationed in Tikrit, Iraq. Captain Smith commented on his father's combat experience: "Before night vision
was a common soldier-issued item, the V.C. owned the night. We
learned from that; now the U.S. military is the most lethal force
on the earth in hours of darkness. When the lights go out in Iraq,
I feel safer than I do during the day."[1] New technologies, such as
thermal imaging, image intensifiers, sniper advanced targeting
pods, laser spot trackers, drones, and satellites, have expanded
the situational overview of today's soldiers and been hailed for
enabling surgical strikes on military targets. This technological
development has altered the visual culture of nocturnal combat
and the social practices of troops toward enemies and civilians.
The night changed from a time of imagination beset with con-
ceivable and illusory threats into a time of image-making, when
human shapes stand out in an unreal world of green hues.

Night vision devices have absorbed nocturnal combat into the
realm of magic. The transformation of ocular observations into

virtual images parallels the visualization of magic's occult workings into material representations. Science and magic meet in illusions of reality through technical interventions, albeit from opposite directions: what is regarded as hidden, mysterious, and irrational in the supernatural becomes concrete and cogent through magical practice, and what is visible, tangible, and comprehensible in the war zone becomes virtual and mesmerizing during mediated nocturnal combat. The world is manipulated in both cases through a deceptive instrumentality that objectifies the subjective powers of mediation in virtual images and imaginary creations. U.S. troops operating in Iraq deliberately sought out this interface of the natural and the supernatural. They resorted to the magic of noctambulation and divination to execute missions and ward off danger. An infantry team leader from the 82nd Airborne Division stationed in Baghdad relied heavily on a magical object that he named the Asset: "The 'Asset' is truly amazing. It has helped guide us along our voyage here in Iraq. It will let us know which route is the safest/least traffic bogged. It will let us know whether we are at the right location for a raid that we must conduct. It is also a great tool for alerting us to potential insurgent activity in the area. We have come to trust the results of the 'Asset' for it is highly accurate. . . . The 'Asset' is a magic eight ball. HAHAH!! Yes I'm dead serious. We use it probably 20–30 times each patrol now that I received it in the mail."[2] The soldiers believed that the eight ball would get them out of tight spots and guide the random swarming operations in hostile areas carried out under the cover of darkness thanks to their night vision capability.

The comparison of nocturnal combat in Vietnam and Iraq reveals the emergence of a mediated hostile gaze through the use of image intensifiers that turned night into day and gave their viewers a sense of real-life ocular vision through immediation. Immediation is the process by which users no longer realize that sight and interaction are electronically mediated, thus "rendering the presence of others so 'real' that the medium recedes into the background" (Eisenlohr 2009:276). Such immediation occurs readily in today's military operations because of the dangers surrounding the night vision–equipped troops and therefore creates a visual combat culture that influences the combatants' practices and insertion in the world. As David Morgan (2005:33) says, "Visual culture is what images, acts of seeing, and attendant intellectual, emotional, and perceptual sensibilities do to build, maintain, or transform the worlds in which people live." In other words, combatants see, think, and act differently in their area of operation with night vision devices, and this condition is magnified by nighttime's celestial qualities, physiological effects, emotional experiences, and cultural meanings. This chapter examines this shift in the visual culture of nocturnal patrols in the wars of Vietnam and Iraq and demonstrates that night vision equipment generated new counterinsurgency tactics in Iraq that caused numerous civilian deaths because of the changing nature of battle space and the dehumanization of civilians and enemy combatants through their magical representation in mediated image-realities.

NOCTURNAL PATROLS AND TACTICAL SWARMS

The arrival of an infantry company in Vietnam was often announced by the sound of Huey helicopters dropping the men in the operation zone. The troops were divided into platoons that spread out across the terrain. Each platoon was organized into a point, flank, and tail-end squad. Humping heavy packs, they walked for days across rice paddies, jungles, or mountain slopes, following compass bearings and counting steps. They might sweep around in a circle or leapfrog with the help of helicopters. Their mission was to find an invisible, hit-and-run enemy. Exhausted by the endless patrols, dehydrated by the tropical heat, and anxious about booby traps and sniper attacks, their destination was as uncertain as the ever-changing intelligence reports. When heavy fire contact was made, the radio-telephone operator passed the map coordinates of the platoon's position to the other units for assistance and called in artillery shelling and helicopter gunships to pound the enemy. Often by the time other platoons arrived, the enemy had already retreated (Appy 1993:172–81; Downs 1978:107–8).

The search-and-destroy missions in Vietnam failed in the end because the Vietnamese revolutionaries refused to enter into open fire fights with U.S. troops during the daytime, and thus turned the visual culture of nocturnal combat into a struggle with the invisible. Soldiers were forced to use touch and hearing rather than sight to find their bearings and fight enemy combatants. Jim Mead wrote about the fear of getting lost on these nocturnal missions: "Our first mission was at night. We were scared stiff. We headed into the jungle without any idea where we were going, or what we were doing. We kept walking for a couple of hours in the dark, praying we wouldn't lose sight of the guy in front of us, and getting lost" (Appy 1993:179). The lack of sleep, visual deprivation, and sound intensification made soldiers likely to feel threatened and out of control, fearing disorientation on these nocturnal missions (Ben-Ari 2003:112).

Because the enemy was so hard to find and did not enter into open firefights, the patrols set up positions in daylight to act as bait and then call in air strikes when they drew enemy fire at night (Appy 1993:182; Bergerud 1993:139–40). They would establish a defensive perimeter by dividing up into groups of three men to protect the position. The fear of falling asleep was palpable in the song taught in basic training: "Vietnam, Vietnam, every night while you're sleepin', Charlie Cong comes a-creepin' all around" (O'Brien 2006:92). Sometimes, a few soldiers formed a listening post beyond the perimeter to detect enemy scouts betraying the approach of the main force. The men would not shoot at suspicious sounds to prevent giving away their position; they tossed hand grenades instead. Listening posts were very dangerous assignments because the men could be caught in crossfire if an attack began, and they could not withdraw for the risk of being shot by their comrades (Downs 1978:179). The results were mixed because the Vietnamese would often retreat, and then the American foot soldiers had to chase them to determine their position for air strikes while running the risk of walking into ambushes and stepping on rudimentary booby traps. The U.S. high command failed to find a successful strategy against the South Vietnamese revolutionaries, and some soldiers took out their frustrations on the civilian population, who were believed to support the insurgency.

U.S. commanders in Iraq were equally at a loss in 2003 and 2004 on how to combat the Iraqi insurgents and foreign mujahideen with deadly surprise attacks. These irregular combatants merged with the social environment by dressing as civilians, placed roadside bombs, and launched suicide attacks without extensive battle plans because they were not trying to assume political power in Iraq, unlike the revolutionaries in South Vietnam. Their principal strategic objective was to create chaos and general insecurity to undermine the authority of the foreign occupying force and increase its death toll to an intolerable level. What made it particularly difficult to fight the insurgents was their lack of a unity of command, as was typical of a classic guerrilla organization like the Viet Cong; they were composed of a network of loosely allied groups (Hashim 2006; Metz 2007:23–31; Robben 2010a).

American military researchers examining future types of warfare had already anticipated this development and had also formulated a response:

"It takes networks to fight networks. Governments that want to defend against netwar may have to adopt organizational designs and strategies like those of their adversaries" (Arquilla and Ronfeldt 2001:15; see also Arquilla 2010). The U.S. military abandoned in 2005 the unsuccessful massive sweeps with tanks, artillery, helicopter gunships, and thousands of troops and switched to small-scale operations, such as random cordon-and-search operations in neighborhoods, surprise raids on houses, and dismounted combat patrols that roamed city streets at will.

The new strategy drew on the counterinsurgency successes of the Marines' Combined Action Platoons in Vietnam, which showed that insurgencies were best fought by imitating rather than carpet bombing or baiting them (Krepinevich 1986:172–77). U.S. troops in Iraq increased their mobility and surprise tactics by deploying small infantry units and allowing them to swarm through battle space in the hope of catching the elusive insurgents unawares. These units did not function as bait for the insurgents, but were predators who actively sought them out. Lieutenant Van Engelen explained this swarming tactic as follows: "I just picked a spot on a map that I thought was a high-volume area that might catch some people. We just set something up for half an hour to an hour and then we'd move on" (Hedges and Al-Arian 2007:27). Swarming was thus antithetical to the cultural mapping of the Human Terrain System because enemy targets were regarded as indistinguishable from noncombatants (see González's chapter in this volume).

The deliberate randomness of the swarming operations imitated the erratic movements of the insurgents and made U.S. combat units out-trump them as chaos-producing forces through a superior situational overview made possible by the latest technology. U.S. combat units were provided with advanced night vision devices and communication equipment, and were backed by formidable rear and air support that allowed them to move separately and freely in battle space, yet were interconnected electronically through interfaced communication systems. The military were trained to exploit this self-induced chaos, as one U.S. Marines manual indicated: "Small unit leaders will be more comfortable working in and through chaos, to the point they can capitalize on the chaos of the operational environment—to the adversary's detriment" (MCCDC 2006:24). Troops were taught to embrace the notion that "war is inherently chaos . . . because, more often than not, conditions on the ground will change so rapidly that original orders and well-thought-out plans become irrelevant" (Campbell 2009:44). Therefore, it can hardly be a coincidence that U.S. General James Mattis chose Chaos as his radio call sign when commanding his marines in Iraq (Ricks 2007:314). Swarming seemed an ideal answer in Iraq's unpredictable battle space because "swarms operate best in chaos" (Honan 2003). U.S. counterinsurgency units thus further enhanced the general disorder created by the insurgency through unpredictable swarming operations.

The upshot of the urban swarming operations was that public space became highly insecure for Iraqi civilians during daytime, and even more menacing after dark because the night "is by and large defined and judged in negative terms, for example, by the absence of light and (and more often than not) warmth, or by chaos, darkness and fear" (Schnepel and Ben-Ari 2005:153). This nocturnal threat was posed by effaced soldiers in camouflage who moved about stealthily. These U.S. troops became so accustomed to seeing in the dark with their high-tech devices that they forgot the night remained pitch black for the unsuspecting civilians. Iraqis did not recognize the poorly marked flash checkpoints erected in towns and cities to capture insurgents and weapons smugglers. U.S. commanders have blamed civilian fatalities on the indiscriminate attacks by enemy combatants, which oblige troops to make split-second decisions to ascertain whether a suicide bomber or a drunken driver is crossing the trigger line. This is certainly true, but the tactics of impromptu checkpoints carry equal blame. Soldiers manning checkpoints want to be in control and therefore changed rules and regulations to induce a "calibrated chaos" that disoriented civilians (Peteet 2010:92).

People's first worry in Iraq was to recognize a checkpoint at all. For example, on the evening of August 7, 2003, at around 9 PM, U.S. soldiers of the 1st Armored Division set up two flying checkpoints with unlit armored vehicles in Bilal Habashi Street in Baghdad for a random weapons search in homes and shops. At around 9:20 PM, Saif al-Azawi and two friends were driving through their neighborhood, with loud music blaring from their car, to pick up a third friend to celebrate Saif's excellent exam results. "At that time," according to one eyewitness, "the electricity in the district was cut off and the interior light of Saif's car was turned on, which prevented him from seeing outside clearly" (Human Rights Watch 2003b:19). A U.S. soldier shouted for them to stop, but the car sped on. Another soldier fired warning shots first, and then impacted the car when it entered the checkpoint. Saif was killed and his two friends injured. The next car was not given any stop signs but immediately fired on, killing the driver, Adil al-Kawwaz, and his three children, while injuring his pregnant wife and his fourth child. The superior officer acknowledged his men's mistake of firing at the second car but insisted that the first car was "loaded with insurgents firing weapons out the windows" (Mansoor 2008:76). A U.S. military investigation concluded that the killings had been a regrettable incident but that the correct engagement procedures had been followed (Human Rights Watch 2003b:18–23).

This tragedy may have been the result of unfortunate circumstance and panic, but such checkpoint killings hint at more structural problems caused by self-produced contact situations and the limited sight of night vision devices. Iraqi public space had become a chaotic environment that bewildered the civilians present in the multimedia panopticon of battle space with its unpredictable tactical practices under the cover of darkness.

NIGHT INTO DAY AND THE IMMEDIATION OF COMBAT

Nocturnal combat was one of the greatest challenges soldiers faced during the Vietnam War because they could not rely on their eyesight to find their way around the battle space. "There were many times you were out on patrol and literally couldn't see your hand in front of your face," recalled Dan Vandenberg. "You'd have to put your hand on the shoulder of the guy in front of you so you didn't get lost or separated. You're walking around through these paddies, and you never know if you're going to step in a well, which were usually dried up and full of snakes. You sure couldn't see any booby traps: You couldn't find your feet, much less a booby trap" (Bergerud 1993:109). Vietnam veteran and novelist Tim O'Brien (1991:248) described this darkness as "the kind of clock-stopping black that God must've had in mind when he sat down to invent blackness. It made your eyeballs ache. You'd shake your head and blink, except you couldn't even tell you were blinking, the blackness didn't change." The darkness and danger of night patrols in Vietnam affected the U.S. soldiers emotionally. "The long night marches turned their minds upside down; all the rhythms were wrong. Always a lost sensation. They'd blunder along through the dark, willy-nilly, no sense of place or direction, probing for an enemy that nobody could see" (O'Brien 1991:249). Soldiers clustered around comrades who had better natural night vision as if they owned some magic that could protect others from harm (Herr 1991:57).

The U.S. armed forces have historically favored day over night operations. Superior firepower and troop numbers allowed for effective daylight action supported by artillery and air attacks (Morris 1985). The tactical advantage of surprise, however, since the 1930s has led to the development of night vision devices for special operations. Small numbers of starlight scopes with limited amplification properties were first used in the Vietnam War in 1965. Only the six-man teams of Long Range Reconnaissance Patrols or Army Rangers, carrying out surveillance and combat missions in enemy territory, and the occasional infantry company were equipped with one starlight scope that quadrupled the available night light. Some soldiers felt uncomfortable. "You aren't supposed to see the night. It's unnatural. I don't trust this thing," remarked Private Bates, who intuited its troubling magical properties (O'Brien 2006:38). Night vision devices were still in their infancy and were useless in the dense Vietnamese jungle (Downs 1978:124; Lanning 1988:132; Stanton 1992:24). Usually, American troops parachuted flares and used tracer rounds to illuminate the Vietnamese revolutionary forces moving about at night. Night vision equipment continued to be uncommon for another two decades. The task force that tried to extract the American hostages from the U.S. embassy in Tehran in 1980 had great difficulty in acquiring enough night vision devices for their ill-fated mission (Kyle 1995:87–89). The standard issuing of night vision equipment around the turn of the twenty-first century has therefore revolutionized warfare.

There are two types of night vision devices: image intensifiers and thermal imaging systems. Image intensifiers amplify the weak light of the moon, stars, and sky glow on a green display. Green is used because the human eye can distinguish more hues in green than in any other color. State-of-the-art devices reach an amplification of 35,000 times but restrict the 190-degrees field of vision of normal eyesight to 40–60 degrees and might dazzle users by strong light sources. Unlike image intensifiers, which require some ambient light, thermal imaging systems can operate in complete darkness by detecting the infrared radiation from heat sources. These devices convert thermal contrasts into visual contrasts but suffer from a lack of detail and the inability to distinguish facial features (Johnson 2004).

Night vision goggles (NVGS) lifted darkness during the Iraq War and allowed troops to see order in the nocturnal chaos by enhancing surprise, mobility, and situational overview, as Captain Danjel Bout of the 3rd Infantry Division wrote in 2005. "These cyclopean sights incessantly tug at your trapezius muscles, but in exchange for their nagging weight they peel away the cloak of night, and reveal the darkness in her naked splendor. The emerald images the NVGs splash across our retinas allow us to move like wraiths across the silent moonscape, dodging and weaving through the murk."[3] NVGs are still beset with technical failures, but their greatest risks are the 40–60-degrees tunnel vision, the difficulties of interpreting the blurry images, and the fear of unknown nocturnal dangers.[4] The website GlobalSecurity.org notes: "Darkness acts as a strong stimulus to the imagination and thus burdens the nervous system; a feeling of insecurity, which might eventually lead to panic, may be the outcome."[5] These circumstances affect a soldier's image assessment.

The misinterpretation of scope-mediated images became clear in an ambush in September 2004 set up to detect the placement of improvised explosive devices (IEDs) along a highway north of Baghdad, described by the soldier Jason Hartley (2005:202–15). Just after the five-man team had settled in, the soldiers heard gunfire from another ambush team farther up the road. They learned over the radio that a man was taking artillery rounds from a van and dropping them along the road for accomplices to bury later as IEDs. The van was fired on but succeeded in speeding away in the hail of bullets. The second ambush team saw the Volkswagen bus appear through the NVGs, pointed their laser-guided rifles, emptied their magazines, and fired a grenade when the driver still failed to stop. Several humvees surrounded the van when it finally came to a halt. After a medic had treated the driver for the nonlethal wounds to his legs and lower back, he was taken into custody and his van examined. To everyone's surprise, it was entirely stocked with crates of baby chickens. The driver had been traveling at night to protect his fragile cargo from the sweltering daytime temperatures, when his engine began to overheat. Noticing water bottles along the highway discarded by military convoys, he stopped to collect those with water to fill the van's radiator and dropped the empty ones. So, as Hartley recalls, "when Ray's team watched this man through their infrared scopes, what he was holding looked to them like artillery shells" (2005:214).

This bizarre incident is just one among numerous misreadings of night vision–aided combat—such as the fatal shooting of a retarded man holding a toy gun, the killing of a girl as her father was rejoicing in the capture of Saddam Hussein's sons Uday and Qusay with celebratory gunshots, the wounding of two boys carrying shepherds' canes mistaken for rifles—let alone the many self-inflicted casualties and civilian deaths at checkpoints (Fick 2006:239; Filkins 2008:203; Gutmann and Lutz 2010:114–15; Human Rights Watch 2003b; Rieckhoff 2007:172–74). Friendly fire and civilian casualties happen in any war, but the chaos-producing swarm tactics enabled by night-piercing equipment hindered civilians in detecting potential threats and made their unwitting behavior vulnerable to misinterpretation by invisible soldiers. Tunnel vision is not unique to NVGs but is also produced by a sniper's telescope, which blocks out peripheral vision and strips the targeted object of its contextual meanings, unlike the bare-eyed scrutiny of an object, which leaves more distant objects visually accessible and intact.

Technical improvements can reduce these mistakes, but the latest third-generation devices cause problems of another order as the conflation of reality and image progresses. Technical sophistication makes viewers forget that images are "the sort of sign that presents a deceptive appearance of naturalness and transparence concealing an opaque, distorting, arbitrary mechanism of representation, a process of ideological mystification" (Mitchell 1986:8). As Lieutenant Ilario Pantano (2006:2) reflected on the experience of being absorbed into the image intensifier's limited field of vision: "The world has shrunk to the shimmering green circle of NVGs." This restricted vision makes killing easier. "Night-vision devices provide a superb form of psychological distance by converting the target into an inhuman green blob," writes Lieutenant Colonel Dave Grossman (1995:169). The decontextualization of human targets observed through NVGs and telescopes adds to their dehumanization by visually isolating people from their surroundings and subjecting them to the rules of engagement that define who is friend and who is foe.

Night vision devices are still uncomfortable to wear, as Captain Bout explained, but better equipment recedes the awareness of mediation only further into the back of consciousness and positions the goggled soldier in the interface of multiple media vectors that absorb his attention during combat when immediacy becomes a matter of life or death. As Jay David Bolter and Richard Grusin (2000:6) have succinctly stated: "Immediacy depends on hypermediacy." Hypermediation causes a sensorial avalanche of multiple media stimuli that are mistaken for immediacy.

The risk of hypermediation was tragically shown in 1988 when a missile launched from the USS *Vincennes* shot down Iran Air flight 655, killing the crew and 290 passengers. According to John Armitage (2003:3), "The *Vincennes* catastrophe occurred because the US navy implicitly trusted the digitally produced visual representations and simulated scenarios, codes and models of its Aegis system during a hazardous foray into the territorial waters of Iran." Similar multiple mediated parameters of enmity dictating tomorrow's soldiers will create an overloaded and overdetermined enclosed experience as they become outfitted with opaque helmets with internal screens beaming filtered image-realities on their retinas that will further dehumanize enemy targets (Vasquez 2009:90–91). As Jay David Bolter and Richard Grusin (2000:53–54) write, "The excess of media becomes an authentic experience, not in the sense that it corresponds to an external reality, but rather precisely because it . . . does not feel compelled to refer to anything beyond itself." Furthermore, the privileged association of truth and sight over the other senses, common in many cultures (Bloch 2008), provides additional credence to the virtual images produced by visual mediating devices.

This authentication of image-realities has its origins in the need for aerial reconnaissance in World War I. Camouflage, powerful cannons, and machine guns made enemy positions invisible to the naked eye. "Just as weapons and armour developed in unison throughout history, so visibility and invisibility now began to evolve together, eventually producing *invisible weapons that make things visible*—radar, sonar, and the high-definition camera of spy satellites" (Virilio 1989:71). The mode of perception on the battlefield changed as commanders gave tactical orders based on mediated photographic and cinematic images, instead of a visual inspection of the battlefield so common before World War I.

The image-realities of tomorrow's sophisticated equipment will further increase the prejudice of mediation. It will preselect targets by narrowing people down to key indicators of enmity in a scopic context that reduces the soldier's weighing of life-or-death decisions to a choice among a small number of fixed options. In this way, the screen "greatly participates in the basic definition of the image itself" (Mondzain 2000:35). Nuanced human and social characteristics are deleted from natural holistic vision, and the battle space is cut loose from a contextual awareness of the world. This is of course not to suggest that natural eyesight provides a neutral knowledge of the world, because vision is always culturally mediated, but only to argue that the composite of thermal images, body scans, and intensified images will create an augmented but selective reality to produce a dehumanized representation defined solely by threat indicators.

Dehumanization by the mediated hostile gaze is preceded by the depersonalization of people in war zones. Soldiers commonly depersonalize both themselves and the enemy as objects to control the emotions brought on by killing other human beings (Ben-Ari 1998:82–88). An infantryman of the 82nd Airborne Division described this emotional detachment as follows: "If there's one thing about being in a war zone it is this . . . the level and intensity of the carnage that I've see is unparallel to anything I will ever experience again in my life. . . . But like all things in life, you become desensitized and used to what you see. That is sadly the point in my life where I am. Seeing another dead body, or executed Iraqi or whatever no long[er] has an effect on me. Nothing . . . cold nothingness."[6] Eyal Ben-Ari (1998:83) has argued that depersonalization turns into dehumanization when the enemy-as-object becomes the enemy-as-demon, and excessive violence becomes justified as morally right. This happened in Vietnam and Iraq. The "Kill, kill, kill the gooks!" of boot camp during the Vietnam War sounds eerily similar to the "Kill! Kill! Kill the sand niggers!" of basic training for the Iraq War (Key 2007:49; Longley 2008:63). American troops regarded the Vietnamese and the Iraqis as savages, and the wars as civilizing missions (Appy 1993:253–55; Silliman 2008). As a result, there was a tendency to consider all Vietnamese and Iraqis as enemies. The point here is that the dehumanization process took an additional step in the Iraq War through the visual mediation of enemy combatants and Iraqi civilians by night vision equipment.

Captain Smith's praise for the greater situational overview of the Iraq War compared to the Vietnam War reveals the questionable reliance on electronically mediated enemy identification: "We have high-tech drones, satellites, planes, thermal imaging devices, and other technology to help us keep an eye on a trouble spot from a safe and unobtrusive distance. We have a much better idea of who the bad guy is in Iraq, when compared to the fields and jungles of Vietnam."[7] Yet this overconfident assessment disregards the fundamental transformation of the battlefield into a "multimedia *field of vision*" by the high-tech capabilities of the twenty-first century (Virilio 2002:136). Battle space has become a sensorium of generative mediation with a distinct visual culture—a composite of mediated combat realities that transforms humans into virtual targets and soldiers literally into killing machines that suspend natural darkness and fade out moving images with lethal force.

The ambivalence of enemies as both human and virtual arises from the mimetic process underlying electronic mediation. According to Gunter Gebauer and Christoph Wulf (1995:2), "Realities are not becoming images here, but images are becoming realities; a plurality of image-realities come into being. Distinctions between realities, images, and fictions break down. The world appears subject to a making in images. Images come into mimetic relation with other images." The trouble with mimetic mediation is that the medium itself disappears from consciousness in the absorbing immediacy of combat and the immediation of night vision technology. Soldiers become so engrossed in the life-threatening environment that they are no longer aware the reality they perceive is mediated and that detection devices suffuse their actions and decisions. Immediation is the denial of mediation that makes soldiers mistake a person's image for the living human being, thus enhancing the dehumanization already at play in the Iraq War through basic training, racial stereotyping, and the Manichaean message from political leaders that the troops were fighting evil and bringing freedom (Robben 2010a:142–46).

The desire for immediacy to react as fast as possible to life-threatening danger magnifies the spectrum of the evanescent media. This contradictory quality of night vision devices makes combat "seem increasingly immediate and realistic so that the act of mediation and the technology enabling it almost appear to vanish," while in contrast, "the ever more pervasive use of such technologies leads to their greater visibility as complex objects and apparatuses that seem increasingly and problematically decoupled from human agency" (Eisenlohr 2009:275). Spectral filters become invisible, images produce new realities, and killing becomes spectacide.

The mediated vision of combat becomes transformed into a hostile gaze because of the particular way soldiers look at human beings as potential targets, the intent with which soldiers judge battle space images, and the power to inflict harm on others. Gazing at human targets with the objective of killing enemies absorbs the viewer's attention in the maelstrom of life-and-death situations and affects a mediated reflection. This surrender to a gaze has been explained by Maurice Merleau-Ponty (1962:226) in terms of the spectacle's selective qualities: "From the point of view of the object, it is separating the region under scrutiny from the rest of the field, it is interrupting the total life of the spectacle. . . . From the subject's point of view, it is substituting for the comprehensive vision . . . an observation, that is, a localized vision which it controls according to its own requirements." The hostile gaze, suffused with the emotions of combat and the fear of dying, creates "a sense of immediacy through the joining of emotion and objectivity" (L. A. Allen 2009:172), while the unmediating object remains oblivious to the perils of the concealed inspection.

The NVGs transform ambient blindness into militarized sight and fuse imagination and experience into image-realities whose virtual veracity acquires cinematographic qualities. The engrossing image-realities produced by night vision devices unfold within a century-old conditioning to the film medium. Motion pictures "inaugurated the distinction between the imaginary and the real," as Friedrich Kittler (1999:118) has demonstrated, by the sequential projection of still images that give the illusion of movement and portray the world through visual codes and theatrical conventions. This cinematographic eye intertwines with the mediated hostile gaze into a virtual reality that becomes emotionally charged with the traumatic experiences of combat.

COMBAT IMAGES AND IMAGINARIES

Soldiers sent to Vietnam and Iraq were fed since childhood with a vast visual repertoire of combat images in movies and newsreels that was expanded with computer simulations by the turn of the century. The U.S. Army has been using video games as a successful recruitment tool since 2002 (see Allen's chapter in this volume) and in 2005 released a computer simulation that navigates combat soldiers through a virtual surveillance patrol in an Iraqi city "populated with civilians, security personnel, NGO's, insurgents, and Improvised Explosive Devices seeking to detect threats of varying significance while attempting appropriate interaction with those they encounter."[8] The array of basic skills training devices ranges from operating machine guns and aerial drones to modules developed to heighten cultural awareness.[9] The proliferation of simulation programs is as likely to confuse virtual and real images in battlefield imaginations for today's troops as movies did for soldiers fighting in Vietnam.

Combat in Vietnam was regularly experienced and remembered by U.S. soldiers in cinematographic terms as if the visual mnemonic encodings were aligned in an edited sequence, as in the following recollection by Vietnam veteran C. W. Bowman: "When we attacked the wood line,

I watched the artillery throw mud and trees up in the air, and the only thing I could think of was, 'Damn, this is just like the movies.' It was like I stepped out of my body and walked around me and then stepped back in myself and then continued the assault" (Bergerud 1993:138–39). Michael Herr (1991:65) described this sensation as an oscillation between real and virtual reality: "Life-as-movie, war-as-(war) movie, war-as-life."

The accustoming to celluloid images made Herr (1991:209–10) confuse film scenes with real combat when he saw his first war casualties in Vietnam: "It was the same familiar violence, only moved over to another medium; some kind of jungle play with giant helicopters and fantastic special effects, actors lying out there in canvas body bags waiting for the scene to end so they could get up again and walk it off." In other words, the eye saw what the mind's eye had recollected from the silver screen.

Iraq veterans also situated combat in cinematographic frameworks. Lieutenant Paul Rieckhoff (2007:191), in the midst of a firefight with insurgents hiding in a house in Baghdad, was reminded of a film set: "It looked like a hostage negotiation scene from a cop movie. I expected a fat cop with a donut in his hand to emerge with a bull-horn and shout, 'Okay, Haji! Come out with your hands up!'" Time stopped for Lieutenant Donovan Campbell (2009:170) when he saw a marine being shot in the stomach and curling up into a fetal position: "At that exact moment, all I remember thinking was *Wow. This is just like in the movies.* Then time kicked in again, the gunfire and the cracking resumed, and I ran like hell to the wounded." Reality may also defy the film images and cinematographic understandings that come to mind readily during combat, as happened to Lieutenant Neil Prakash at an air strike against insurgents during the battle of Fallujah. "Explosions went up 5 to 10 stories. Huge gray clouds shot upwards. It looked like volcanoes were erupting. But that wasn't what shocked me. On top of the explosions, bodies were thrown straight up into the sky. It wasn't like the movies at all, where the explosion goes off and the guy is airborne, flailing his arms and legs. It looked like a child threw some action figures straight up in the sky. They didn't flail at all" (Burden 2006:182).

Combat lends itself well to the confusion of the real and the imaginary. Violent situations are overdetermined experiences that can never be encoded entirely in memory (McNally 2003:190). "Combat is a form of vertigo," says Lieutenant Nathaniel Fick, who participated in Operation Iraqi Freedom. "I was trained to thrive on chaos, but nothing prepared me for the fear of doubting my own senses. Frequently, I found that my memory of a firefight was just that—mine. Afterward, five Marines told five different stories" (Fick 2005:219). Some of the many visual, tactile, olfactory, auricular, and palatal sensations may enter memory and are then transformed into remembrances, sensations, narratives, smells, visualizations, and imaginations that are hard to disentangle. "In any war story, but especially a true one, it's difficult to separate what happened from what seemed to happen," reflects Tim O'Brien (1991:78).

The troubling experiences of American and Vietnamese veterans are the staple of psychic trauma and might reappear in flashbacks, nightmares, and the sighting of ghosts, which are dealt with in different cultural ways. The North Vietnamese veteran and novelist Bao Ninh (1993:42), one out of ten survivors of the five-hundred-men-strong 27th Youth Brigade, showed how traumatic memories troubled him with intrusive associations: "I am watching a US war movie with scenes of American soldiers yelling as they launch themselves into combat on the TV screen and once again I'm ready to jump in and mix it in the fiery scene of blood, mad killing and brutality that warps soul and personality. . . . My heart beats rapidly as I stare at the dark corners of the room where ghost soldiers emerge, shredded with gaping wounds." War correspondent Michael Herr (1991:68–69) became burdened by the death and destruction he had witnessed: "One night, like a piece of shrapnel that takes years to work its way out, I dreamed and saw a field that was crowded with dead. I was crossing it with a friend, more than a friend, a guide, and he was making me get down and look at them." These traumatic images wove themselves through Herr's everyday reality: "Worst of all, you'd see people walking around whom you'd watched die in aid stations and helicopters" (Herr 1991:252).

Vietnamese soldiers were also haunted by ghosts. Bao Ninh (1993:24) described in his novel *The Sorrow of War* how the ghosts of dead soldiers troubled his alter ego, Kien: "At midnight, shadows slipped silently from the hammocks. Gently creeping to the hut doors, making signals to the night guards, they disappeared in single file into the dark jungle. The shadows slipped quietly into the stream and headed, in teeming rain, towards the great dark mountain."

The ghosts seen by Kien were the wandering spirits of people who had suffered tragic or grievous deaths. The Vietnamese believe that a person has a spirit consisting of a material soul that senses and feels and a spiritual soul that thinks and imagines. If a person experiences a violent death and is not ritually buried and remembered, then the material soul will perpetually relive the agonizing death, and the spiritual soul will suffer from traumatic memories. These spirits linger around the place of death and the bodily remains. Fallen soldiers are regarded as having died a tragic death, but their suffering is attenuated by their sacrifice for the greater good of the nation. Massacred civilians, in contrast, have suffered grievous deaths because they died both tragic and unjust deaths. Villagers living near the killing sites of the My Lai massacre of 1968 "claimed that they had seen old women ghosts licking and sucking the arms and legs of small child ghosts, and they interpreted the scene as an effort by the elderly victims to ease the pain of the wounded children" (Kwon 2006:85). Only a proper reburial and periodic ritual commemoration of these dead can put their souls to rest by bidding farewell to a painful past (Kwon 2006:120–25). Such ritual intervention is also beneficial for the living who are reunited with their deceased relatives, commemorates their presence in domestic ancestral rituals, and makes survivors come to terms with their own predicament during and after the Vietnam War.

The anxiety of the Vietnamese people about the grievous deaths and troubled afterlives of their massacred relatives mirrors the post-traumatic stress disorder (PTSD) of American veterans of the Vietnam War. The PTSD concept was developed by American psychiatrists working with Vietnam veterans and became officially recognized in 1980 in the American Psychiatric Association's *Diagnostic and Statistical Manual of Mental Disorders*. Patients were treated with medication and various kinds of psychotherapy, including behavioral flooding or prolonged exposure therapy. They were exposed incrementally to traumatic cues by seeing a video of a jungle tour, feeling a rifle in their hands, or smelling gunpowder to desensitize them to their traumatic memories (Young 1995:177).

Computer simulations made their entry into the treatment of Vietnam veterans in 1997 with the experimental program Virtual Vietnam. Virtual reality exposure therapy was also used for victims of the terrorist attacks of September 11, 2001, and has been helping the treatment of traumatized veterans from the Iraq War since 2005. The treatment program Virtual Iraq consists of custom-made computer simulations. Clinical interviews with soldiers diagnosed with PTSD are analyzed for traumatic cues. The psychologist's cut of virtual images is then further enhanced with sounds, smells, and vibrations. Traumatized veterans sit on a raised platform and are outfitted with a head-mounted display, a collar that releases scents, and headphones that allow them to relive their most harrowing experiences through virtual remediations. The patient controls his progress through the simulated dismounted patrol or convoy, and the therapist can add disturbing stimuli—such as the sounds of gunfire, incoming mortars, and radio; the sight of wounded soldiers and civilians and night vision imaging; the scent of burning rubber, cordite, and spices; and the feeling of wind or the vibrations of a vehicle or explosion by shaking the platform with bass speakers. A series of sessions serves to habituate the patient to the stimuli that activate traumatic memories to reduce anxiety and avoid adverse behavioral reactions (Halpern 2008; Reger et al. 2011).

Soldiers are now coming close to running the entire gamut of their combat careers in virtual reality—from recruitment, basic training, mediated combat with night vision devices, and wartime memories recalled in cinematographic or computer game images to PTSD treatment by splicing together traumatic cues and mind frames into a simulated illusion intensified with scents, sounds, and vibrations.

CONCLUSION

Battle space changed in World War I from face-to-face combat informed by sight and sound to the so-called empty battlefield with long-range machine guns, mortar attacks, and artillery shelling. World War II expanded warfare from terrestrial operations to sea and air battles with submarines and bombers. Face-to-face combat continued to take place throughout the twentieth century, as became painfully clear during the Vietnam War, but the trend to mediate operations through electronic devices was favored by standing armies around the world. The 1991 Gulf War marked a new revolution in conventional warfare by being the first stealth war in which aircraft and cruise missiles defied detection and "arms of communication prevail for the first time in the history of combat over the traditional supremacy of arms of destruction" with the result of few allied casualties (Virilio 2002:112). The 2003 Iraqi Freedom invasion and its shock-and-awe bombing of Baghdad seemed to perfect this cyberwarfare. Yet the low-tech resistance of Iraqi insurgents with their homemade explosive devices made of simple electrical switches and discarded ammunition crippled the superior technology and entangled the U.S. armed forces in an irregular and deadly war, just as the Vietnamese revolutionary forces had done four decades earlier. Precision bombing during the Iraq War made way for proximity killing as in nineteenth-century conventional wars but with a twist: soldiers observed their targets up close in a multimedia battle space, as if in face-to-face combat, but they spotted the people unawares in the area of operations through electronically mediated image-realities. This advanced spectral technology revolutionized the combat tactics and visual practices of nocturnal operations in Iraq. Swarming counterinsurgency units heightened battle space chaos for enemy combatants and civilians alike.

Night vision devices produce an immediation of combat that mistakes night for day and human representations for the people themselves. This visual practice generates a hostile gaze endowed with a cinematographic eye wrapped in the rush of battle. The ensuing dehumanization turns the killing of human targets into spectacides. In fact, experimental eye-tracking systems incorporated in specially wired contact lenses will allow future warriors to shoot by looking fixedly at the human target without physically pulling a trigger as eye movements respond to weapon systems, and "eyeshot will then finally get the better of gunshot" (Virilio 1989:2; Ben-Ari 2003:121). This engrossing gaze creates an image that through its very materialization invites spectacide by producing a perceived threat and evoking hostile emotions. Spectacide contains an emotional and visual contradiction that seems to bear the cost of trauma. The killing is virtual because of the hostile gaze, but real because of the immediation of combat. This contradiction cannot be as easily reconciled in consciousness as in virtual reality when soldiers come face to face with the wounded and the dead, the destruction and havoc of human settlements, and the suffering inflicted on societies.

NOTES

I thank Robertson Allen, Patrick Eisenlohr, Sverker Finnström, Martijn Oosterbaan, and Neil Whitehead for their stimulating comments and valuable references.

1. Both quotes from the *New York Times* blog *Frontlines: Dispatches from U.S. Soldiers in Iraq*, http://frontlines.blogs.nytimes.com, posted April 11, 2006; accessed November 12, 2009.
2. From the blog *Eighty Deuce on the Loose in Iraq*, http://airborneparainf82 .blogspot.com, posted April 25, 2007; accessed August 15, 2008.
3. From the blog *365 and a Wakeup*, http://thunder6.typepad.com/365_arabian _nights/page/3, posted October 24, 2005; accessed November 12, 2009.
4. The spatial disorientation of night vision devices raised the accident rate of helicopter flights in 1996–97 from 9.3 per 100,000 flying hours of unaided night operations to 15.8 for operations with night vision equipment (Johnson 2004:1).

5. "Night Operations," http://www.globalsecurity.org/military/ops/night.htm; accessed March 3, 2011.

6. From *Eighty Deuce on the Loose in Iraq*, http://airborneparainf82.blogspot.com; posted September 2, 2007; accessed August 15, 2008.

7. From *Frontlines*, http://frontlines.blogs.nytimes.com, posted April 11, 2006; accessed November 12, 2009.

8. "Army Releases 'Every Soldier a Sensor' Training Tool," 2005, http://www.global security.org/militar/library/news/2005/10/mil-051027-army01.htm; accessed March 8, 2011. "Self-Directed Learning Internet Module," 2010, USC Institute for Creative Technologies website, http://ict.usc.edu/projects/print/496; accessed March 8, 2011.

9. Singer 2010. Also see http://www.americasarmy.com; accessed August 20, 2012, and "Cultural and Cognitive Combat Immersive Trainer," 2012, http://ict.usc.edu/prototypes/c3it; accessed August 20, 2012.

VIRTUAL SOLDIERS, COGNITIVE LABORERS

ARRIVAL: CIVILIAN WORK, SOLDIER PLAY

On my first morning at the development offices of the official U.S. Army video game, *America's Army*, I was met by the game's executive producer. He showed me around the office, which housed a thirty-four-person workforce of electronic entertainment industry professionals.[1] After this brief tour, we gravitated toward the office kitchen, the intuitive choice for coffee and morning conversation. "Coffee is a big deal here. It fuels the team," he told me. We were met in the kitchen by a group of four uniformed men—some in full U.S. Army fatigues, others wearing digitized camouflage pants with regular T-shirts. Naturally, I assumed they were soldiers; it was the U.S. Army's video game studio, after all, and they were dressed in army gear. As conversation continued, I asked one of them how long he had been in the army, adding that I did not know that actual soldiers worked on the video game. He laughed and said, "Oh, we're civilians. We like to play at being in the army."

This statement stuck with me long enough to record it in my notes precisely because of its glibness and salience in achieving a blending between worlds that are typically talked about in contemporary American discourse as being oppositional and discrete: the separate worlds of work and play, and those of the soldier and the civilian. Of course, the actual boundaries between these spheres (if they exist at all) are porous and eroding, and they have been becoming less visible for quite some time through multiple channels (Virno 2004). The corporate adoption of the "play-at-work" mantra (and its darker double, the imperative to "work-at-play") has only accelerated in the past decade and seems not to be abating (de Peuter and Dyer-Witheford 2005; Kline et al. 2003). A huge variety of social networking tools problematize the work–play binary even further as employees continue to use networked technologies during work while extending working hours beyond discrete activities and temporally bounded segments of time. This has led some to describe these sets of practices as being a primary characteristic of a post-Fordist "regime of high technology capitalism—the sort of capitalism in which video and computer games are right at home" (Kline et al. 2003:65).

Similarly, as detailed in the introduction to this volume, the rhetorical distinction that once existed between the world of the civilian and that of the soldier has become increasingly vague through a wide variety of media representations (Gregory 2006; Halter 2006; Lenoir 2000, 2003) and militarized practices (Lutz 2001, 2002b; Maček 2009; Nordstrom 2004a). As a video game that touts one of its goals as "compet[ing] in the electronic entertainment space for youth mind share" to encourage the consideration of military enlistment at an early age, *America's Army* seems to actively and effectively perpetuate this ambiguity—more so than many other forms of military recruitment and media campaigns.[2] This free online game was imagined with the intention of providing a relatively unintimidating game space for younger male video gamers to also "play at being in the army." In a sense, many had already done so through an array of other hugely successful military-themed combat games in the commercial market.[3] But whereas these commercial military games sought to gain a market share among the demographic of teen to thirty-something males through increasingly sensational, cinematic, and technophilic combat gaming scenarios, the purpose of *America's Army* hinged on gaining headway within a separate market—future military recruits. Because the target demographic for both markets was essentially the same, creating a video game developed and produced by the U.S. Army was, to the calculating minds of military economists, a logical opportunity to leverage a preexisting demand for militarized games by coopting messages about the army that were already in circulation in the electronic entertainment industry.

This type of play enlists media users as *virtual soldiers*—not only in the popular sense that they are soldiers playing in a virtual or simulated environment, but also in the sense that they are potential soldiers (in other words, virtually soldiers) who might fight in Iraq, Afghanistan, or elsewhere in the future. Throughout this chapter, when I refer to "virtual soldiers" I use the term interchangeably, sometimes to connote one or both of these meanings simultaneously as they are not mutually exclusive. But the latter meaning of *virtual* is especially salient given the fact that versions of *America's Army* are also used in training enlisted soldiers for weapons familiarization and cultural awareness role-playing exercises (not unlike those discussed in Roberto González's contribution to this volume). Actual enlistment or the aspiration and ability of an individual to do so are not the only determining factors that make a virtual soldier, however; instead, the institutionalizing force of the army acting on individual subjectivities enlists persons as virtual soldiers. In this way, a person who does not have even the slightest desire to join the military might nevertheless be a virtual soldier.

In this chapter, I illustrate how the video game developers of *America's Army* became virtual soldiers and how their example, while unique, points to larger trends in global war that problematize the easy binaries between war and peace, work and play, soldier and civilian, and battlefront and home front. Both the finished product of their labors and their individual work experiences highlight the kind of magic that is at play—literally, in this case—in creating and perpetuating these tacit ontological binaries that obfuscate the actual grayness between them.

The game the developers were creating, *America's Army 3* (see figure 7.1), was the latest in the *America's Army* franchise, an ongoing army recruiting experiment since 2002. In this free online first-person shooting game—essentially a continuous immersive advertisement for the U.S. Army—players cooperate with teammates to compete against an opposing squad for the purposes of achieving objectives like capturing or defending a building and protecting or killing a VIP. *America's Army 3* puts players through virtual boot camp and combat experiences and awards them with medals and career advancement points if army-sanctioned rules of engagement are followed. Players use these points to specialize their soldier characters to specific combat roles. Although one goal of the game is educating the American public about the army—"winning their hearts and minds" through simulating heroic narratives of combat (see Sluka, this volume)—this goal has always been superseded by the recruit-

7.1 A marketing image of the in-game environment of *America's Army 3*. Source: U.S. Army image database, http://www.americasarmy.com/media/ssViewer. php?xmlImageName=screenshots, accessed June 18, 2011.

ing goal, aimed at enlisting teenagers (target age seventeen and implicitly young men) familiar with computerized interfaces and navigation within virtual spaces. The game essentially has sought to recruit a cognitariat workforce (Berardi 2009a), possessing qualitative leadership skills and technological know-how, to join the army.

As I have detailed elsewhere in closer examinations of the game's technology and presentation (R. Allen 2009, 2011), the enemy in *America's Army* is a flexible and amorphous one that vaguely references actual cultures, languages, and ethnicities while simultaneously maintaining a critical distance from events and places. As an object of othering, it is a tabula rasa onto which any actual enemy can be conjured into virtual existence. This works in tandem with personalized accounts of U.S. Army combat medal recipients—called "Real Heroes" in the game—to create a binary configuration between the living soldier and the virtual, anonymous enemy. This configuration constructs what Catherine Lutz calls a "mythic enemy" (2001:87) by dehumanizing and distancing the enemy, relegating it to the realm of the hyperreal and the virtual (see also Robben, this volume). Like a virtual soldier, this virtual, mythic enemy evokes a potentiality that refers to more than mere technological simulation; it participates in a prefigurative process of othering (Baudrillard 1994), which James Der Derian summarizes in his claim that "how we prepare for future enemies might just help to invent them" (2001:108). This creation of a virtual enemy could be viewed as working in tandem with other systems of human terrain mapping (Price, this volume) because both create dehumanizing mechanisms that enable a prefigurative and oversimplified objectification of humans and cultures.

Like the enemies of their creation, the designers of *America's Army* underwent a similar imperative to flexibly adapt their labor to the mythic narratives of war. Through their work and basic training experiences, the game designers became a kind of hybrid soldier-civilian, possessors of expert military knowledge who worked within a liminal space between so-called military and nonmilitary spheres to translate this knowledge to video gamers and the larger public. In doing so, their labor not only produced a finished software product but also projected an affective, militarized ethos for marketing and public relations. I show how this type of work—characterized by some as "affective labor," "immaterial labor" (Hardt and Negri 2004; Lazzarato 1996), or, as I prefer, "cognitive labor" (Berardi 2009a, 2009b)—was mobilized to soften the stark distinctions between the categories of the gaming civilian and the working soldier.

Digital games, the increasingly dominant form of entertainment in the United States, are especially ritualized forms of media magic that takes place when users sit in front of computer screens. The sheer amount of games, gamers, and time spent playing games validates Victor Turner's statement that "for every major social formation there is a dominant type of public liminality" (1979:468; see also Huizinga 2002 [1949]). Though digital games are "magic circles" with self-contained rules, logics, and even cultures, they nevertheless shape—and are shaped by—the outside world (Boellstorff 2006), and *America's Army* is an example par excellence of this process. The dehumanization of the anonymous enemy other is one way in which the game is able to do this, blending the techno-modern with the magico-primitive (see the introduction to this volume) by conjuring an enemy into existence when none previously existed. The technological process of game development is seemingly magical to most people, and as a developer indicated in an interview (see below), even the U.S. government managers of the game regularly viewed the development of their outsourced product as "this magic that happens behind the scenes." Overshadowing these forms of magic is the biopolitical apparatus of the military—ever focused on recruitment, return on investment, and public relations—and the privileged, prophetic place that virtual simulation holds in determining actual outcomes. In the context of these magical processes of virtual war, I argue that the amalgamation of categories between gaming civilian and working solider (evident in the figures of the *America's Army* game developers and central to the creation and maintenance of virtual soldiering) engages in a playful but serious liminality, which is an effective vehicle of militarization; it is a post-Fordist magical construction that perpetuates war.

RED PHASE: COGNITIVE MILITARY GAME LABOR

A post-Fordist economy is generally distinguishable from its Fordist predecessor by the economic privatization and deregulation of formerly state-run industries and social service programs; shorter production cycles; more networked and less hierarchical structures of organization; greater mobility of jobs, coupled with increased instability in long-term employment; and the centrality of new technologies in all of these processes (see Virno 2004).[4] Among the starkest characteristics of post-Fordism is the increase in the ambiguity between work time and leisure time; there is no longer "a clean, well-defined threshold separating labor time from non-labor time. . . . Since the 'life of the mind' is included fully within the time-space of production, an essential homogeneity prevails" (Virno 2004:103). Bifo Berardi refers to the individuals working under this state of affairs as members of the "cognitariat" (2009a, 2009b).

These general conditions describe the cognitive workplace of the early twenty-first century. Once the separation between work and nonwork time becomes ambiguous, other qualities of human labor power become privileged. While the ability to carry out manual tasks has remained essential, other skill sets have grown in importance: "Just as in [the industrial] phase all forms of labor and society itself had to industrialize, today labor and society have to informationalize, become intelligent, become communicative, become affective" (Hardt and Negri 2004:109). Although specific types of labor have always compelled or required employees to project an emotional tenor in their work (e.g., flight attendants, service work), types of cognitive labor more extensively privilege and capitalize on these affective, mental, and social qualities of employees. For these reasons, in contrast to Fordist industrial laborers who primarily sold their time in exchange for "a temporary death from which s/he could wake up only after the alarm bells rang," cognitive laborers "tend to consider labor as the most essential part in their lives, the most specific and personalized" (Berardi 2009a:76–77). As I will show, this projection of affect, sociability, and apparent candidness is also a central characteristic in the "soft sell" marketing and recruiting efforts of *America's Army*.

Video games, as a rising part of the contemporary global information-entertainment culture industry, operate as an exemplary industry of the post-Fordist cognitariat, emphasizing "scientific know-how, hi-tech proficiency, cultural creativity, human sociability, and cooperative interactivity" (de Peuter and Dyer-Witheford 2005). It is an intensely cyclical industry that has always entailed a significant amount of labor precariousness, with studios commonly laying off a majority of employees after major releases of games. This trend became more pronounced following the economic recession beginning in autumn 2008. In this highly competitive trade that has blended work and nonwork time almost seamlessly, even artists, designers, and engineers receiving unemployment benefit checks have had to continually labor to keep their skills up to date and their portfolio fresh.

This was the industry in which the game developers of *America's Army* worked; they were, by and large, a group of individuals in pursuit of careers in game development or similar fields. As is often the case with soldiers who enlist in the U.S. military, it was principally economic and career advancement opportunities that led most *America's Army* game developers to choose work for a military contractor. Although a few of them had experiences with the military through previous enlistment or employment, for most their work was the first extended period of contact they ever had with a military organization. It was a young group, with the vast majority of employees having less than five years of game development experience; many were fresh graduates from Bay Area universities with degree programs in graphic arts, design, animation, and other software- and skills-related programs. Even by the standards of the demographically skewed video game industry employment norms, this was a beardy group of mostly twenty- to forty-year-old white male game developers.[5]

Most of the developers were avid video gamers. Some typically stayed at the studio for hours after the end of the workday to use the computers and facilities for their personal enjoyment. One person told me, "All of these new games come out and you need to go check 'em out. For me, I feel like it's a part of my research and development. But if I didn't do this for a living, I would still [play games]." Sometimes they played as an individual activity, but very often it was a collective, social enterprise of net-worked gaming that kept employees of *America's Army* playing together, either at the studio's computers or at home.[6] Because such activities directly fed back into their development of the game, keeping them up to date about new games, news, technologies, and memes, these practices were encouraged by the game's producers, who sought to maintain the studio as a comfortable and stress-free space. During "crunch time," an unspecified period prior to the game's release when tasks compressed into smaller windows of time, many would forgo their gaming and would stay late to work at the studio, sometimes sleeping there. In these experiences, the game developers of *America's Army* differed little from the rest of the game development industry.

WHITE PHASE: RECRUITING THE DESIGNERS

The labor of *America's Army* game designers went beyond the mere development of the game and entered a resocializing, institutionalizing, and militarized process that crafted them into virtual soldiers. This emerged in part as a result of the subject material of their game, as designers and artists necessarily had to be knowledgeable about the minute details of army uniforms, weapons, and doctrine. As I describe shortly, efforts undertaken to include the team under the institutional umbrella of the army further achieved this. Several developers also brought their past experiences and interests in the military to the development offices: Two were veterans of the U.S. armed forces, and several others were gun enthusiasts, volunteer participants in live simulation training exercises for Bay Area police forces, and, of course, enthusiastic players of games, which were often military-themed. One developer even left the team to run a successful business designing military gear and reviewing new weapons for sale on the civilian market.[7] With these influences, the design team embodied a remarkable mix of militarized libertarian principles, coupled with a hefty dose of Berkeley liberalism, hipster irony, and a sardonic disdain for almost anything to do with the Republican Party, especially Sarah Palin.

In this work environment, the developers adopted to varying degrees the subjectivities of soldiers. This was especially true in their thinking about their employment. The HBO mini-series *Generation Kill* (2008), based on Evan Wright's book (2004) about his experiences as an embedded reporter with a marine unit during the 2003 invasion of Iraq, was one of many shared narratives that shaped how several developers envisioned their work relations and relationships with outside institutions in terms of the military. Off-site managers at military bases in Alabama were compared to incompetent leaders in the film series, such as Captain America. Colonel Casey Wardynski, the director of the Army Game Project, was the Godfather, another character in the series. And I, the anthropologist, was clearly in the position most analogous to Wright: "I don't think of you as a spy anymore," an artist, Walker,[8] told me after my first week in the office; "you're more like an embedded journalist, and that means we need to keep you alive." When I joined developers during countless in-studio play tests of their game, I came to understand that this sense of camaraderie was also brought about and sustained through the shared and patently fun experiences of virtual military combat in video games.

Later in an interview, Walker expanded his analogy between the development team and army units, explaining to me that "this is an elite team. We are an elite squad of individuals. We have been chosen by the army to make this game. That's a big deal and I think a lot of team members take that for granted. . . . There are thirty people on-site here and four people off-site. That's a tight squad; that's a platoon-sized unit. That's exactly what that is, a platoon-sized element, and [the producer] runs around like the platoon sergeant. We got a design squad, an art squad, and [the executive producer] is like the lieutenant." For many army game developers, their exposure to some of the specialized experiences of soldiers became a meaningful way for them to include themselves within the greater institution of the army and identify with the situations of enlisted soldiers. Walker went as far as envisioning his work on the game in terms of an extended deployment overseas, as he was living in California, away from many of his friends and family in Georgia.

This metaphor of the team as a military unit continually resurfaced to explain other situations and employment experiences throughout my time at the game development studios. But it was a metaphor that had some grounding in real experiences as well, for many on the team had trained together as a unit when the army sent them to boot camp.

As it turned out, so many people were dressed in combat uniforms on my first day of fieldwork because about a third of the developers—one woman and twelve men—were freshly returned from a voluntary five-day job-related excursion to Fort Jackson's Army Training Center.[9] Along with employees from other Army Game Project offices, they underwent

7.2 Civilian *America's Army* video game developers at mini Basic Combat Training. Source: http://www.americasarmy.com/about/blogImages.php?xmlImageName=Dev BlogsGreenUpImages&blog=true, accessed June 18, 2011.

five days of "mini Basic Combat Training," otherwise known as "mini BCT." During this short time, they endured many of the same ordeals of resocialization as new entries to boot camp—buzz cuts, obstacle courses, pushups, cafeteria lines, weapons training, and obnoxious drill sergeants. They were assigned to squads, slept in barracks, and were issued their own equipment and uniforms, complete with an *America's Army* arm patch. Describing it later, one participant claimed, "The first day was one of the worst days of my life" (see figure 7.2).

This ordeal had manifold purposes. At its core, it was intended to give the game developers an experiential taste of boot camp for the purposes of integrating their new familiarity with army life into the video game. Many developers approached the event as an opportunity to build their professional skills as artists, sound technicians, level designers, programmers, and producers. Developers indicated that their mini BCT experiences aided in the creation of an introductory framing segment of *America's Army 3* involving a virtual boot camp in which users learn how to play by navigating an obstacle course, completing weapons familiarization, and running through a live fire shoothouse. In this way, the developers' experiences at mini BCT came to be portrayed as a kind of halfway mark in a referential sequence pointing from the virtual boot camp of the game to the mini boot camp of the game developers, to the "true" boot camp of the enlisted soldier.[10]

In emphasizing this sequence of representational fidelity, press releases claimed the game as a "virtual test drive" of the army and that it is "as close to being in the Army as you can get without enlisting."[11] Taglines for the game also revealed this rhetorical device quite succinctly, declaring that *"America's Army* is a game like no other, because of its detailed level of authenticity" and that the game, although mostly created by subcontracted civilian developers, was "designed, developed, and deployed by the U.S. Army."[12]

The army was quick to advertise the fact that they had sent its game developers to boot camp, enlisting them as virtual soldiers. The mini BCT event was used for marketing to generate hype among video game players prior to the release of *America's Army 3* in June 2009. The *America's Army* marketing agency put together a video and photos of the event, taking on-site film recordings and interspersing it with retrospective interviews of developers and video game footage.[13] Two developers were asked to blog about their experiences at mini BCT, which they extensively describe in online forums at http://americasarmy.com.[14] Short video blogs with various developers enabled fans to take behind-the-scenes looks at the work and offices of the development team. And, adhering to a promotional language of realism, a press release for *America's Army 3* advertised how its developers became transfigured into the roles of soldiers, implying that players can also undergo a similar transformation through the game: "Nobody knows military simulations like the world's premier land force, the United States Army. So, when the Army began making the America's Army game to provide civilians with insights on Soldiering from the barracks to the battlefields, it sent its talented development team to experience Army training just as a new recruit would. The developers crawled through obstacle courses, fired weapons, observed paratrooper instruction, and participated in a variety of training exercises with elite combat units, all so that you could virtually experience Soldiering in the most realistic way possible."[15]

Despite the unexpected physical intensity of mini BCT, nearly all developers who attended the event remembered it as an occasion that contributed to their personal growth and understanding of the army. One developer wrote on the *America's Army* online forums that he and other co-workers "were yelled at, chided, [and] pushed beyond our physical and mental limitations, but came out all the stronger for it in the end because we endured."[16] After his return to the office, another developer told some colleagues, "It has changed me. I don't know if for good or bad, but it has changed me." Yet another described the experience as being "really moving, even though it wasn't the full blown experience. [It was] as much of a taste as you really can get without actually being in the Army. I would never have opted to do it, knowing what I know now [about how difficult it was], but I'm glad that I did. I wasn't going to be the only person on the team that quit."

Often, these personal reasons for attending accompanied professional ones. This was the case with one individual (from another Army Game Project office) who stated that "the short answer as to why *I* want to go and do it is that I'm about to turn forty and I'd really like to know if I can handle it." He went on to articulate why he thought the army sent the game developers, telling me that "they believe the more we know about what it takes to turn civilians into soldiers the better we will be able to depict that in the things that we build. I think also that the more we know about tactics, techniques, trainings, and procedures, the more lifelike we can build scenarios, and the more effective we can be."

As this person implied, "turning civilians into soldiers" no longer happens solely in the institution of the military but has become a process that happens during the everyday life of media consumers in the United States (Der Derian 2001; Hardt and Negri 2004; Sumera, this volume). Nearly every American has become (in some cases unwilling or unwitting) consumers of war and participants in the national mediated narratives of war (Lutz 2009). "Soft sells" such as *America's Army* further contribute to production of this militarized subjectivity by adding the dimension of interactivity and the veneer of agency through the medium of the game. By relying on user-generated interest and discovery of the army through the game and other *America's Army* material online, the messages of the game (which might be dismissed as heavy-handed statist propaganda in other contexts) instead morph into impressions that can be readily accepted. Such processes of subjectification, which originate from institutions but operate as if they derive from individual motives, exemplify how biopower capitalizes on the ostensibly liberatory nature of social media, interactive entertainment, and networks of information sharing in the early twenty-first century (Berardi 2009a).

The marketing and media efforts of mini BCT capitalized on the affective performance of the game developers as soldiers. This worked to translate and reconfigure military power for gamers, suggesting to players that they also can possess the knowledge and expertise that was imparted to the game developers by the army—either by participating within the liminal space of the game or, even better, by enlisting and joining the army. Through these diverse methods, both developers and players of *America's Army* became virtual soldiers.

BLUE PHASE: SELFLESS SERVICE DURING CRUNCH TIME

Following the developers' return to California, stories of mini BCT continued to periodically effervesce through conversations, and the experience became one of many in the folklore of *America's Army* game development. For some, it was a high point in their employment at the studio, for in the year following mini BCT the team went through difficult times. There was a general lack of direction and vision—both internally and externally—as to what the new *America's Army 3* was supposed to be like. One root of these problems was a frustrating and convoluted system of military contracting and subcontracting that separated the development team from much army institutional support. In a networked arrangement that was confusing at best, the team's offices near Berkeley communicated with a variety of other offices across the United States. In name, the development team worked for a private company. This company was contracted to develop *America's Army* by another large private military contractor, SAIC, which was, in turn, contracted by the U.S. government. But there was minimal contact between the game developers and these private employers; instead, their customers, the U.S. Army and the U.S. government, oversaw the majority of project operations from offices in Alabama and West Point.

This arrangement led to many difficulties. Nearly everyone in the office felt that the management of the project from the Alabama offices was inept. The demands placed on them to perform their work, they felt, did not match the amount of monetary and institutional support that trickled down to the office after the prime contractor (SAIC) and the subcontractor had taken a substantial portion of the funding allocated to the development of the game. Often, they felt, the team became a scapegoat for problems that originated elsewhere. In one exchange during an interview with a developer named Benjamin, I asked what he felt about the project management outside of the team in regard to their understanding of the process of game development.

> **B**: I don't think they have any idea. It doesn't seem uncommon, this sort of understanding as to what actually goes into producing this stuff. These people just don't understand how [games] are made.
> **R**: Do you think they are like, "They just play all the time!"
> **B**: "Yeah, they're just messing around!" They don't really understand what goes into it all and the nuts and bolts—how much work is actually required.

The development process, he told me, was seen as a kind of obfuscated, occult work from the perspective of these outsiders: "The end product is all this fun, all this cool stuff, so for them it's just this 'magic' that happens behind the scenes and for them it must seem rad doing it because playing the product is fun. I don't think they have any idea as to how tenuous everything still is."

Following a series of employment shakeups that eliminated most of the experienced members of the development team, they became demoralized and doubtful of their own job security. This created a considerable level of hostility toward project management, but also a closer level of camaraderie among team members. "No one is here out of loyalty to the product at this point," Benjamin went on to tell me, "Everyone who is still here after all of those firings took place is here out of loyalty to each other and to the people who got let go. We're not going to disgrace their efforts that they put in to trying to get this game out the door; we're not going to screw over each other by abandoning this project so that people don't have the credit to put on their résumés." When this came to a head near the lowest point of the 2009 economic recession, Walker assessed the team's situation in terms of troop morale: "All of us—the team as a whole—would feel much, much better if we could see a year into the future. But that is a well-guarded secret. That is a problem, a *huge* problem. It is a problem with our management; it is a problem with the army. It is a problem that will have to be solved if they want to continue to do this, because it is *horrible* for morale. . . . If they don't want people to continue to look for jobs all day long, then they need to make them feel like they are going to be taken care of in the future, and that is something that is *severely* lacking."

When it was useful to their purposes, members of the army sought to militarize this discontent by continuing to project to the subcontracted development team a sense of inclusion within the larger organization of the army. In a team meeting, a visiting senior officer sought to encourage the overworked and understaffed office as they entered crunch time a few months prior to the release of *America's Army 3*. Speaking to them as if they were soldiers and framing their work in terms of "selfless service," one of the seven core army values, he told them, "Thank you for putting up with the drama . . . but you can't quit, because you represent an organization that doesn't quit. This country wouldn't be here if the organization that you represent had a quitter's attitude. I don't care who pays you, you work for the army. You're going to have to be like the Special Forces and do more with less. You have the Special Forces mentality. . . . Everybody wanted to have a piece of the bad guy after 9/11. You guys are serving the war effort in a huge way."

Though the senior officer's ploy did not appear to work in terms of motivating the designers, his words were not visibly dismissed for their reliance on cheap platitudes and patriotic appeals. The developers took pride in their work, and most were pleased to be creating something noncommercial and for the army. For this reason, despite their disagreements with individuals at the project management level, the office's orientation in regard to "big army" at the institutional level was positive. But the pressing needs of job security, more competitive salaries, and better benefits—in addition to receiving much-needed resources to ensure the timely release of the game—were on the minds of nearly everyone at the time. When these issues were mentioned to the officer, he dismissed them, telling the team, "That's not a big problem, I think." But some developers persisted, petitioning to him, "We've lost talent, and can't attract talent because we can't pay competitively. We want to continue to work for the project, but [management] has screwed us." Choosing not to take into account these realities, the senior officer instead interpreted this as a threat and asked the team, "Is this a 'let's have a walkout' kind of problem?"

In eliding the fact that the game developers were laborers by implying that they were developing the game purely for patriotic reasons to help "get a piece of the bad guy," the officer re-created the situation of many who join the military for primarily economic reasons but nevertheless feel compelled to speak of their enlistment in terms of national service. The language of selfless service mystifies the economic reasons underlying employment in the military and by military contractors. Andrew Bickford writes that "if we think of the U.S. military as a labor market, and its soldiers as workers, these are people who find themselves in coercive and exploitative situations [which] can compel soldiers to fight and soldier on; it is a form of labor rationalization . . . that ultimately does little for the soldier" (2009:151). His description of soldier labor applies to that of the game developers' work as well, for these virtual soldiers were essentially asked to continue projecting the affective qualities of a soldier by pushing through crunch time in the service of their nation.

GRADUATION: LAYOFFS

Crunch time abruptly ended on June 17, 2009, when the completed *America's Army 3* was released to the public for free download. At the end of the workday, the developers went to their favorite bar for a celebration. The next morning, they came to their offices to find the usually dark studio brightly lit and their computers locked. On that day, all but a handful of employees were laid off without prior warning and the Emeryville development office was shut down. Referring to the move as a "consolidation," an Army Game Project representative told reporters that the layoffs "will allow us to gain efficiencies between our public and government applications."[17] According to other unofficial sources, though, there simply was not any money for the program; due to the economic downturn, enlistment in the army was up. Even though *America's Army* had generated a considerable number of recruiting achievements and publicity over the years, such novel efforts had simply become less of an immediate fiscal priority. Funding for the Army Game Project, typically cobbled together from previously reliable annual budget surpluses from a variety of army organizations, did not materialize. Though operational still in 2011, the project pulled back many of its ventures in addition to the game, including the Virtual Army Experience (see R. Allen 2009).

Largely due to preexisting external issues that were beyond the control of the Emeryville development office, the free game was critically broken and essentially unplayable for several weeks after its release. Frustrated players, many of them soldiers and veterans, had waited expectantly for months to download the game, and they naturally equated news of the layoffs as retribution for the broken *America's Army 3*. In an angry retort to players' mounting criticisms of the game and its developers, one of the former developers posted a comment (quickly deleted by forum moderators) at the americasarmy.com forums. He implored fans "to imagine trying to build a game with an impossible deadline, steadily declining workforce (via firings), a hiring freeze, constantly being fed misinformation, having the 'higher ups' completely ignore your weekly plea for either a) more time, or b) more manpower, working a ton of unpaid overtime, pouring your heart and soul into a misadventure only to have the uniformed community scoff at you for uncontrollable variables . . . RIGHT when you've just lost your job."[18]

Through multiple channels it had become painfully and abruptly clear to all of the developers that despite the similitude of their experiences to actual soldiers, they were, in the end, ex-employees of a subcontractor to a contractor to the U.S. military. "The army takes care of its own" was a phrase that was ironically repeated during the days following the layoffs. They had always understood that they were not a part of "its own," and that, anyway, the army rarely adequately takes care of even "its own" veterans. But there was an expressive bitterness in their words that seemed unusually high, even for freshly laid-off workers. A great deal of this rancor derived from a growing realization that the closest parallel between their experiences and the experiences of many U.S. soldiers was, ultimately, in how they ended up feeling forgotten, unappreciated, and discarded by the military.

Much ado could be made about the uniqueness of the developers' situation. But my primary reason in writing this chapter has not been to elicit sympathy for them or show how their situation was anomalous. Their abrupt joblessness was unfortunately not an abnormality, especially in California during June 2009, when the state unemployment rate was fast approaching 12 percent (U.S. Bureau of Labor Statistics 2010). Fluctuation in the video game labor market, punctuated by mass layoffs, has been an industry norm and post-Fordist principle for years.

My purpose, instead, has been to explain how the circumstances of the developers might illuminate general trends in the militarization of popular culture in the United States. The enlistment of the developers' labor to perform as virtual soldiers highlights a pervasive mobilization of the culture industry and the cognitive capacities of its laborers as vehicles of war. The corporatization of the military (and the militarization of corporations) is one underlying engine of this trend, which is only accelerating.

As more private mercenaries become employed in U.S. foreign occupations and counterterrorism attempts; as more businesses become contracted through Pentagon funding initiatives; as the capabilities of digital technologies increase the immersive qualities of military entertainment; and as social scientists weaponize culture and ethnography (see the chapters by Ferguson, González, Price, and Whitehead in this volume), new forms of virtual soldiering will emerge. Sooner or later, it might behoove everyone to ask of themselves, "How am I a virtual soldier?"

NOTES

1. Over the course of twenty months (2007–9), I spent approximately seven months at the Emeryville, California, development offices of *America's Army* in addition to shorter visits to several institutions affiliated with the Army Game Project.
2. The quote is from Col. Casey Wardynski, "Army Game Project Results Overview (2009)," p. 15. Unpublished document; manuscript provided by the author on May 26, 2009.
3. For example, the hugely commercially successful iteration in the *Call of Duty* series of games, *Call of Duty: Modern Warfare II* (2009), grossed over $310 million in its first week of sales in the United States and the United Kingdom, making it the largest release for any form of entertainment media ever. By mid-January 2010, the game had grossed over $1 billion in revenue (see Cork 2009; BBC News 2010).
4. This chapter is rhetorically structured according to the phases of basic combat training (red phase, white phase, and blue phase).
5. For the industry employment norms, see Duffy 2007.
6. Valve's *Team Fortress II* and *Left 4 Dead* were popular studio favorites.
7. See http://www.milspecmonkey.com, a site that designs and sells military gear and patches.
8. All individuals referred to by only proper names are aliases. To preserve anonymity in this and other articles, I have sometimes created composite aliases, combining two or more individuals into a single alias or interspersing an individual's quotes and identifiable markers across multiple aliases.
9. See Hamacher 2007.
10. To use Jean Baudrillard's terminology, this sequence of representations is intended by the army to be interpreted as a simulacrum of the first order (1994:6) in which the in-game boot camp serves as an artificial placeholder for the real army boot camp. I would contend, however, that the representational process of *America's Army* is much more complex than this. I prefer to think of the game as part of a hyperrealistic narrative of what the army desires itself to be, a narrative that *produces*, rather than reflects, realities (see Allen 2011). This would place *America's Army* in Baudrillard's schema as a simulacrum of the third order in which the original is preceded by its copies (1994:6), much in the same way the

contemporary boot camp experiences of many new army enlistees are preceded by an abundance of narratives (i.e., virtual boot camp experiences) populating the military-entertainment culture industry.

11. Such claims are also made for other Army Game Project products, like the Virtual Army Experience (R. Allen 2009).

12. See "America's Army Operations Update," January 2009, http://www.americas army.com/press/newsletters/enewsletter_2009_01.php, accessed March 23, 2011.

13. For the video, see http://www.americasarmy.com/media/videoViewer.php?xml ImageName=allVideos, accessed March 23, 2011.

14. See http://www.aa3.americasarmy.com/about/article.php?blogid=1, accessed March 23, 2011; http://www.americasarmy.com/about/blogs.php?blogid=2, accessed March 23, 2011.

15. See "America's Army Game," http://www.goarmy.com/downloads/americas_army .jsp, accessed March 23, 2011.

16. See http://forum.americasarmy.com/viewtopic.php?t=269828, accessed March 23, 2011.

17. See Faylor 2009; "America's Army 3 Devs Let Go Day after Launch," http://kotaku .com/5296131/americas-army-3-devs-let-go-day-after-launch, accessed March 23, 2011.

18. See "America's Army Launches New Version, Sacks Developers, Moves HQ," June 20, 2009, http://www.gamepolitics.com/2009/06/20/america039s-army -launches-new-version-sacks-developers-moves-hq, accessed March 23, 2011.

VIRTUAL WAR IN THE TRIBAL ZONE

Air Strikes, Drones, Civilian Casualties, and Losing Hearts
and Minds in Afghanistan and Pakistan

"They were killed right here [in an air strike]; they were 10 and 17 years old," he said.
In the compound next to his, he said, four entire families, including those of his two
brothers, were killed. "They bombard us, they hate us, they kill us," he said of the
Americans. "God will punish them."

—**Afghan civilian cited by Carlotta Gall,** *New York Times***, 2008**

Today, the central focus of the anthropology and ethnography of
war is the effect on local populations and communities of living,
frequently for extended periods of time, under war conditions
(e.g., Nordstrom 1997; Tishkov 2004; Richards 2005; Lubkemann 2008; Finnström 2008; Maček 2009). Here, I consider the
civilian casualties caused by the use of air strikes by planes, helicopters, and especially remote-controlled drones in the "global
war on terror" in the tribal zones of Afghanistan and Pakistan.
I argue that these tactics of virtual counterinsurgency, touted as
being highly discriminate and effective (literally able to "put war-
heads on foreheads") and as representing the technological cutting edge of a revolution in advanced modern war-fighting capabilities, have in actual practice resulted in a collateral disaster
that has effectively ensured that the battle for "hearts and minds"
among these communities in the so-called Af-Pak theater of war
has been lost.

"Virtual warfare" is the characteristic form of emerging postmodern warfare. Modern impersonal and depersonalized warfare emerged as a result of the Industrial Revolution in Europe during the eighteenth century and the evolution and spread of cannons and firearms, which made killing from a distance the normal form of combat. Wikipedia defines virtual war as "the increased utilization and dependency on technology during the course of warfare. It includes the time/space separation between an attacker and the intended target which results in the 'sanitization' of war."[1] According to Alexander Moseley, "Virtual warfare involves the abandonment—perhaps total—of face to face combat, in favor of wars fought from safe shelters hundreds and even thousands of miles away from the actual 'battlefield.' There, pilotless planes and guided cruise missiles hone in on targets. Virtual war constitutes the next progression in battlefield technology, a path that began with the first thrown implement" (2002:33–34).

At the time of this writing, the war in Afghanistan—Operation Enduring Freedom—which began in October 2001, had entered its ninth year. The war had steadily escalated and grown worse for the occupying forces. The Taliban was growing in numbers and expanding with alarming success. They were described as "resurgent," and their attacks, funded mainly by the expanded opium trade, were increasingly sophisticated and well coordinated and exacting a rising toll on U.S. and coalition troops (Hedges 2008). As the war grew and spread to Pakistan, it increasingly relied on air power; consequently the number of civilian casualties rose rapidly, such that in 2008, Human Rights Watch reported that "civilian deaths in Afghanistan from US and NATO airstrikes nearly tripled from 2006 to 2007, with recent deadly airstrikes exacerbating the problem and fueling a public backlash." Even the generals in command agreed that the U.S. counterinsurgency campaign was failing in both Afghanistan and Pakistan. It was not only failing to defeat the Taliban and Al-Qaeda, it was actually doing the opposite—undermining the Afghan and Pakistan governments and stimulating support for the insurgents.

In Afghanistan, in response to the increasing Taliban attacks, in 2008 the U.S.-led forces retaliated with massive aerial bombing campaigns and large-scale house raids. The number of insurgent attacks increased nonetheless, and the number of civilian casualties skyrocketed, such that in the fifteen months of the surge more civilians had been killed than in the previous four years combined. "During this same period, the country descended into a state of utter dereliction—no jobs, very little reconstruction, and ever less security. In turn, the rising civilian death toll and the decaying economy proved a profitable recipe for the Taliban, who recruited significant numbers of new fighters" (Gopal 2008). Once confined to the deep Afghan south, by the end of 2009 the insurgents were operating openly right at the doorstep of Kabul, the capital. Although this counterinsurgency surge, little noted by the media, failed miserably, the newly elected Barack Obama administration immediately planned another one.

The military moved to a strategy involving pulling back from the countryside and focusing on protecting more heavily populated areas, and the less populated parts of the countryside were left to Hellfire missile–armed drone aircraft. This was a reprise of the strategic hamlet strategy that failed badly in Vietnam and also represents the classic situation in guerrilla wars where the army controls the cities but the insurgents control most of the countryside. By the end of 2008, the Taliban controlled 72 percent of the country, up from 54 percent the year before (Moncrieff 2008), and the Afghan government was nearly nonexistent in the countryside. At night the Taliban controlled the roads, and they were moving in on Kabul. The city itself was in tatters, with poor Afghanis living in crumbling warrens with no electricity and often without safe drinking water. A city designed for about 800,000 people, it now held more than 4 million, mostly squeezed into informal settlements and squatters' shacks (Gopal 2008).

The Afghan government was corrupt from top to bottom, and in 2009 the president, Hamid Karzai, sometimes referred to as "the mayor of Kabul" for his government's lack of reach, "won" a fraudulent election. The words *occupation* and *puppet government* rang ever truer in Afghan ears. All this was a Taliban bonanza, and there was mass popular opposition to the United States in Afghanistan, just as there was in Iraq and Pakistan. The majority of Afghan people had come to regard the American and coalition troops as occupiers, and they strongly opposed sending in more troops. They regarded the U.S. and coalition forces "as they did the Russians, as foreign, anti-Muslim invaders," and believed that the government the United States was backing was "corrupt and rapacious" (Polk 2009:15).

At the end of 2009, the majority of Afghanis felt *occupied* by the American and allied foreign troops and *threatened* by the Taliban. Although the majority opposed the Taliban, underlying conditions enabled the organization to grow stronger. Increasingly, Afghanis were convinced that the foreign forces could not bring security, and they yearned for stability more than anything else, regardless of whether it was under the Taliban or the Western-supported government. There had also been a steady decline in support for the U.S. and allied forces. In 2005, 80 percent of Afghanis supported the presence of foreign troops; by March 2009 fewer than half did (*The Week*, February 27, 2009, p. 14). A BBC/ABC survey taken in February 2009 showed rising anger among the Afghan population over the U.S. assaults, and 77 percent said air strikes, particularly by unmanned drones, were unacceptable because they endangered civilians (McGivering 2009).

For the previous four years, Pakistan had also been a nation in turmoil, run by a shaky government supported by a corrupt system, dominated by a blatantly criminal security service, and threatened by a large fundamentalist Islamic population with strong ties to the Taliban in Afghanistan. The war in Pakistan escalated in May 2009, when the Pakistan army, under pressure from the United States, launched large-scale counterinsurgency operations in the tribal borderlands in the northwest of the country, which killed and maimed thousands of civilians and created a huge humanitarian catastrophe. At the same time, the CIA stepped up a campaign of airborne attacks by unmanned drones in the Federally Administered Tribal Areas (FATAS) of Pakistan, begun in January 2006, which by the end of 2009 had killed an estimated seven hundred civilians. The Pakistan army's assault against Islamic militants in the Buner District flattened villages, killed civilians, and sent thousands of villagers fleeing from their homes to escape the fighting. In Swat, the offensive displaced up to three million mainly Pashtun people, more than half the population of the country, risking the destabilization of the entire northwestern region of the country. As Shibil Siddiqi (2009) observed at the time, "Already the squalid refugee camps are seething with anger at the military offensive and have turned into ideal recruiting grounds for the Taliban."

At the end of 2009, the majority of Pakistanis also opposed their country's participation in the war on terror, and they were particularly critical of the use of drone strikes. The drone attacks on targets in the tribal areas killed innocent civilians, uniting the Pashtun against the United States and recruiting and increasing popular support for the Taliban. The strikes were deeply unpopular, and the tactic backfired by sowing public anger and fueling anti-Americanism, while failing to defeat the militants. A poll in July and August 2009 showed that Pakistanis were increasingly distrustful and suspicious of America, with 80 percent opposing cooperating with the United States any longer in its war on terror, and 76 percent opposing the use of the drone strikes (Zaidi 2009:18), and the poll excluded the country's tribal areas, where the opposition was even greater (Hayden 2009:23). The Pakistan government strongly opposed and routinely protested such strikes, but the Pakistan military was secretly cooperating with them. By the final months of 2009, a war by machine assassins—remote-controlled airborne drones—was visibly provoking terror and terrorism "as well as anger and hatred among people who [were] by no means fundamentalists," and destabilizing the country (Tom Engelhardt, cited in Feffer 2009).

In an earlier publication, I argued that the United States has lost the battle for hearts and minds in the war on terror, that civilian casualties are the main factor that loses the support of the people during guerrilla wars or insurgencies, and that that was losing the wars in Iraq and Afghanistan as well (Sluka 2009). The deaths of civilians, which the military refers to as "CIVCAS" and "collateral damage," are not a sideline or incidental to the result of these wars (Engelhardt 2008b). In Afghanistan and Pakistan, as in Iraq, the killing of civilians by foreign forces is the biggest source of tension. Civilian casualties caused by foreign forces has sapped support for the troops' presence in Afghanistan, been a major source of friction between the Afghan and Pakistan governments and the West, and resulted in a growing number of increasingly violent demonstrations shouting anti-U.S. slogans and calling for the foreign troops to leave. Experts agreed that a key reason for the Taliban resurgence was growing popular sympathy for the militants because of overreliance on the use of force, especially air power, by the U.S.-led occupation forces that had killed thousands of civilians (Landay and Shah 2009).

THE AF-PAK WAR BODY COUNT

We have no idea exactly how many civilians have been "blown away" by the United States and its allies in the wars in Afghanistan and Pakistan, but there is no doubt that so-called collateral damage has been widespread and far more central to the conduct of the war than the authorities have acknowledged (e.g., see Thompson 2008). In Afghanistan, civilian casualties have come in myriad ways—from artillery fire, from shootings of civilians in vehicles at checkpoints, from troops blasting away from convoys, during raids on homes, in village operations, and, most significantly, from the air (Engelhardt 2008a).

The "fog of war" makes counting the dead difficult, and all official figures on civilian casualties are likely to be significant undercounts, but by November 2009 official figures indicated that there had been approximately 21,250 total civilian casualties in Afghanistan. According to the United Nations, in 2008 some 2,118 civilians were killed, a third (828) by Afghan and international forces (Engelhardt 2009e), including 522 from airstrikes, which represented a 40 percent increase in casualties from the previous year. But the United Nations also admitted they were hampered in their research by lack of access to all parts of the country because of poor security, and the independent Kabul-based human rights group Afghanistan Rights Monitor presented much higher figures. They reported that 3,917 Afghan civilians were killed in 2008, more than two-thirds in rebel attacks and 1,100 by foreign forces. They also reported that more than 6,800 had been wounded, around 120,000 were forced from their homes, and about 680 died in air strikes that year.[2]

In July 2009, a UN report said that so far that year about 1,800 civilians had been killed in Afghanistan. The Taliban and warlords were responsible for about 1,000 of these, and 700 were killed by international and Afghan forces, including 455 who died in air strikes (*Dominion Post*, February 5, 2009). It also reported that the war was spreading into residential areas; that the number of civilian casualties was steadily escalating as more people were being killed by air strikes, car bombs, and suicide attacks; and that the number of civilians being killed in the fighting was doubling every two years (*Sunday Star-Times*, July 19, 2009).

There is no website comparable to Iraq Body Count (http://www .iraqbodycount.org) that monitors all civilian casualties in Pakistan, and it is difficult to determine how many there have been. The best figures indicate that by November 2009 the war on terrorism in Pakistan had killed 7,000 civilians and 2,600 military personnel since 2003 (Zaidi 2009). Pakistan sources reported that 916 civilians had been killed and 310 wounded in drone strikes, but U.S. sources said the figure was 700 killed (Bergen and Tiedemann 2010).

WAR IN THE TRIBAL ZONE

The concept of war in the "tribal zone" was introduced by R. Brian Ferguson and Neil Whitehead (1992a) for the analysis of warfare that occurs in the context of the encounters on frontiers between expanding states and indigenous peoples. They showed that the "frequent effect" or impact of foreign intrusion into the territory of "tribal" or indigenous peoples "is an overall militarization; that is, an increase in armed collective violence whose conduct, purposes, and technologies rapidly adapt to the threat generated by state expansion. That area continuously affected by the proximity of the state, but not under [effective] state administration, we call the 'tribal zone'" (1992a:3). Imperialism or "expanding states" induce and aggravate violence and armed conflict in the tribal zone among and between tribes and between tribes and the state. It not only stimulates such warfare, it changes its causes and conduct.

In understanding the dynamics of the tribal zone, Ferguson and Whitehead suggest that imperial states employ a blend or mix of "coercion" and "seduction" to achieve their ends: "The primary means of coercion are military threats; those of seduction are gifts, trade opportunities, and pledges of political support" (1992a:7). It is not a coincidence that this is exactly the basis of the still-dominant "two fronts" counterinsurgency theory, which advocates a combination of military repression and political reform. For indigenous peoples, "the three basic options in regard to state agents are resistance, cooperation, and flight" (Ferguson and Whitehead 1992a:17), and all three of these are apparent in the "antiterrorism" wars in the tribal zones of Afghanistan and Pakistan.

Two other characteristic aspects of war in the tribal zone apparent in the Af-Pak war are the tendency for formerly divided tribes to unite in resistance against the state, and for the state to seek to divide and conquer the tribes by playing them off against each other. Ann Jones (2009) has shown that attributing all resistance in Afghanistan to the Taliban is a mistake. She argues that it is not actually a Taliban insurgency per se, but a very localized and complex one with more than a dozen groups operating in the country: "It's very much tribal-based; they come together against a common enemy, as they did with the Soviets. What unifies all these people is us" (2009). Building that unity is made easier for the Taliban when U.S. forces or those of its allies are heavy-handed in their operations. Air strikes that kill innocent civilians are a classic example. With regard to divide and conquer, U.S. military commanders were studying how to recruit Afghan tribesmen against the Taliban and Al-Qaeda: "Taking a page from the so-called 'Sunni Awakening' in Iraq, which turned Sunni tribesmen against militants first in Anbar Province and then beyond, the strategic about-face in Afghanistan sought to extend power from Kabul to the country's myriad tribal militias. Likewise, the Pakistani government has attempted to deploy tribal fighters against the Taliban in the Federally Administered areas" (Cole 2009).

DEATH FROM ABOVE: DRONES AND VIRTUAL
WARFARE IN THE AF-PAK THEATER

The U.S. Air Force has been increasingly relying on unmanned aerial vehicles (UAVs) or drones, particularly the MQ-1 Predator (figure 8.1) and larger MQ-9 Reaper (figure 8.2). The first UAVs were used in Yugoslavia, where in 1998 the Kosovo war became history's first virtual or postmodern war. The seventy-eight-day campaign achieved its objectives without a single NATO combat fatality (Ignatieff 2000). Drones were used again during the 2001 invasion of Afghanistan and since 2004 in the tribal borderlands of Pakistan. During this time they have also been used to assassinate people and bomb vehicles and buildings in several other countries (e.g., Yemen in November 2002). Now, they are "preying" on people and "reaping" death and destruction in Iraq, Pakistan, and Afghanistan.

The drones are in use "24/7" over Afghanistan and the Pakistan tribal borderlands. These ghost planes are launched from Afghanistan, but mainly flown by joystick pilots located halfway around the world at air force bases in the United States. As Washington and the military see it, the ideal use of Predator and Reaper drones is to pick off terrorist leaders. Most of the drones are armed with Hellfire missiles or smart bombs, which the pilots can fire with the push of a button once they have spotted targets on their video screens. Killing is just a matter of entering a computer command; to the drone pilot, it is like pushing Ctrl-Alt-Del and the target dies. Ctrl-Alt-Del, also known as the "three-finger salute," is computer jargon for "dump" or "do away with," as in the Weird Al Yankovic song "It's All About the Pentiums": "Play me online? Well you know that I'll beat you / If I ever meet you, I'll Control-Alt-Delete you." The UAV pilots "have an almost godlike power. Their job is to survey a place thousands of miles distant (and completely alien to their lives and experiences), assess what they see, and spot 'targets' to eliminate—even if on their somewhat antiquated computer systems it 'takes up to 17 steps— including entering data into a pull-down window—to fire a missile' and incinerate those below" (Engelhardt 2009d).

In 2007, these hunter-killer drones were performing twenty-one combat air patrols at any one time, by the end of 2009 they were flying thirty-eight, and by 2011 they were expected to increase to fifty-four. In 2009,

8.1 MQ-1 Predator, armed with Hellfire missile. Public domain photo. Source: http://www.af.mil/photos/media_search.asp?q=predator. Provided as a public service by the U.S. Air Force.

8.2 MQ-9 Reaper landing after a mission in support of Operation Enduring Freedom in Afghanistan, 2007. Public domain photo by Sgt. Brian Ferguson. Source: http://www.af.mil/photos/media_search.asp?q=predator. Provided as a public service by the U.S. Air Force.

8.3 Predator on patrol, 2010: Maj. Rick Wageman operates the virtual cockpit of an MQ-1 Predator at a base in southern Afghanistan. Public domain photo by Sgt. Samuel Morse. Source: http://www.af.mil/photos/media_search.asp?q=predator. Provided as a public service by the U.S. Air Force.

the air force reported that for the first time they would be training more joystick pilots than new fighter and bomber pilots, creating a "sustainable career path" for air force officers. One Predator pilot-from-afar commented that "job satisfaction [manning a joystick] is very high. Every day we're doing this, we're in the thick of the fight. We fly 38 [combat air patrols] a day. Where they're happening, the hottest 36 things are going on" (Kaplan 2009) (see figure 8.3). Other joystick pilots have described fighting from an air-conditioned cubicle as "antiseptic. It's not as potent an emotion as being on the battlefield," but "it's like a video game. It can get a little bloodthirsty. But it's fucking cool." Though the pilots are no longer at risk, the experience of fighting from home bases has brought new psychological twists to war: "You see Americans [or civilians?] killed in front of your eyes and then have to go to a PTA meeting," said another pilot (cited in Singer 2009), raising the issue of whether this might lead them to suffer from post-traumatic stress disorder (Saletan 2008).

Fearing unpopular U.S. and coalition casualties, drones have become the weapon of choice in the fight against Al-Qaeda and the Taliban, and they are reportedly "knocking off the bad guys right and left" (Engelhardt 2009c). By November 2009, at least fourteen Al-Qaeda and Taliban leaders (a.k.a. "high-value targets") had been killed by drones, and many more insurgent fighters had been "taken out" as well. Tom Engelhardt (2009c) observes that the drones are the "wonder weapon of the moment," and "you can already see the military-industrial-robotics complex in formation." In fact, as James Der Derian (2001) describes, they are already part of a massive and expanding "military-industrial-media-entertainment network."

The hype and hubris surrounding this technology is immense. The mainstream media has been full of glowing reports on the drones, some of which imply that their use could win the war on terror all by itself, such as a report from April 2009 that the drones were killing Taliban and Al-Qaeda leaders and "the rest have begun fighting among themselves out of panic and suspicion. 'If you were to continue on this pace,' counterterrorism consultant Juan Zarate told the *LA Times*, 'al Qaida is dead'" (*The Week*, April 3, 2009, p. 7). In an uncritical *60 Minutes* television report on U.S. Air Force drone operations in May 2009, the officer in charge was asked if mistakes were ever made in the drone attacks: "What if you get it wrong?" His response was: "We don't" (CBS Interactive Staff 2009).

The air force claims that its priority is to precisely target insurgents while avoiding civilian casualties. They strongly assert that they are very concerned about civilian casualties and take extreme measures to avoid them, and that "casualty avoidance can be the targeting team's most time-intensive task" (quoted in Mulrine 2008:26). At the Combined Air and Space Operations Center, Middle East, there is always a military lawyer on duty, whose job is to provide advice reflecting the Law of Armed Conflict, the international treaties that prohibit intentional targeting of civilians and requires militaries to minimize risks to civilians. Supposedly, a strict NATO protocol requires high-level approval for air strikes when civilians are known to be in or near Taliban targets, and when civilians are detected, strikes are called off. The military claims it is extremely precise, and that they have called off many operations when it appeared that civilian casualties might result (Mulrine 2008:28).

Today, the drones are hyped as "the future of war," the "only good thing to come out of the war on terrorism," and an effective and highly discriminate counterterrorism and counterinsurgency weapon. Future Combat Systems, the army's $160 billion modernization effort, calls for a host of unmanned vehicles and combat drones, and virtually no one doubts that robots will eventually occupy a central role in the U.S. military. As P. W. Singer (2009) has shown, it is an unprecedented revolution in military affairs (also see Yenne 2004 and Zaloga 2008). UAVs are touted as being more cost-effective in lives and money and as being able to take American soldiers entirely out of harm's way using tele-operated systems. There is virtually no limit to the extraordinary hype about these weapons as the "greatest, weirdest, coolest, hardware in the American arsenal" (Satia 2009), and this was recognized in an article in *Newsweek* in September 2009 that categorized the drones as "weapons porn" (Graham 2009).

CRITIQUE OF THE DRONE WAR

However, the evidence shows that this hype is sheer fantasy, if not literally science fiction. There have been *many* mistakes. One typical example occurred in June 2009, when U.S. drones launched an attack on a compound in South Waziristan. When locals rushed to the scene to rescue survivors, drones then launched more missiles at them, leaving a total of thirteen dead. The next day, when local people were involved in a funeral procession, the drones struck again, killing seventy of the mourners (Kelly 2009). The drone strikes have caused thousands of civilian casualties and have had a particular affinity for hitting weddings and funerals, and they are seriously fueling the insurgency (Engelhardt 2009a). Rather than present them as nearly single-handedly winning these wars, it would be more consistent with the facts on the ground to suggest that they are almost single-handedly losing them. A UN report in 2007 concluded that U.S. air strikes were among the principal motivations for suicide attackers in Afghanistan, and at the end of 2008 a survey of forty-two Taliban fighters revealed that twelve had seen family members killed in air strikes and six had joined the insurgency after such attacks. Far more who haven't joined have offered their support (Gopal 2008).

In particular, the drone attacks in Pakistan, which have been touted as the most successful, have in fact been responsible for significant civilian casualties. Of the sixty Predator strikes there between January 14, 2006, and April 8, 2009, only ten hit their actual targets, a hit rate of 17 percent, and they killed 687 civilians. In total, the website Pakistan Body Count, which only tracks drone casualties, said in November 2009 that 916 civilians had been killed and 310 seriously wounded, and that this represents just a 3 percent success rate against Al-Qaeda.[3] Even David Kilcullen, author of *The Accidental Guerrilla* (2009b) and dubbed by the media a "counterinsurgency guru," told the U.S. Congress in April 2009 that the drone attacks in Pakistan were backfiring and should be stopped. He said, "Since 2006, we've killed 14 senior Al-Qaeda leaders using drone strikes; in the same period, we've killed 700 Pakistani civilians in the same area. The drone strikes are highly unpopular. They are deeply aggravating to the population. And they've given rise to a feeling of anger that coalesces the population around the extremists and leads to spikes of extremism. . . . The current path that we are on is leading us to loss of Pakistani government control over its own population" (quoted in Naiman 2009). Kilcullen said that the kill ratio had been fifty civilians for every militant killed, a hit rate of 2 percent, or 98 percent civilian casualties (see figure 8.4), which could hardly be considered "precision."

Kilcullen argues that the appeal of the drones is that their effects are measurable, killing key leaders and hampering insurgent operations, but the costs have far outweighed the benefits for three reasons. First, it creates a "siege mentality" and casualties among Pakistani civilians, which leads to support for the insurgents. Second, it generates public outrage not only in the local area but throughout the country, not to mention internationally and at home in the United States (see figure 8.5). Third, it represents a tactic—more accurately, a form of technology—substituting for a strategy. He concludes, "Every one of these dead noncombatants [creates] an alienated family, a new desire for revenge, and more recruits for a militant movement that has grown exponentially even as drone strikes have increased" (Kilcullen and Exum 2009).

It has also been reported that the drone strikes in Pakistan "are creating turmoil in the tribal areas. A witch-hunt against suspected spies

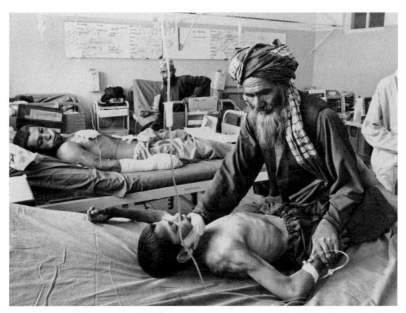

8.4 February 2005: Wounded Afghans receive treatment at a Kandahar hospital after an American air strike. Photo: Allauddin Khan/AP. Reprint permission granted.

has resulted in the deaths of at least a dozen people in North Waziristan, many of them beheaded" (Yousafzai and Hosenball 2009:35). This is another typical consequence of imperial "war in the tribal zone." Furthermore, even when the air strikes have succeeded in killing militant leaders, in many cases this has simply turned them into martyrs. For example, more than five thousand people attended the funeral of rebel commander Ghulam Yahya Akbari, killed in a U.S. air strike in October 2009. Reports said that "thousands wept" and "women wailed from the rooftops" as a long procession accompanied his body to the grave site near his native village in Herat Province (MacKenzie and Saber 2009).

The reliance on air power has served to undermine public support in Afghanistan and Pakistan, and continued aerial bombing will result in more civilian casualties, leading to more resentment, resulting in more support and recruits for the insurgents, leading to a long, losing war. As Engelhardt (2008b) argues,

> Force creates counterforce. The application of force, especially from the air, is a reliable engine for the creation of enemies. It is a force multiplier (and not just for the US forces either). Every time an air strike

8.5 April 2009: Demonstration against a U.S. drone missile strike on Pakistan's tribal areas. Photo: Shakil Adil/AP. Reprint permission granted.

is called in anywhere on the planet, anyone who orders it should automatically assume that left in its wake will be grieving, angry husbands, wives, sisters, brothers, relatives, friends—people vowing revenge, a pool of potential candidates filled with the anger of genuine injustice. From the point of view of our actual enemies, you can't bomb, missile, and strafe often enough, because when you do so, you are more or less guaranteed to create their newest recruits.

As Singer recognizes, "We are now creating a very similar problem to what the Israelis face in Gaza. They've gotten very good at killing Hamas leaders. They have in no way shape or form succeeded in preventing a 12-year-old in joining Hamas" (quoted in De Luce 2009).

In military operations, targeting decisions must be made to minimize civilian casualties, otherwise it is a war crime, and because most victims are civilians, hunter-killer drones are terrorist weapons. In the United Kingdom, Lord Thomas Bingham has compared them to cluster bombs and land mines, weapons that have been deemed too cruel for use, and Kilcullen judged their hit rate as "immoral" (Satia 2009:16). As Robert Naiman (2009) observed: "Since it is manifestly apparent that, 1) the drone strikes are causing civilian casualties, 2) they are turning Pakistani public opinion against their government and against the US, 3) they are recruiting more support for insurgents and 4) even military experts think the strikes are doing more harm than good, even from the point of view of US officials, why shouldn't they stop? Why not at least a time-out?" The answer is because the military believes they are "the only game in town," they are seen as an alternative to more troops on the ground, they reduce U.S. casualties, and there is now a huge and powerful multibillion-dollar military-industrial-media-entertainment complex developed around them and pushing them.

To President Barack Obama and most Americans, the drones are seen as terrorist-killers, but in Afghanistan and Pakistan they are viewed as fearsome indiscriminate killers of civilians. From the imperial top-down perspective, remote-controlled "terminator" drones are perceived as a fantastically successful new weapon, right out of science fiction. But from the bottom-up perspective of the targeted populations in the tribal zones, they have been experienced as a flawed weapon that they fear, resent, and despise because of the collateral damage they have caused. In actual use, they have been prime recruiting agents for the militants and have lost the hearts and minds of the population (see Landay 2009 and Mujahid 2009).

Furthermore, the psychology of aerial attack—death from above—is a psychology of terror. "Many Afghans now say they would rather have the Taliban back in power than nervously eye the skies every day" (Gopal 2008). A villager who survived a drone attack in Pakistan explained that "even the children, at play, were acutely conscious of drones flying overhead" (Kelly 2009). During the 1980s, the use of helicopter gunships by the Soviets in their war in Afghanistan, and by the militaries armed by President Ronald Reagan in El Salvador and Guatemala, generated discussion of the psychology or even sociobiology of fear of threats from above, and Bruce Cockburn's 1983 song "If I Had a Rocket Launcher," which he wrote after visiting a Guatemalan refugee camp in Mexico: "Here comes the helicopter—second time today / Everybody scatters and hopes it goes away / How many kids they've murdered only God can say / If I had a rocket launcher . . . I'd make somebody pay."

For many, the much touted sophistication of this technology only makes the civilian deaths more galling. They ask: If it's so sophisticated, how come in practice it's so indiscriminate and kills so many innocent people? That is the experience on the ground. As one local politician in Afghanistan expressed it, "They are bombarding villages because they hear the Taliban are there. But this is not the way, to bomb and kill 20 people for one Taliban. This is why people are losing hope and trust in the government and the internationals." Like many Afghanis and Pakistanis, he was starting to suspect a more sinister meaning behind the civilian deaths: "The Americans can make a mistake once, twice, maybe three times," he said. "But twenty, thirty times? I am not convinced that they are doing this without intention" (quoted in Baker 2009). Psychologically, Afghanis and Pakistanis in the tribal zone view the drones as dangerous predators, and they are never going to see them as their protectors.

Michael Ignatieff observes that the media's "failure to report what the true face of war looks like has caused the public to be detached from the carnage wrought by the occupation of Iraq and the war in Afghanistan," and he warns that virtual war is a dangerous, seductive illusion: "We see ourselves as noble warriors and our enemies as despicable tyrants. We see war as a surgical scalpel and not a bloodstained sword. In so doing we mis-describe ourselves as we mis-describe the instruments of death. We need to stay away from such fables of self-righteous invulnerability" (2000:214–15). The wars in Afghanistan and Pakistan, as well as Iraq, were already distant and virtual, even before the arrival of virtual weapons like hunter-killer drones. Americans are disconnected from these wars by half a planet and the mainstream media. With no connection there is no understanding and little empathy or consciousness, and we—the public—are easily misled and rendered manipulable by those C. Wright Mills (1956) so aptly described as "the power elite." As Ignatieff observes, "If war becomes unreal to the citizens of modern democracies, will they care enough to restrain and control the violence exercised in their name? Will they do so, if they and their sons and daughters are spared the hazards of combat?" (2000:3–4).

Virtual war dehumanizes the victims, desensitizes the perpetrators of violence, and lowers the moral and psychological barriers to killing. For example, the people who develop, build, operate, and deploy virtual weapons—that is, those who are part of the weapons industry and military-industrial complex—do not care what these weapons do in Iraq, Afghanistan, and Pakistan. At the same time, in the United States today, young people play video games developed by the military—such as *America's Army* and *Close Combat: First to Fight*—that enable them to casually kill the simulated human beings whose world they control. In this way, the militarization and weaponization of culture is directly reflected in the conjunction of entertainment and military media. This socialization for virtual war means that the step to killing real human beings is very small, because the only change is psychological and moral; the physical process of remote-controlled violence is exactly the same, regardless of whether the victims are real or simulated. Basically, by walking through the process in virtual reality, players are being conditioned (or deconditioned) to do the same process in real life.

CONCLUSION

Civilian casualties are not a sideline or incidental to the result of the war on terror—they lie at its heart (Engelhardt 2008b). They are the single biggest issue in Afghanistan and Pakistan, because everyone agrees, including the generals running the war, that there is no purely military solution and success is impossible without winning the hearts and minds or allegiance, trust, and confidence of the people. In July 2009, in response to the rising number of civilian casualties, General Stanley McChrystal sought to change the emphasis from killing insurgents to protecting civilians, and he ordered his troops to avoid calling in air strikes if civilian lives were at risk to show the local people that the U.S. forces were there to protect them. However, the military's effort to be more humane and reduce civilian casualties still consisted of stepped-up aerial bombing, beefed-up special forces, and the widespread use of unmanned aerial drones (Youssef 2009). But the fact that the war effort itself now fuels the insurgency and continues the cycle of violence proves that there is no military solution in Afghanistan or Pakistan. The U.S. military presence in Afghanistan greatly contributes to the legitimacy of the Taliban, Al-Qaeda, and the Pashtun insurgency. The "resurgence" in the power of the Islamists, even though they are despised by a majority of the population, is a direct result of the counterinsurgency tactics being employed. That is, the United States and its allies are losing the battle for hearts and minds in Afghanistan and Pakistan, as they did in the war in Iraq.

The United States is scrambling for another surge solution based on escalation of the conflict, and relying on sending in more troops and using more drone and other airborne attacks. These tactics are bound to fail, because they are what got us where we are now. The use of air power has already undermined public support for the governments in Afghanistan and Pakistan, and continued aerial bombing will result in more civilian casualties, leading to more anger, resulting in more support and recruits for the insurgents, leading to a long, losing war. Dropping bombs and killing civilians anger whole populations and create ill will, and, as John Paul

Lederach has asserted, bombing Taliban and Al-Qaeda targets "is like hitting a mature dandelion with a golf club; it just ensures another generation" of insurgents (quoted in Dodge 2009).

In Afghanistan, U.S. and allied troops are perceived as bringing death and destruction wherever they go. The increase in U.S. troops is inciting resistance in many areas, not quelling it, because the majority of Afghanis now regard the U.S. and coalition forces as foreign, anti-Muslim invaders and occupiers. The insurgents are not blustering when they say that more troops mean more targets for their fighters and suicide bombers. As William Polk reminds us, "As the history of every insurgency demonstrates, the more foreign boots there are on the ground and the harder the foreigners fight, the more hatred they engender. Substituting drone attacks for ground combat is no solution" (2009:14). He also notes that what actually brought most insurgencies to a halt, including the one in Vietnam, was the withdrawal of the foreigners (2009:12): "US military intervention in Afghanistan has not only solidified the Taliban as an organization but has also created increasing public support for it. There is much evidence in Afghanistan, as there has been in every insurgency I have studied, that foreign soldiers increase rather than calm hostility. The British found that to be true even in the American Revolution" (2009:14).

The Taliban and other insurgents remain formidable foes, and the chances of defeating them are poor and growing poorer because, although they are not necessarily becoming more popular, the occupying forces are becoming less popular every day. Moreover, they see the government we back as corrupt and rapacious. Observers report that it is deeply involved in the drug trade, stealing aid money, and even selling U.S.-supplied arms to the Taliban. Many Afghanis, and Pakistanis as well, believe that their government is just a puppet of the United States, and the presence of U.S. troops and drones only bolsters that belief. Afghans are famous guerrilla fighters, and history teaches that they are a fiercely independent people who will continue fighting as long as it takes to drive out the foreign occupation. Without an end date for U.S. military intervention, there is little chance of winning Afghan hearts and minds, whether by coercion or negotiation. Those who argue that the United States cannot leave until Afghanistan is peaceful have it exactly backward: Afghanistan will never have peace as long as it is occupied by unwelcome foreign troops.

At this point, Afghanistan is almost certainly a failed state, and nuclear-armed Pakistan has being dangerously destabilized as well. Thus, the crucial factors the U.S. government and military identify for a successful counterinsurgency campaign—a stable and popularly supported government, and winning the support or hearts and minds of the people—are never likely to be achieved. At the end of 2009, General McChrystal optimistically claimed that it would take at least five to ten years to "win" the war, but British general Sir David Richards predicted that bringing peace and stability to Afghanistan might take as long as thirty to forty years. But even should that happen—which is doubtful—if, as William Astore (2009) suggests, "the cost of victory (however defined) is hundreds, or even thousands, more American military casualties, hundreds of billions of additional dollars spent, and extensive 'collateral damage' and blowback, will this 'victory' not be a pyrrhic one, achieved at a price so dear as to be indistinguishable from defeat?"

After being elected to office in 2008, President Obama took "ownership" of the war and described it as "a war of necessity" fundamental to the "defense of our people" (Leon 2009). He rebranded previous President George W. Bush's global war on terror as "overseas contingent operations," which is a virtual expression for "wars" because it sounds innocuous and does not even mention the military or violence. On the other hand, the U.S. military now refers to it as "the Long War." This exhibits a good dose of realism, given that after October 2011 the war in Afghanistan became *the longest war in U.S. history*. Obama also chose to follow the example of the previous administration by introducing another surge solution based on escalation of the war. Norman Solomon (2009) has identified six ways the Af-Pak War is expanding: more troops, more drone attacks, more political interference, more war in Pakistan, more civilian casualties, and more political blowback this is causing. As Engelhardt (2009b) observes, "All we know, based on the last year, is that 'more' in whatever form is likely to prove a nightmare, and yet anything less than escalation of some sort is not in the cards." In the Vietnam era, there was a shorthand word for this—*quagmire*.

This then, is the future: The Obama administration has chosen to up the ante on troop numbers and drone use in Pakistan and Afghanistan, "ensuring not the end of Al-Qaeda or the Taliban, but the long life of robot war within our ever more militarized society" (Engelhardt 2009c). The most likely outcome is that the war against the Taliban will lead to the further deterioration and destabilization of Afghanistan and Pakistan, rather than eradicate terrorism and Al-Qaeda. The United States and its allies are not even close to winning these wars, and, as Stephen Walt (2009) observes, the bottom line is that "staying in Afghanistan will cost many more dead American soldiers—and, inevitably, Afghan civilians—and hundreds of billions of additional dollars." The tragic but inescapable reality is that as long as this long war goes on, Afghan and Pakistan civilians will be the ones paying the heaviest price.

Anthropology has a long tradition of discourse concerning rationality and of using occult metaphors—magic, sorcery, and witchcraft—to highlight the frequent unreason characteristic of systems of authority and domination. For example, as Bruce Kapferer observes, Max Gluckman applied magic and witchcraft as general metaphors for faulty reasoning or bad thinking:

> [He] used Azande witchcraft logic to explain why poor scientific theories were upheld despite contradictory evidence. The answer was in the biasing and selection of evidence, the fact that the theory as a whole was never put to question, and so on. . . . Gluckman had in mind the shameful commitment to unreason of his native South Africa, then bound by the chains of apartheid. He was concerned with the circumstances whereby it would come to its rational senses and escape the prison of its particular logic of the absurd. But the main features of witchcraft and magic he concentrated on were their appearance at points of social conflict. . . . They were the forms of reason which appeared in those spaces where other modes of reasoning failed. (2002:8)

Today, the shameful misapplication of the pseudo-science of counter-insurgency in the wars in Iraq, Afghanistan, and Pakistan demonstrates the same characteristics of a logic of the absurd: a fatally flawed military theory touted as the apex of reason but in fact based on misapplied social science and flawed thinking—that is, unreason—emerging in a context of social conflict where reason has failed.

Anthropologists have observed that the virtual space of killing and war is akin to the magical because sorcery or magic and cyberspace are both "virtual realities." As Neil Whitehead has shown, in tribal societies war shamans were believed to be capable of physical assassination by remote means—killing their enemies at a distance by occult methods. "The native idea of a separation of body and spirit allows for men to transform into or enter the bodies of animals, insects, and birds" (2002:77)—or even inanimate objects such as drones. In the native context, there is "a shadow

8.6 Virtual fieldwork on virtual war: Author "flying" the Microsoft UAV Predator flight simulator. Real drone pilots also train on simulators. Photo by Kate Sluka.

war in which enemy shamans contend with each other through the use of spirit proxies," and "each shaman has a number of such familiars disguised as *predators* and *raptors* who will seek out their foes" (2002:131; emphasis added). In shamanic warfare, conflicts are "enacted in the spirit domain for the night sky is replete with the souls of contending shamans" (2002:128). Now the sky is replete with the virtual presence of joystick pilots of remote-controlled drones searching for victims to kill. The culture of the U.S. Air Force is changing, the definition of "warrior-airman" is expanding, and the drone pilots are emerging as the dark shaman of the military (see figure 8.6).

Today in our postmodern world, war zones have literally become theaters of conflict that feed the imaginary of military violence and the practice of its material enactment, and virtual warfare has created a new form of killing in war—spectacide, that is, *virtual* killing, such as by remote-control drone pilots. Similarly, Ignatieff has argued that the conditions of virtual war transform war into something like a spectator sport: "As with sports, nothing ultimate is at stake," and thus "war affords the pleasures of a spectacle, with the added thrill that it is real for someone, but not, happily, for the spectator" (2000:191).

Finally, as Ferguson and Whitehead have observed with regard to war in the tribal zone,

> More formidable tribes can lead to a shift in imperial strategy, away from hegemony to a more fixed territorial defense. In the long run, this may mark the beginnings of the dynamics of imperial collapse. The possibility of tribal peoples meeting and defeating state forces in set-piece battles was dealt a severe blow by the revolutionary technology of the nineteenth century; but that may be changing, as demonstrated by the Soviet experience in Afghanistan. It seems a real possibility that tribal peoples armed with modern weapons and using set military practices will pose a greater challenge to state armies in the future. (1992a:27)

The warrior tribesmen opposing the imperial U.S. war against terrorism in Afghanistan and Pakistan are fulfilling this prophecy.

NOTES

1. "Virtual War," Wikipedia, http://en.wikipedia.org/wiki/Virtual_War; accessed August 9, 2010.
2. "Civilian Casualties of the War in Afghanistan," Wikipedia, http://en.wikipedia .org/wiki/civilian_casualties_of_war_in_Afghanistan_(2001%E2%80%93present; accessed October 25, 2010.
3. "Iraq War," Wikipedia, http://en.wikipedia.org/wiki/Iraq_War; accessed November 14, 2010.

PROPAGANDA, GANGS, AND SOCIAL CLEANSING IN GUATEMALA

The violent image of unrestrained power in Guatemala in the 1980s was an army soldier or tank confronting unarmed civilians. Today, armed power in Guatemala is represented by a heavily equipped police officer in a black uniform and a ski mask driving a four-wheel-drive truck that may or may not have license plates. Nonetheless, violence in Guatemala today has its roots in the period of military dictatorship and civil war. As during the dictatorship, everyone has the recourse of violence. But some people, because they are very rich or powerful, or because they are important to people who are very rich or powerful, have more recourse to more violence. And because violence has magical qualities, this violence is structured in such a way that these same people, who might be aware of the power of their recourse, can claim innocence or ignorance of its deployment just as terror imbues each moment of everyday life.

This chapter challenges simplistic explanations for current violence that place the growth of police power solely as a response to the escalating homicide rate driven by the rise of street crime, drug trafficking, and gangs—a contemporary discourse that resonates with an official history explaining past state terror as the "necessary" response to armed subversion, thus leading to a form of virtual war through propaganda to secure legitimacy for state violence. My exploration of feminicide, social cleansing, and extrajudicial executions in contemporary Guatemala reveals the nexus of violent relationships among gangs, drug traffickers, organized crime, the army, police, political parties, and elite capital.[1] It illustrates the multilayered ways in which impunity feeds lawlessness, which in turn reinforces impunity, creating a seemingly magical realm of chaos, guaranteeing freedom from punishment or legal sanction for perpetrators of violence. It demonstrates that contemporary violence is inextricably linked to past violence and impunity itself is shored up through the systematic violation of law by those charged with upholding it. Last, it demonstrates the ways propaganda is used to justify human rights violations.

In December 1996, the Guatemalan Army and Union Revolucionario Nacional Guatemalteca (Guatemalan National Revolutionary Union) guerrillas formally signed peace accords ending more than three decades of armed conflict. The establishment of a truth commission, the Comisión para el Esclarecimiento Historico (CEH, Commission for Historical Clarification), was one of the outcomes of the peace accords. CEH findings included 626 villages massacred, 1.5 million people displaced, 150,000 people fled to refuge in Mexico, and more than 200,000 dead or disappeared (CEH 1999). Although these numbers of dead indicate savagery on a massive scale, particularly in a country that had a population of approximately eight million at the height of the violence in the early 1980s, more shocking still was the attribution of responsibility for these horrific crimes. The CEH determined that the Guatemalan army was responsible for 93 percent of all human rights violations and the guerrillas responsible for 3 percent, with the remaining 4 percent of violations committed by unknown assailants. Government forces were also found responsible for 99 percent of acts of sexual violence. Furthermore, the CEH concluded that the army had carried out genocidal acts (CEH 1999:5:42). Although there are regional, national, and international cases haltingly winding their way through the courts, to date only three low-ranking military commissioners have been brought to trial (Sanford 2003a).

If the generals and their genocidal cronies are the winners with impunity, the citizens of Guatemala are not. The Guatemala homicide rate doubled from 23 murders per 100,000 inhabitants in 1999 to 45 in 2006, reaching 108 in Guatemala City, nearly three times as high as Baghdad's current rate. As a point of comparison, the murder rate in the United States is currently 5.9 per 100,000 people (Casas-Zamora 2009).

If the number of murder victims continues to rise at the current rate, more people will die in the first twenty-five years of peace than died in the thirty-six-year internal armed conflict and genocide (Sanford 2008a). Although the female population increased by 8 percent between 2001 and 2006, the female homicide rate increased by more than 117 percent (Alston 2007:11). In 2008, seven hundred women were killed. All told, two thousand women were murdered in the past three years, and there have been only forty-three convictions for murder—that is, 2 percent of the murders—giving Guatemala a 98 percent impunity rate for female homicides (Castresana 2009). Indeed, the mortality rate of women in peacetime Guatemala has already reached the very high levels of female mortality in the early 1980s at the height of the genocidal war that took 200,000 lives.

Though peace accords were signed in 1996, the structures of the military and their paramilitary agents continue to dominate Guatemalan politics. The main legacy of that period, popularly known as *La Violencia*, is that power and violence are inextricably linked to one another. Moreover, violence and the threat of violent death by clandestine groups or agents of the state continue to dominate the public imaginary. The daily enactment of the cultural elaboration of fear is what Michael Taussig (1987) has noted is so effective in controlling massive populations.

The ongoing elaboration of fear is possible because the structures of La Violencia did not end with the signing of the peace accords. Thus, one might consider that rather than a "postwar" manifestation of violence, these structures elucidate Sverker Finnström and Neil Whitehead's concept of war with no beginning or end. As the military dictatorship ended, the hierarchies and interactions within the military, organized crime, and death squads remained in place, even as their power was transformed and rearranged at all levels of Guatemalan society. As one high-ranking Guatemalan army officer told me, "We have the most organization, so we win" (author interview 1994).

One day after the U.S. Department of State identified Guatemala as the "epicenter of the drug threat" in its annual narcotics report, Baltazar Gomez, director of the Policia Nacional Civil (PNC, National Police), and Nelly Bonilla, commander of the PNC antinarcotics unit, were arrested on drug charges. The previous PNC director, Porfirio Perez, was arrested for stealing cocaine and cash in August 2009 (Malkin 2010:A11). These most recent arrests confirm the entrenchment of drug trafficking interests within the highest ranks of the PNC. Furthermore, these arrests illustrate the very real state involvement of security forces with transnational drug trafficking and the fluidity of these links between trafficking and "global war" (see Whitehead and Finnström's introduction to this volume), in this case the global war "on drugs."

Within Guatemala, these violent groups constitute a parallel power structure, which continues to dominate the country now, just as it did during La Violencia. This parallel power structure influences the country a great deal. Former generals and other high-ranking officials from the dictatorship have taken on roles in the civilian government and through political parties; at the same time, they have branched out into their own individual organizations, where they continue to use violence to pursue their own ends. Some dominate particular geographic areas. Others are involved in drug trafficking or high-level organized crime. The gangs control territories and the people who live there.

All of the elements of the parallel structure interlock with one another, in vertical as well as horizontal relationships. For instance, the gangs make payments to the police so that the police do not interfere with their operations in their territories. Those payments flow upward: the local police officers have to pay a certain amount of the money to their boss, who in turn has to pay off his boss. At the higher levels, there are the drug traffickers, who might buy the services of someone much more senior in the police, who might then send some of the payments downward to individual officers. At the same time, the narcotraffickers and organized crime syndicates are often paying off the local gang members for doing contract jobs to support illicit trafficking and existing power structures. These jobs range from violent work as hit men, kidnappers, extortionists, arsonists, and car jackers to recruitment of low-level traffickers and other support networks for narcotraffickers and organized crime. In short, these are not just informal, local arrangements. They are extensive structures of violence, bribes, threats, and patronage.

It is important to understand this interlocking power structure, because its influence means that threats and violence that might appear minor from a U.S. or European perspective are actually extremely dangerous. The parallel power structure of interlocking violent groups has the effect of amplifying, strengthening, and sustaining violence.

In Guatemala today, groups gain power by violence, wield it by violence, and lose it by violence. This is true not only of the gangs, drug traffickers, and other criminal organizations but also of the police and even members of the government. Even protection from harm is accomplished by brute force. The only way to stay safe is to "trump" anyone who threatens you by responding with greater violence.

The state is aware of this parallel structure. Although some brave members of different government branches have sought to rein in these parallel powers, the government and its agencies continue to be implicated in drug trafficking, corruption, and the violence that sustains these illicit enterprises. Government involvement ranges from toleration of what goes on to corrupt acceptance of it to actual complicity in the crimes. These violent practices represent the incarnation of Giorgio Agamben's (2005:22–23) exceptionalism. Members of the elite still work within and dominate this violent power structure because it is their structure. The only difference is that their status and resources sometimes give them the means to trump violence more frequently than poorer, average citizens. The cost for government officials who seek justice can be high. Lawyers' Rights Watch Canada reported that forty judges and lawyers were killed in Guatemala from 2005 to 2009 (Lawyers' Rights Watch Canada 2009).

GANG CONTROL OF NEIGHBORHOODS AND OTHER GEOGRAPHIC TERRITORIES

The gangs, or *maras*, play a key role in the parallel structure of violence in Guatemala. The two most common gangs are MS-13 and Mara-18, both of which have operations all over Central America. Mexican drug cartels have taken advantage of this situation and moved some operations into Guatemala. A recent U.S. Department of State report noted that "Entire regions of Guatemala are now essentially under the control of DTOs [drug trafficking organizations], the most visible of which is the Mexican group known as the 'Zetas'" (2010:305). Moreover, the "Mexican cartels consolidated their control of trafficking routes in the northern and eastern rural areas of Guatemala" (2010:307). The report also points to ineffective law enforcement on the part of Guatemalan authorities, including the failure to make any arrests in a major drug trafficking case in 2008 because suspects fled before search warrants were executed (2010:308). Most likely, they were tipped off by the authorities—this is an example of where democratic procedures (such as search warrants) get blamed for the flight of suspects, rather than internal corruption that leaks information of pending arrests to criminals. The Department of State report also acknowledges "widespread corruption in the Guatemalan prison system that allows prisoners to conduct and direct criminal activities during their incarceration" (2010:308).

The MS-13 and Mara-18 have their roots in the United States and have come to prominence recently, but gangs in general have played a role in organized violence in Guatemala for decades. During La Violencia, the government often employed assassins, or death squads, to murder people whom they saw as enemies or guerrilla sympathizers. Gang members informed on factory workers, union organizers, teachers, and students involved in political protest. In exchange for this information, the police acceded neighborhood territory to gangs for their illicit activities.

After the peace accords, clandestine groups with ties to former and current police and army officials used the army routes, landing strips, and heliports for the movement of weapons and drugs. These routes were previously used for army counterinsurgency operations, which interlinked to every municipality in the country. Today, the narcotraffickers control drug supplies and smuggling routes, and other groups are involved in high-level corruption. Meanwhile, the gangs continue to get most of their power from controlling neighborhoods and the people who live in them.

While gangs dominate urban areas, they can also be found high in the mountains in small indigenous villages as well as coastal communities. Rural or urban, their operations are based on the territories they control. The borders between one gang's territory and another's are incredibly dangerous. The gangs have checkpoints on their borders (a tactic initially used by the military and the army-controlled civil patrols during La Violencia), making it impossible to pass unnoticed from one area to another. They focus particular efforts on public transportation because most Guatemalans have to travel by bus, making that an effective point of control, regulation, and "taxation."[2] Most Guatemalans have to pass through many different territories to get to work or school, which makes everyday life extremely risky.

Similarly, drug traffickers, cartels, and organized crime are extremely dangerous. They engage in rape, murder, and other violent crimes, and their ties to the police and to other illegal and extralegal violent groups allow them to operate with impunity. Drug traffickers, cartels, and organized crime are the elite employers of gangs and their members. Shifting allegiances between these groups or their gang proxies can result in street warfare as well as targeted or massive inter- or intragroup killings.

Language and propaganda are developed to reflect new realities of terror (Feitlowitz 1998). In Guatemala, the twenty-first-century lexicon has expanded to include the term *narcomatanza* (narco-killings), which refers to massive killing within or among drug trafficking organizations. Propaganda about killings has moved from the dropping or posting of leaflets to the use of the latest communication technology. The new language and technology of propaganda augment the cultural power of these killings, which are seen and not seen. For example, in early December 2008, sixteen people were killed in three different locations in the neighborhood of Agua Zarca in the town of Santa Ana Huista, in the northern department of Huehuetenango, which borders Mexico. A few days later, YouTube user *soyelcoyotecojo* ("I am the crippled coyote" or "I am the coyote who fucks you") posted a video recording showing graphic images of the dead under the title "this is circulating throughout Huehuetenango" (*Prensa Libre* 2008c). Ultimately, the Mexican Golfo Cartel was blamed for the killings and the Guatemalan president expressed fear that Mexican cartels were taking over the nation (*Prensa Libre* 2008b). This sentiment was shared by the U.S. Department of State, which reported that Mexican cartels had consolidated control of northern regions of Guatemala (including Huehuetenango) (2010:308).

It is essentially unheard of for the police to conduct actual investigations or valid operations against the gangs, drug traffickers, or organized crime syndicates. When they do act against them, it is generally not because they have done an investigation, responded to a complaint, or gathered evidence. Usually, it is a signal that someone with more power than that particular gang is wielding it against them, through the police. The occasional arrests and big raids are about these types of exercises of power, not controlling the gang problem or protecting innocent citizens from crime. Sadly, it is just another example of one group trumping another with violence, fear, or threats. It could be that the gang has angered someone more powerful than they are, or that another group is trying to take over their territory and have paid off the police to do their work for them. Or it could just be a show—it is very common for gang members to be "arrested" but released within hours. Or, it could be an investigation that is forced on the Guatemalan state by external actors, such as the United States or neighboring El Salvador, as was the case with the PAR-LACEN investigation in 2007 to which I return shortly.

CONTROLLING THEIR NEIGHBORHOODS

The transmutation of the neoliberal new world order and the "war on terror" in the global "war on drugs" is experienced from the kingpins of drug cartels down to the gangs on the streets where there is no room for neutrality: you are either with them or against them. For people who live in gang-controlled areas, this means that any interaction, no matter how seemingly minor, can escalate into a situation that threatens their lives and their families' lives. When a gang member gives an ordinary citizen an order or makes a request, it's not just about that situation itself—it's about the gang's power and control.

The gangs seek stability and to maintain their own security. They seek to control revenues, as well as risks to themselves from the government, the police, or other armed groups. That means they need to control *people*: the people who live in their territories, the people who work in industries they seek to dominate (such as bus drivers), the people who are witnesses to crime or victims of it, the press, and so on. This need for control is what can transform an ordinary interaction, such as being asked for a ride or invited to a party, into a life-threatening situation. Saying "no" to a member of one of these violent organizations is perceived as a threat to their control.

For instance, when a gang asks neighborhood residents to pay the gang "tax," they might want to enrich themselves, but they are also proving they have control over those people. It is a way of constantly reestablishing power. If a person refuses to pay the tax, the gang does not perceive that merely as a person depriving them of a dollar; they see a person who is challenging their authority. If someone challenges their authority, they punish them, and often their families as well.

In other words, any interaction between gang members and regular citizens carries two meanings. The first is about the immediate situation itself: "will you give me that money?" The second meaning is about the gang's power: "do you accept my control over your life?" Answering "no" is seen as a direct challenge to the gang's power, and that means that refusing to give up even a dollar can be enough to designate a person as an enemy of the gang, which is a very dangerous position.

This is not unlike the daily enactment of the National Security Doctrine established under the military dictatorship of General Efrain Rios

Montt, who came to power through military coup in March 1982. Under the National Security Doctrine, anyone who questioned army repression was seen to be challenging the legitimacy of the state itself, and the state was envisioned as the embodiment of common good. Any threat to the army was a threat to the state and thus a threat to common good. Anyone who questioned or challenged the military regime was immediately labeled subversive and subject to elimination (Sanford 2003a, 2003b, 2003c).

Guatemala's parallel structure of violence serves to amplify and reinforce the dangers to ordinary citizens. First, it allows the gangs to operate with impunity. They can attack those whom they perceive as threatening their control without fear of punishment. Second, it gives them a national network of other people they can call on to help them kidnap, harm, or kill someone, even if that person flees from the city or town where they live. Finally, it leaves the gang's victims helpless, because other people are too afraid to help them out of fear that they will be targeted themselves.

Ultimately, the most important point is that the gangs are powerful, organized, and highly skilled at what they do. They may be marginalized in the greater society, but that does not mean they are stupid. They are putting their skills to productive use in the underground world of the illicit economy because the formal economy has no place for them. They have been raised in a violent society where whoever holds the most recourse to violence has the most power. So they make use of those existing structures to get what they want. They know how to find people. They know how to move things. They know how to make things happen.

POLICE CORRUPTION AND INEFFECTIVENESS IN GUATEMALA

The police in Guatemala are corrupt and ineffective. They do not investigate crimes or patrol the streets. When a crime occurs, they see it only through personal terms. Was the victim someone important, someone with influence? Was the perpetrator someone who pays bribes, or someone powerful? If the answer to both of those questions is "no," then why should it be their concern?

The *Washington Post* reported: "Speaking on condition of anonymity, a Guatemalan policeman described a highly structured shakedown and payoff system. Police officers bully business owners into paying bribes, he said, and the bribes are split with supervisors, who withhold promotions if rank-and-file officers don't deliver. Narco-traffickers sometimes pay $4,000 to $5,000 or more each month to ensure their shipments get through, the officer said. 'They break people,' he added. 'There are officers who are 10 percent corrupt who become 100 percent corrupt'" (Roig-Franzia 2007, A10).

Police corruption goes further than bribes to look the other way when a crime occurs or payments in exchange for information. The police are often involved in extrajudicial killings and "social cleansing," and they have ties at many levels to gangs, organized crime, and other elements of Guatemala's parallel system of violent groups.

Though gangs have ties to the PNC, they can also be hunted by police, especially if they have not paid their quota of protection money or have become too big of a liability. In much the same way, gangs also have ties to drug traffickers and organized crime, which, in turn, also have ties to the police and military. In this way, clandestine structures within Guatemala are embedded in the military and police and run by its officers and former officers. So deeply embedded are these parallel powers that the Comisión Internacional Contra la Impunidad en Guatemala (CICIG, International Commission against Impunity in Guatemala) was established through a joint agreement between the United Nations and the government of Guatemala with a mandate to investigate and name the illegal groups, parallel powers, and clandestine security structures; their funding sources; and their ties with government agencies and officials. The PNC and the penitentiary system were among the key institutions identified as priority targets for the CICIG investigation, which began its mandate in January 2009 (Nonviolent Peaceforce 2007).

Let me share testimony from Juan, a young man who narrowly escaped a social cleansing:

> I was coming home from work at about six in the evening. The gang had stopped me to ask for money. There were about six gang members. Suddenly a blue pick-up truck with tinted windows appeared driving directly toward where we were standing. There were three armed men sitting in the back of the truck. The gang members immediately began to run. Four of the gang members ran up into the hills. The two I knew ran in the other direction. I ran down the highway toward where I lived. I was terrified because I knew the pick-up was carrying out a "social cleansing" and that if I was caught, they would kill me because

they would assume I was a gang member because I had been standing with those men. I am sure the men in the pick-up were police officers.

The pick-up stopped and the men in the back jumped out [and] grabbed two of the gang members and threw them into the pick-up. Then they started to run toward me. I kept running, but the pick-up kept following me. It followed me as I turned off the main road. I ran down a narrow alley near a river. The alley was too narrow for the truck to pass and I saw it stop. I didn't see what happened next with the truck because I begged a woman to let me hide in her house. She reluctantly let me in but she was terrified the men in the pick-up would hurt her family if they knew I was in her house and she begged me to leave in the middle of the night when no one would see me.

I ran to the sugarcane fields across the river and stayed there for a whole day until night came again. That next night I returned to my house and got my *cedula*, birth certificate, and the little money I had and fled.

There was no way I could ask for police protection since they were the very ones who had just been after me. I didn't trust the police in any case because even if I had sought the police's help against being harmed by the gang, I knew they would not protect me from being killed by the gang as a snitch. Gangs have networks all over the country. If a gang member is on the run in one area, they go elsewhere and hide with the local gang there. Because gang members who might have survived the social cleansing would have taken refuge in another nearby town, I knew there was no safe place to go. (Author testimony, March 2007)

There are a few key points to be garnered from Juan's story of survival. (1) Regular citizens are extorted by gangs and pay unregulated taxes to gangs to move in and out of their own neighborhoods. (2) The police are aware of this practice. (3) The police carry out extrajudicial killings of gang members. (4) Gangs have networks throughout the country. (5) Regular citizens are vulnerable to gang and police violence. (6) There is no safe haven from gang or police violence once one is targeted.

COMPARING SOCIAL CLEANSING TO GANG VIOLENCE

While Guatemala, like Mexico, El Salvador, and other Latin American countries, has a serious gang problem, there are markers to gang activity that are quite different from those of social cleansing. Gangs tend to practice violence in their territories and generally carry out violence over territories, markets, resources, partners, or membership. This means that gangs carry out violence, such as murder, within their territories or on the peripheries of their territories (ERIC et al. 2001, 2004). These types of violence are exacerbated when gangs become linked to organized crime—in the case of Guatemala, to drug traffickers. In many ways, Guatemalan gangs today resemble the *sicarios* of Colombia—local thugs for hire who act independently but are also tied to drug trafficking and paramilitary groups.

Gang violence generally involves firearms and knives. There is little that is professional or technical in the handling of the murder. There are usually few shots fired due to limited capacity and resources (PDH 2006). Gangs carry out murders in the least complicated and most immediate way possible because of these limited resources, as well as the insecure environment in which they operate. Whereas social cleansing includes intense managing of the crime scene, gangs make no effort to remove the evidence. When there are disputes between gangs, age is an important variable, and the victims are generally young. Cadavers of people murdered by gangs generally appear in the territory where the gang dominates, which also tends to be where the murder takes place. The pattern of targeting, sequestering, transporting, confining, and torturing a victim prior to murder only to transport and dump his or her cadaver in yet another locale is not a modus operandi of gang violence—it is the hallmark of social cleansing (Sanford 2008b).

The infrastructure and resources that sustain social cleansing allow more complicated, long, drawn-out murders that usually include torture. Social cleansing seeks to generate terror by leaving signs of torture to warn others of what could happen to them. Gangs target their victim, not a larger group. Whereas gangs kill in their own territories, social cleansing victims are generally taken to a different location, a clandestine jail, where they are tortured and killed. Later, they are dumped in another location, which is often not gang territory. Murders by gangs indicate low use of resources. Social cleansing requires resources. For example, a car is indispensable, as are a place to confine the victim, modes of communication, and a highly coordinated team. When social cleansing is carried out, there are efforts made to sway public opinion to accept this method of social control. There have been banners, flyers, stickers, and posters circulating in the country that support social cleansing methods.

For example, presidential candidate and former General Otto Pérez Molina used the "Mano Dura" (The Strong Hand) as his election symbol while claiming to have been a general of "peace." The mano dura was also a symbol of death squads in the 1980s and is understood to represent the (unlawful) elimination of "undesirables." Though Guatemalan election law forbids any campaign advertising earlier than six months before an election, Perez Molina began an advertising campaign in October 2006 that continued through the election in November 2007. The raised fist (mano dura) and orange shirt were emblematic of his campaign (see figures 9.1 and 9.2).

VIGILANTES, DEATH SQUADS, AND LOCAL JUSTICE

Of course, one might argue that the paramilitary groups are not tied to the state and are probably just rogue vigilantes. In *Vigilantism and the State in Modern Latin America: Essays on Extralegal Violence*, Martha Huggins defines vigilantism as comprising activities that include "lynching, murders by *justiceiros* [justice-seekers], death squad and paramilitary/parapolice violence, and violence by on-duty police" (1991:6). These types of activities most frequently target citizens and are understood to be "essentially conservative or reactionary" (1991:6). Positioning the actions of "lynch mobs" and other more or less spontaneous groups of civilians alongside extrajudicial violence by paramilitary groups, Huggins argues that violence and "justice" in Latin America are conditioned at all scales by the region's dependent, peripheral status. As I have argued elsewhere, these peripheries are then reproduced at the margins of the state within nation-states (Sanford 2004).

The neoliberalizing state has played a central role in creating the conditions for these forms of violence (Goldstein 2003). In Guatemala, where lynchings have risen as a local practice since the signing of the peace accords, a state response has been mostly absent. Indeed, a comprehensive investigation conducted by the United Nations Mission in Guatemala (MINUGUA) concluded that the state's weak response to lynchings had become a factor of both legitimation and justification for lynchings: "the idea that lynchings are outside the reach of the law is viewed as a guarantee of impunity by those participating" (MINUGUA 2004:27). In this way, the state distances itself from "local" violence and at the same time creates a virtual space of violence to avenge violence.

Likewise, the rise of urban gang violence and organized crime has ob-

9.1 Otto Pérez Molina, candidate for president for the Partido Patriota, on the campaign trail in 2007. In 2007 he lost in a runoff election, and in 2011 he once again ran for president (successfully). A former general, Pérez Molina is implicated for crimes against humanity in multiple court cases. Used by permission of Jonathan Moller, photographer.

9.2 General Otto Pérez Molina presidential campaign propaganda. October 2006. Photo by Victoria Sanford.

scured ongoing death squad activity tied to the PNC, which continues to take the lives of Guatemalan citizens through extrajudicial executions and social cleansing. International attention was drawn to the nefarious practices of the PNC in February 2007 when an international investigation determined that three Salvadoran members of the Central American Parliament (PARLACEN) and their driver were kidnapped near a major shopping center in Guatemala City, held in a clandestine jail, and taken to a rural location in the direction of the Salvadoran border, where they were beaten, shot, and burned alive in their vehicle. A joint FBI/Salvadoran police investigation revealed the perpetrators of this extrajudicial execution to be none other than the PNC's elite "antinarcotics" unit designated to investigate organized crime. Five officers were arrested and later slaughtered while being held in a maximum security prison (Sanford and Lincoln 2010).

Government officials claimed the implicated officers were killed by gang members in the prison. Families visiting inmates witnessed the arrival of heavily armed men in black uniforms, who stormed the prison shortly before rounds of machine gun fire were heard from within the prison. The chief prosecutor's response to the prison slaying was to conclude that the investigation of the extrajudicial execution of the Salvadorans was over because the implicated officers had been killed (EFE 2007). Minister of Gobernación Carlos Vielman and the PNC director Erwin Sperisen resigned and later fled to Switzerland. Sperisen was arrested in Geneva and charged with a prison massacre in Guatemala. He will be tried in Geneva because he is a Swiss citizen (*El Periodico* 2012). Vielman, a Spanish citizen, is now being processed in Madrid for the same prison massacre and other crimes committed in Guatemala. Dr. Javier Figueroa, subcommander of investigations, fled the country and is believed to be in Austria. Victor Soto, the director of criminal investigations, initially fled, but three years later he turned himself in; he is now awaiting trial in Guatemala City (Herrera and Galeano 2012:1). Prosecutor Juan Carlos Martinez, who was investigating the extrajudicial killing of the police in prison, was assassinated in July 2008 (*Prensa Libre* 2008a).

The former director of the PNC indicated how deeply entrenched death squads are in the police after the PARLACEN killings. Seemingly unaware that he was implicating his own special antinarcotics unit as a group of assassins for hire, then PNC director Sperisen suggested, "The police officers might have been hit men tricked into believing that the Salvadoran politicians were Colombian drug dealers posing as representatives to the parliament" (Roig-Franzia 2007:A10). Despite the fact that visiting families saw armed men enter the prison and heard machine gun fire before the men left, Sperisen insisted to the *Washington Post* that imprisoned gang members killed the implicated police (Roig-Franzia 2007).

Beyond illuminating the state's willingness to assassinate its own employees or dismiss them as hit men, the Salvadoran case also shed light on the government's tendency to deploy "gang violence" as a red herring to obscure the political roots of violence. Rather than investigate murders, government officials tend to blame multiple deaths of young men on gang violence—thus blaming the victim for being a gang member, having ties to gangs, or simply being in the wrong place at the wrong time. Occasionally, the social cleansing is so flagrant that it produces national outrage, as did the case of five young men who were eliminated by PNC officers in September 2007. This crime gained notoriety because the witnesses who reported it were a small army patrol, and the PNC officers who carried out the social cleansing turned out to be the bodyguards of the PNC director (Acuna 2007). Not surprisingly, an April 2007 poll of Guatemalan citizens found that 90 percent do not trust the police (Cereser 2007).

According to several international diplomats speaking under condition of anonymity in 2007, Otto Pérez Molina, Javier Figueroa, Victor Soto, and Victor Rivera each had their own death squads (author interviews, Guatemala City 2007). After the PARLACEN killings, Soto, who headed the Division of Criminal Investigations and was the direct supervisor of the antinarcotics unit charged with carrying out the PARLACEN killings, fled and initially moved to Ocos, San Marcos. Local rumor had it that he was both bodyguard and companion of Ocos mayor Edilma Elizabeth Navarijo, who is under investigation for drug trafficking (*Redaccion Prensa Libre* 2009). Rivera, a Venezuelan national, arrived in Guatemala in the late 1990s from El Salvador as a private security consultant to elites on kidnapping cases. Though he never had an official title, he had an office and staff in the Ministerio de Gobernación. Rivera was with the implicated officers after their arrest and later testified in court about the case (Redacción El Faro 2007).

Who are these killers, and where do they come from? Social cleansing is nothing new. Those army and police responsible for some 50,000 disappearances and assassinations in the 1980s have largely escaped investigation and prosecution. Indeed, one of the only arrests for social cleansing in the 1980s was the 2009 arrest of Subcomisario Abraham Lancerio Gómez, twenty-five years after he participated in the 1984 forced disappearance of student leader and union activist Fernando García (Reyes 2009). As the arrest of Lancerio Gómez indicates, cases like these still matter because the intellectual and material authors of these crimes continue to hold powerful positions in the army and police. Indeed, Fernandez García was the husband of Nineth Montenegro García, who founded the Grupo de Apoyo Mutuo (Mutual Support Group) for families of the disappeared. Montenegro has served in the Guatemalan Congress since the late 1990s and has remained a powerful advocate for human rights and justice. In March 2010, she received death threats and a plot for her assassination was uncovered. CICIG investigated the case and determined that the would-be assassins sought to make her killing an example to disrupt the functioning of government institutions and democratic society (Reyes 2010).

Adela Torrebiarte was named to replace Carlos Vielman as the new minister of Gobernación. A member of one of Guatemala's elite families, Torrebiarte had distinguished herself in the early 1990s as the founder of Madres Angustiadas, a group of mostly elite women seeking recognition of their suffering because of kidnappings for extortion. Her son was kidnapped in 1995. Many Guatemalans told me that Torrebiarte had invited Victor Rivera to Guatemala in the mid-1990s to help her resolve this kidnapping. Rivera was a shadowy figure of Venezuelan origin who had been working with the Salvadoran regime before the peace accords, and he arrived in Guatemala ready to use his skills and training to help resolve kidnappings. It appears his record was pretty strong in terms of finding the victim, who sometimes survived the attack by Rivera's antikidnapping squad. Though Rivera never had an official position within the Ministerio de Gobernación, more than a decade later, when I visited his office in 2007, he had a large office with his own conference room adjacent to the office of the then vice minister Vinicio Gómez. When I arrived, the interactions between Rivera and Gómez were such that I initially believed Gómez to be Rivera's secretary, not the vice minister of Gobernación. In any case, it appears that Torrebiarte placed Rivera and his resources on the trail of the PARLACEN case. In April 2008, Rivera was assassinated (Sas 2008). His killing sent shockwaves throughout Guatemala because if Rivera could be killed, then no one was untouchable.

Torrebiarte also promoted Julio Hernández Chávez to be director of the PNC after the PARLACEN slayings. Hernández Chávez had been second in command after Sperisen and directly above Figueroa as chief of the Criminal Division. His promotion followed closely on the heels of the extrajudicial execution of the implicated police, the resignation of Vielman and Sperisen, and the flight of Soto and Figueroa. At the time, his experience and seniority in the PNC were hailed.

Meanwhile, the human rights community sustained a wave of attacks directed at human rights workers and lawyers representing local activists against corrupt and abusive police. The Guatemalan public was overwhelmed by the general lawlessness as homicide rates continued to climb and government officials continued to blame gangs for the slayings. In such a relentlessly violent ambience, many believed that Otto Pérez Molina would win the elections with his mano dura campaign. Rumors of social cleansings began to spread throughout Guatemala.

One year earlier, in July 2006, Guatemalan Human Rights Ombudsman Sergio Morales met with representatives of the Inter-American Commission for Human Rights. He presented a list of 293 human rights concerns. Among them was the concern about the participation of state security forces in social cleansing operations. Included with this concern was the observation that the PDH (Procuraduria de Derechos Humanos de Guatemala) had not been able to determine whether this was a policy of security forces or an activity in which some forces were involved (Cereser 2006).

On September 21, 2007, five young men were abducted from the marginalized barrio El Gallito in Zone 3 of Guatemala City. They were thrown in the back of a pick-up truck. Their beaten, tortured bodies were later found in a marginalized neighborhood in Zone 7. This case caught national attention because the parents of the young men went to the local police station to see their sons. The police station had no record of any arrest. The parents insisted they had seen their sons violently arrested by two police officers, and they had the license plate number of the truck. Later, a small army patrol confirmed having seen the young men in the back of the pick-up. They explained that they thought it was a police action. After reviewing the police vehicle's GPS record, it was confirmed that the vehicle had been in El Gallito, then to the station of Division of Special Police Forces, then to El Naranjo in Zone 7, where the boys' bodies were found (Acuna 2007). This case stunned Guatemalans because there were army witnesses and because the implicated officers were bodyguards of the PNC director Hernández Chávez (Sas 2007). At the request of Torrebiarte, Hernández Chávez resigned. He also suggested that it was not his responsibility to "control" the bodyguards; rather, this responsibility fell to another unnamed officer of the PNC. Reminiscent of Sperisen's analysis of the PARLACEN killings, Hernández Chávez suggested three hypotheses for the social cleansing: (1) the police were contracted by a rival group of the five victims; (2) the police were seeking revenge for the rape of some girlfriends of police officers; or (3) it was a deliberate action to destabilize the image of the PNC and its director (Sas 2007). It is interesting to note that Hernández Chávez never expressed doubt about the guilt of his bodyguards, nor did it seem to trouble him that each hypothesis painted his subordinates as assassins for hire. Also absent from his comments was any recognition of the injustice of killing five young men or even an acknowledgment that they were the victims of a premeditated social cleansing. Hypothesis 1 implicates the victims as gang members, hypothesis 2 implicates them as rapists, and hypothesis 3 does not even acknowledge their existence. These justifications hearken back to the discourse of the Guatemalan army during the 1980s, when its generals claimed soldiers fired on civilians in self-defense, blamed the victims of massacres as "self-immolating," and claimed that the disappeared had gone to Cuba (Sanford 2003b).

CONCLUSION

Impunity—from the Latin *impunitas*, meaning free from punishment—is the cornerstone of violent power relations in Guatemala today and appears to be part of a wider trend, as indicated by other chapters in this volume (see Sluka, Robben, and Finnström). In Guatemala, one might suggest that the culture of terror that produced genocide in the 1980s has become a culture of impunity in "peacetime." This culture of impunity is systemic and systematic. It begins with the inefficiency of a legal system that has never been able to overcome the formalism of past authoritarian regimes that privileged procedures over facts. Thus, the legal system as it is currently constituted locates the truth of a case in the execution of written procedures that are filed in the court, rather than in actual court hearings. Although the transitional postwar revamping of the judicial system included a new emphasis on judicial transparency through the prominence of oral arguments that included USAID-funded trainings for lawyers and judges alike, a decade later, the courts have largely reverted back to written cases with little or no oral argument (FDPL 2007:5). Thus, oral arguments and their accompanying transparency clash with an intransigent legal culture that demands form over content and ritual over justice. In such a system, it is difficult to assign responsibility for the resolution of a case when the goals are defined not in terms of legal resolution but in terms of procedural completion (Sanford and Lincoln 2010). Thus, the prosecutor concluded his investigation into the PARLACEN slayings after the implicated officers were themselves slaughtered.

This bureaucratic proceduralism is constituted within a judicial power that is increasingly exercised on the whims of the court and its agents. This ambient power founded in proceduralism and shrouded in ambiguity is then institutionalized in corruption where "justice" can only be achieved after all parties have agreed on a price. The end result is a juridical system based on bureaucratic proceduralism, rather than rule of law.

Impunity in Guatemala is an absence of rule of law. The guarantee of no punishment means the those who commit genocide walk freely, as do those responsible for thousands of murders since the signing of the peace accords. Impunity is also an invitation to commit crime in an ambience of lawlessness—certainly, it is void of any possible deterrence. As the cases I have highlighted here have shown, impunity is the violation of the law by those charged with upholding it.

NOTES

Support from the John Simon Guggenheim Foundation and Lehman College gave me the time to research and write this chapter. The opinions expressed herein are mine as are any errors. Special thanks to Neil Whitehead and Sverker Finnström for their patience. Neil, you are missed.

1. Feminicide is the killing of women by men because they are women. *Feminicide* is a political term because it holds responsible not only the perpetrators but also the state and judicial structures that normalize misogyny through the commission or toleration of feminicide as well as the state's omission of its responsibility to guarantee the safety of all citizens.

2. For a fascinating study of these types of nonstate border regulations, see Roitman (2004).

THE SOUNDTRACK TO WAR

The soundtrack to war has been variously imagined for thousands of years. In the Bible, trumpets sound, helping bring down the walls of Jericho. Homer populates the *Iliad* with pipes and flutes; Achilles, himself, plays the lyre, singing the feats of previous hero-combatants. Sun Tzu writes about the importance of gongs and drums to strengthen the spirit and signal warriors during battle. In *The Song of Roland*, music assumes a particularly vivid role, as advancing Muslim soldiers sound drums and horns while the French Roland dies, the veins on his forehead bursting from the exertion caused by blowing his ivory horn to signal for Charlemagne's return.

Such are the roles of music in the premodern, bellicose imagination. It signals, rallies, emboldens. It moves people, emotionally as well as physically, prepping minds and bodies and situating both in battle. In these early accounts, the soundtrack to war—full of trumpet calls and marching rhythms, urging on and directing belligerents—is an implicit part of warfare itself, and the role of martial calls and signals is an important part of its power. In this version of war's soundtrack, music organizes combatants through signals and cadences, its successful use defining the structure, pace, and rhythms of war. It is neither tangential to nor merely representative of combat. War is musical through and through.

Beyond simply urging and signaling, military music and

marching cadences have had a more significant impact on the history of warfare. As William H. McNeill argues, the development of martial music played an essential role in the formation of close-order drill, an event he credits with the "modern superiority of European armies over others" (1995:3). "Prolonged drill created obedient, reliable, and effective soldiers," he writes, but its importance does not end there (1995:127). Such musically defined drill also and most crucially enabled what McNeill calls "muscular bonding," or the "euphoric fellow feeling that prolonged and rhythmic muscular movement arouses among nearly all participants in such exercises" (1995:2–3). Drill, and the cadences at its center, altered military history not simply because it helped soldiers move in ever-tighter formations. Its impact, rather, is best located in the way it aided in the crystallization of community in the esprit de corps (1995:3). Drill, muscular bonding, synchrony, morale. These are some consequences of the soundtrack to war.

There is something magical, subtle, even insidious about the intersection of war and music from the start. Imbued with the power to convert, with the ability to help formulate collectivities and define morale, to help shape bodies and forge minds, the soundtrack to war is integrated into the very fabric of the modern military as well. It should come as no surprise, therefore, that the U.S. Army Bands bill themselves as the largest and oldest employers of musicians in the country. According to their website, "Army Bands provide music throughout the spectrum of military operations to instill in our soldiers the will to fight and win, foster the support of our citizens, and promote our national interests at home and abroad."[1] Music traverses all aspects of the modern U.S. military, from convincing and urging combatants to winning hearts and minds (at home and abroad). Today, as before, war remains musical through and through.

The ideological reach of military music and drill defines a conspicuous site of what Catherine Lutz has called America's "military normal"—the "massive investments in war and in the public relations of war, and the assorted beliefs that sustain them all" (2009:26). Nowhere is this role more observable than in the parading months throughout the United States, when the sound and sight of military music and drill permeates cities large and small, situating military spectacle, music, and pomp at the center of summer family entertainment. Such events, simultaneously ceremonial and relaxed, are a potent index and literal re-creation of American militarism, their Sousa-inspired soundtracks a customary, audible tribute to U.S. military power. Parades and their music naturalize U.S. militarism, making it an unquestioned part of the social. In these events, musical articulations and their performative splendor in turn amplify the espirit de corps that McNeill locates in close-order drill, forging bonds and drawing communities together. Parade music radiates sonically in the enactment of these military-civil rituals, implicating countless listeners in its siren call. Even if, as is often the case in the contested, sectarian parading tradition in Northern Ireland, music here is not directly imbricated in immediate physical conflict, U.S. parades are nevertheless a powerful site of mobilization. This is total war.

Far from monolithic, the soundtrack to war assumes numerous forms. If marching bands and cadences, trumpet calls, and "Taps" define one aspect of war's soundtrack, others can be heard in countless representations featured in media as diverse as documentaries, video games, feature films, recruitment advertisements, and the evening news. Again, specifically coded martial music, full of trumpet fanfares and marching rhythms, are the most obvious examples of this version of war's soundtrack, especially common in U.S. news reports after September 11, 2001, in which military-coded music literally drummed up retributive fervor (Engstrom 2003). Also part of this soundtrack, however, are the now iconic militarized sounds of Richard Wagner's "Ride of the Valkyries" and Samuel Barber's *Adagio for Strings*. Through their deployment in the films *Apocalypse Now* and *Platoon*, respectively, both pieces have been rearticulated and reframed as testaments to what Anthony Swofford calls in *Jarhead*, his account of soldiering in the first Gulf conflict, "the magic brutality" of war (2005:6–7). This other soundtrack, realized and defined by blending martial sight and militarized sound, is an equally important part of U.S. militarism, subtly and not so subtly redefining the role and meaning of countless musical genres and their attendant uses. Here musical culture itself, even that which may seem quite remote from military matters, is mobilized for war. Not limited only to martial music, even purportedly "resistant" genres like hip hop are implicated, too, as evidenced by the video game *50 Cent: Blood on the Sand*, in which you can play the "war on terror" as rapper 50 Cent in an unnamed Middle Eastern country in the grip of an intractable urban war. In this version of war's soundtrack, music's mysterious, magical powers are developed and deployed to convince, cajole, and inspire, its persuasiveness and pervasiveness nothing less than the militarization of sound itself.

Though the process of militarizing cultural knowledge through the Human Terrain System is now well known, the kind of musical mobilization evidenced here is less commonly recognized even if the end results can be as pernicious. In any case, in recent decades, the U.S. military has come to understand music's potency, something that it now wields in increasingly shamanic-like ways. Early, successful deployments of loud music campaigns against Manuel Noriega in 1989 and the FBI's similar use of music against the Branch Davidians during the Waco, Texas, siege in 1993 functioned as proofs of concept, in turn ushering in a new era of sonic warfare in which sound and music have been routinely deployed as forms of aural deception, coercion, and domination (Goodman 2009). In some instances, the sonic is turned inward, and music functions as a kind of talisman for U.S. troops. Soldiers jerry-rigging tanks and hummers to play music from their iPods while on patrol is just one example—the sound of music psyching warriors up for the kill (Pieslak 2009). In other instances, music is deployed outwardly against enemies in increasingly devastating ways, and the invisibility of sound is harnessed and cultivated as a ruinous weapon. The use of music as a form of so-called no-touch torture, in which detainees are held in stress positions, sometimes exposed to extreme temperatures and strobe lights, and blasted with songs at exceedingly loud volumes for extended periods of times is the most notorious of examples (Cusick 2006, 2008). In both instances, whether internally or externally directed, the weaponization of sound is complete, and the digital technologies that have led to effortless musical portability are now deployed in explicitly militarized ways. The digital-magical is at once the terribly real. Sound, the ineffable, has become sound the destroyer. And while the future of such use is unclear, technological enhancements in the militarization of sound continue apace, with instruments like long-range acoustic devices, also known as "sound cannons," being used both on enemy combatants in Iraq and Afghanistan and, notably, on protestors at the 2009 G-20 meeting in Pittsburgh. "Where is war?" this volume's editors ask. When considering its soundtrack and the weaponization of the aural, the answer is resounding: everywhere.

The connections between music, magic, and war, as can been seen even in this admittedly brief overview, are manifold. The kind of weaponization of music just addressed maps profitably to historical ways of imaging the power of music in relationship to the occult—from conceptions of the sonic excesses of early modern English witches (Williams

2011) to practices of possession, shamanism, and soul loss in Renaissance Italy's musical culture (Tomlinson 1993). While contemporary Western beliefs continue to champion the power of music (as in the marketing language the military uses to describe its band programs), parallel interpretive moves also seek to explain away such influence through appeals to neuroscience and the brain, effectively legitimating and neutralizing the embarrassment of emotional excess and musical transport (Sacks 2007). Such approaches, however, also work to cordon off "our" ways of being moved musically from those of "others," leaving the more extreme musical practices of trancing, for example, left to those on the global periphery. As Jonathon Pieslak usefully suggests in his analysis of soldiers listening to music as an inspiration for combat, however, trancing is exactly what these warriors engage in during practices of collective listening prior to going out on patrol (2009:164–65). In similar fashion, the magic of music is leveraged by soldiers and civilians alike in countless homemade war music videos, compilations of combat imagery from the battlefields of Iraq and Afghanistan, edited to fit the contours of some form of popular music, and posted online. Here, again, the magic of music is deployed, and potent combinations of militarized sound and musical image are transported to computer screens throughout the world.

In what follows, I turn my attention to these videos, addressing issues of video creation, editing technologies, and audience reception. My goal is to advance a more concrete understanding of the role of music in contemporary warfare and the ways music's power is imagined and unleashed. Functioning as they do as part of the trajectory of war's soundtrack, the magic of these videos—striking new forms of subjective engagements with war's felt imaginary—can best be located in their war-making power. Created for the most part by individuals rather than by military institutions, these videos leverage premodern ways of imaging the role of music in war with decidedly modern technologies of annihilation and control, amplifying and harnessing sound's destructive potential. As such, they are crucial sites in which virtual war and magical death are intertwined and made operational.

AESTHETICS AND MEANING

In examining the broad resonance, appeal, and deployment of war's contemporary soundtrack among a host of social actors, I have found various approaches to aesthetics and aesthetic theory to be invaluable. I am especially indebted to writings that expand understandings of "the aesthetic" beyond the realm of art, representation, and questions of the beautiful or sublime and instead grapple with the role aesthetics as symbolic forms assume in everyday, sociopolitical life. Among such works, Bruce Kapferer and Angela Hobart's understanding of the productivity and power of aesthetics is especially helpful. They write, "The aesthetic and its compositional forms are what human beings are already centered within as human beings. This is to say that human beings are beings whose lived realities are already their symbolic constructions or creations within, and through which, they are oriented to their realities and come to act within them" (2005:5).

What is particularly important about this formulation of aesthetics for my purposes is the way Kapferer and Hobart attribute agency to aesthetic forms. For them, aesthetics possess a profound explanatory and effective power. Rather than simply being responsive to some external reality, aesthetics have the potency to define the lived realities and contexts in which they are in turn operational. In other words, aesthetics are best understood as having both epistemological and ontological significance. Neither simply reactive to events nor limited to the world of art, the museum, or the stage, aesthetics are part and parcel of the full scope of life, defining the contours and logics of understanding and acting, and in turn responding to, defining, and making intelligible life as lived.

Leveraging these insights into the nature of aesthetics, I am interested in the ways in which war music videos implicate both ways of knowing and ways of fighting war. A focus on the aesthetics of war music videos—that is, the ways they are arranged and constructed as well as the ways they are understood and acted on—helps us better understand the symbolic constructions and imaginative spaces that explicate and are constituent of collective violence and militarized killing. These videos are not simply watched and listened to. They are weaponized and wielded in a variety of complex ways, and I attend to these in what follows. As such, war music videos are not about war as much as they are part of it. Exploring their war-making capabilities, and the ways in which they continue to rearticulate the function of music in war, is where I now turn.

MUSICAL MEDIATION

Shortly after the 2005 launch of the video-sharing website YouTube, several journalists began writing about the purportedly new forms of war representation appearing there. Most commonly referenced were count-less homemade combat videos, ostensibly filmed by military personnel. In initial media attempts to make sense of these depictions and the locations in which they were circulating, reporters quickly dubbed the war in Iraq the "YouTube war," situating such an appellation within the context of CNN's coverage of the first Gulf War and common conceptualizations of the "living-room war" of the Vietnam era. While usefully identifying part of the distinctiveness of these videos, such a naming convention never-theless fails to capture what is most unique about them. Simply put, most are little more than combat footage set to some form of predominantly Anglo-American popular music. As reporter Ana Marie Cox notes about an *MTV News* program devoted to these representations, "the [television] special closes a loop in pop culture, since these clips are essentially music videos" (2006).

Combat videos, the most common war music videos, typically feature scenes of U.S. forces in battle scenarios. These are the main referenced productions in media accounts of these representations and are conse-quently the kinds of depictions invoked in the phrase the "YouTube war." Writing about one such video, reporter Michael Hedges provides a now standard interpretive response: "As the video clip picks up momentum, driven by a heavy-metal soundtrack, U.S. Marines pour a hailstorm of bullets and grenades into a housing complex while ducking return fire" (2006). It is a salient, if oversimplified, observation.

In reality, combat music videos typically feature heavy-metal music, although hip hop and alternative rock are also common. More specifi-cally, such videos tend to focus on nu metal, a metal/hip hop crossover subgenre that rose in popularity in the mid-1990s (concomitant with the events of the first Gulf War) to nearly dominate hard rock airplay, the summer tour circuit, and MTV's *Total Request Live* by the end of the decade. Dispatching with lengthy guitar solos and replacing them with guitar-driven noise, samples, turntables, and screamed vocals, nu metal also features drumbeats and rhythms borrowed from hip hop, giving the music a heavy, immediate groove while still remaining harsh and discor-dant. Nu metal's groove is particularly important to the mainstream suc-cess of the subgenre, making it palatable to a wide variety of listeners and distinguishing the music from more extreme forms of metal that make extensive use of extremely fast drumming sections and more atonal guitar sounds. Nu metal's groove, moreover, is central to the deployment of the subgenre in war music videos, a point I take up more fully later.

For many fans, musicians, and commentators alike, nu metal is summed up in a few words: "skull-crushing," "nightmarish," and most of all, "intense" (Kitts and Tolinski 2003). Although lyrical themes often reinforce these interpretations, the overall sonic impact of the subgenre—including the sound of the instruments, recording and production values, and so on—mostly leads to such conclusions. As two music journalists write, the timbre of a nu metal guitar "has to sound like a Mack truck being crushed by a collapsing skyscraper" (Kitts and Tolinski 2003:145). Here, even the definition of nu metal's guitar sounds invokes themes of violence and destruction, and the discursive field in which the genre is formed and realized rarely strays far from issues of power and domination.

Korn and Limp Bizkit are the most internationally popular nu metal groups, and Drowning Pool is the best known outside of the subgenre's fan base. Indeed, the latter band's song "Bodies"—with its repetitive chorus, "Let the bodies hit the floor"—has been mapped more than any other to current U.S. warscapes through its use in numerous movies and documentaries including *Stop-Loss*, *Fahrenheit 9/11*, *Soundtrack to War*, the mini-series *Generation Kill*, and others. The band has also developed a large following among U.S. soldiers both at home and abroad, performing on USO tours and teaming up with the Iraq and Afghanistan Veterans of America on the "This Is for the Soldiers Tour" of 2007 and in support of veteran-related legislation. Journalist David Peisner, in an article about music and interrogation practices, observes, "If the military had its own People's Choice Awards, Drowning Pool would win top honors. Nearly every interrogator and soldier I spoke to mentioned the agro-metal outfits 2001 hit 'Bodies'—with its wild-eyed chorus, 'Let the bodies hit the floor'—as a favorite for both psyching up U.S. soldiers and psyching out enemies and captives" (2006:91). Here, again, the internally and externally facing nature of war's soundtrack and its inherent flexibility define its magic and power. Nu metal has become yet another weapon in the military arsenal, and it is deployed to both inspire and destroy.

Indeed, the phrase "heavy metal is war" has become common enough among soldiers that it is worth understanding literally. While the musical avant-garde has for nearly a century turned to the sounds of combat as inspiration for ever-more discordant creations—most famously explored in futurist composer Luigi Russolo's *The Art of Noise* (1986)—soldiers have increasingly turned to metal as a way of understanding the meanings and experiences of war. Metal's influence is not limited to the lyrical themes often featured in the genre. More important, it is again the sound itself—the rapid-fire bass drum patterns; dissonant, distorted guitars; relentless speed; and screamed vocals—that has made metal a metonym for war. As one soldier somewhat hesitantly observes about the sounds of combat, "The explosions and machine guns, and the shooting that's going on, that's the music. It's kind of like listening to Slayer [an American speed metal band], like that sort of shit. Listening to a 240 [machine gun] fire off rounds, or a TOW missile hit something, that's music to your ears kind of. And that sounds all twisted and wrong, but that's music in itself" (quoted in Pieslak 2009:56). Music's role in defining the aesthetics of war is here made manifest.

The use of nu metal and particularly Drowning Pool's song "Bodies" in countless combat videos is best understood within this specific genre, interpretive, and functional history—a musical style that rose to prominence during the first Gulf War, has been routinely tied to themes of violence and destruction, and has most recently been used to inspire U.S. warriors and psychologically break detainees. Through repetition and the mapping of nu metal to a variety of images and practices of war, the genre has become a powerful, affective marker of current U.S. warscapes, implicating a wide range of the listening public in its militarized sound. As Bruce Johnson and Martin Cloonan write, "particular forms of sonority and musical genres . . . can function for specific categories of emotion," creating "affective platforms" for representation and meaning (2008:153). This is a particularly useful way for understanding the representative power of the genre, in which the sound of nu metal has come to represent war.

VIDEO CREATION

The militarized significance of nu metal is consequently crucial to the existence and meaning of war music videos. Indeed, the selection of music marks the starting point for formal video creation; this is where the creative process begins and accounts for a video's auditory essence. Among the editor-producers I have contacted, all begin with a song first, choosing and editing video imagery afterward. "I always select the music first, the music will set the mood and pace of the video," writes one U.S. civilian editor-producer.[2] Another editor, Ryan Hickman, writes tellingly about the motivations behind his video "Taliban Bodies," likely the first of such war music videos and one of the most viewed and circulated: "every time 'Bodies' by Drowning Pool, came on the radio, I always pictured military equipment blowing things up to the beat of the song."[3]

Other editor-producers express a range of reasons for creating their videos. One I interviewed, a marine combat correspondent who was attached to a battalion of soldiers fighting in Fallujah, Iraq, in 2004, noted that the idea for creating a war music video was partly in response to requests from the soldiers he was assigned to and filming. Once he decided to make a video, he petitioned these soldiers for recommended songs so he could begin the process of selecting imagery to match the song's musical features. Though several suggested Drowning Pool's "Bodies," he ultimately decided to choose a different piece because he was concerned the song "glorified violence."[4] Pulling together what he considers to be a "G-rated highlight real," he informed me that his primary goal in creating the video was to get soldiers "thinking about being young and bulletproof."[5] Here the combat correspondent blends with the shaman, someone capable of creating talismans to keep combatants safe. The techno-modern and magico-primitive are indivisible, and the premodern meanings of war's soundtrack retain their power and appeal.

War music videos have also simply become commonplace. In some instances, they function as a kind of souvenir, especially for soldiers tasked with more desk-bound, administrative responsibilities. One combat veteran I interviewed spoke disparagingly about these kinds of video productions, ones that feature more "downtime" activities, firing range practice, or simply images of soldiers posing with weapons: "I actually saw one of these guys rolling around in the dirt in his gear, so that it would get dirty. . . . If you see these pictures of soldiers clean out in the middle of nowhere, it's completely staged."[6] The aesthetic power of war music videos defines the meanings and reality of warfare, portraying an ideal that some soldiers invariably work to manufacture. Even soldiers like to play soldiers.

As noted, the selection of music marks the beginning of combat video creation, and the formal elements of the song selected are routinely deployed throughout the process of production. Without musical logic as a productive guide, most videos would be little more than sequences of

randomly shot images, a mishmash of combat scenes or images of weaponry devoid of any cohesion or narrative arch. Typical videos, however, are
heavily edited to highlight numerous musical elements. Imagery (sometimes recycled across multiple video productions) is often synchronized
to a variety of musical features, mostly rhythmic (in which images or the
sounds of explosions or gunfire are aligned to a song's beat), timbral (in
which images are aligned to changes from sung to screamed vocals or
from "clean" to distorted guitars), or formal (in which images are aligned
to transitions from chorus to verse). Video editor-producers excel in the
development of these synch points, a term I borrow from Michel Chion's
theorization of film sound. Chion writes, "synch points naturally signify
in relation to the content of the scene and the film's overall dynamics. As
such, they give the audiovisual flow its phrasing" (1994:59). The rhythms
of war are once again defined by the magic of music.

If synch points describe the flow of these video creations, they define
their normalization as well. War music videos, despite the huge range and
diversity of raw materials at editor-producers' disposal, are remarkably
homogeneous in their formal structures. Nu metal tempos routinely fall
between 110 and 140 beats per minute, a moderately fast to fast tempo.
Unlike the sometimes wide-ranging speeds exhibited in other metal
subgenres, nu metal songs do not routinely diverge from these tempos.
Videos based on nu metal therefore routinely exhibit a finite range of
tempo variation, and the rate at which images change tends to be pre-
dictably based on these tempos as well as periodically emphasized musical elements, such as drum fills or vocal screams. Video creations do not
offer a diversity of audiovisual experience. Rather, and importantly, they
suggest a rhythmic predictability, a tempo and groove that makes combat
familiar, even comfortable. The accessibility of nu metal's tempos trans-
lates into the accessibility of war itself, making of it something directly
controllable. The soundtrack to war here suggests a powerful mode of
cultural imagination, one in which the complexity and chaos of combat is
made orderly, neat, and composed.

"TALIBAN BODIES"

To understand better the formal properties of war music videos, it is
worthwhile to examine one in significant detail. Pursuing this approach
will help explicate video meaning and appeal, explaining how these videos
define ways of knowing and in turn provide editor-producers and audi-

ences alike with profound cultural frames for understanding the meanings of war. In addition, such an approach will help clarify the reasons why these videos circulate and come to assume their war-making power. With this goal in mind, I have chosen to examine "Taliban Bodies," created in October 2001 and therefore likely the first of such videos.[7] Although it diverges somewhat in terms of a more rapid-fire editing approach than other videos, its overall aesthetic and the fact that it was the precursor to countless other similar productions make it a useful example.

"Taliban Bodies—Special Edition," a revised edit of the original video, created and uploaded shortly after the U.S. invasion of Afghanistan, begins with a minute-long scrolling textual introduction, using an English translation of copy from leaflets dropped by the U.S. military on the Taliban (and others) in Afghanistan. The soundtrack to *Terminator 2* provides video sound at this point in the video. Because the leaflet text helps situate the moral universe in which the video operates, it is worth quoting in its entirety.

> Attention Taliban! You are condemned. Did you know that? The instant the terrorists you support took over our planes, you sentenced yourselves to death. The Armed Forces of the United States are here to seek justice for our dead. Highly trained soldiers are coming to shut down once and for all Osama bin Laden's ring of terrorism, and the Taliban that supports them and their actions.
>
> Our forces are armed with state of the art military equipment. What are you using, obsolete and ineffective weaponry? Our helicopters will rain fire down upon your camps before you detect them on your radar. Our bombs are so accurate we can drop them right through your windows. Our infantry is trained for any climate and terrain on earth. United States soldiers fire with superior marksmanship and are armed with superior weapons.
>
> You have only one choice . . . Surrender now and we will give you a second chance. We will let you live. If you surrender no harm will come to you. When you decide to surrender, approach United States forces with your hands in the air. Sling your weapon across your back muzzle towards the ground. Remove your magazine and expel any rounds. Doing this is your only chance of survival.[8]

Themes of retributive violence and the technological superiority of the U.S. military are noteworthy here. The threat of military precision—"our

bombs are so accurate we can drop them right through your windows"—
is particularly salient, especially because, as I argue later, war music videos
highlight a similar fetishism of surgical precision, idealizing the power of
the distanced kill.

The video proper begins with the lyrical chant of Drowning Pool's
song "Bodies," "let the bodies hit the floor," whispered and repeated three
times through (video time 1:01–1:06). Throughout this hushed repetition, images of Osama bin Laden, Ali Saed Bin Ali El-Hoorie, Ayman
Al-Zawahiri, Anas Al-Liby, and others flicker across the screen. Notably,
none are members of the Taliban, even if some are associated with the
group. For the purposes of the video, these images appear to be random
and interchangeable. Regardless, the connection between lyric and image
is unmistakable—these are the bodies that are meant to hit the floor. A
fourth repetition of the lyrical refrain is highlighted by two quick hi-hat
cymbal hits, interrupting "the" and a screamed "floor"; each hi-hat note,
in turn, is synchronized to images of fighter jets (video time 1:07). A
screamed "floor" begins on the downbeat of the next measure, at which
point the entire band (bass, drums, guitars) enters. The screamed vocal
extends four measures, as a barrage of military plane images accompa-
nies its sound (video time 1:09–1:16). This brief passage is immediately
followed by a guitar break, lasting two measures, distorted and played
with the use of a wah-wah pedal, a guitar effect common in hard rock and
popularized by musicians like Jimi Hendrix. The solo guitar corresponds
to the longest-lasting film sequence yet, what appears to be the test firing
of a ground missile, intentionally sped up so that it explodes exactly on
cue at the beginning of a drum fill (video time 1:16–1:20). The fill, lasting
two measures (accompanied once again by a flurry of combat images),
sets up the return of the entire band to the main theme (video time 1:20–
1:23). The coordination of sound and vision in twenty seconds of "Taliban
Bodies" corresponds to that mapped out in table 10.1.

The entire video, in fact, comprises little more than synch points, creating an overwhelming audiovisual density and sense of speed. The analogical relationship these points assume within a video devoted to military
might and power is noteworthy. The speed of the video and the intensity
of the song buttress the meanings of the military imagery flashing by.
Nearly every musical component—guitar effects, rhythmic flourishes,
percussive hits, vocal screams—is matched with a specific image of mili-

TABLE 10.1

Coordination of Sound and Vision in "Taliban Bodies"

TIME	MUSIC	IMAGES
1:01–1:06	"Let the bodies hit the floor" whispered three times	Photographs of bin Laden and others
1:07–1:08	"Let the bodies hit the . . . FLOOR!" Two beats of hi-hat between "the" and "FLOOR!"	Fighter jets synced with the two hi-hat hits
1:09–1:16	Full band introduction; screamed "FLOOR!" through next four measures	Fighter jets; missiles; complex flight formations
1:17–1:90	Unaccompanied guitar, distorted and processed with a wah-wah pedal	Test missile firing, sped up to explode exactly on the downbeat of the next measure
1:20–1:23	Beginning of drum fill; full band entrance to set up next section	Missile explosion in sync with drum entry; barrage of battle images throughout drum fill

tary hardware and combat technologies. Drowning Pool's song, therefore, is essential in providing these images with their meaning, crammed as they are so close together that it is impossible to count the number used. As Chion writes, synch points can be singularly crucial in film sound because often "what we hear is what we haven't had time to see" (1994:61). This holds especially true for the blending of sound and vision in "Taliban Bodies" and suggests a key poetics of its militarized audio-vision. Music defines what we see as much as what we see defines what we hear. Or, as Nicholas Cook argues, music and image alter each other to create a "blended space," one in which "attributes unique to each medium are combined, resulting in the emergence of a new meaning" (2001:181). Music functions as more than the sound of these depictions; it actively shares in the construction of video meaning and defines, in turn, one of the primary reasons people choose to watch and listen.

EDITING TECHNOLOGIES

Given the importance of synch points in war music videos, editing practices and technologies, not surprisingly, are a fundamental component of video creation. As Carol Vernallis writes in her analysis of music videos more broadly, "editing . . . places the video's images and the song's formal features in close relation" (2004:49). Ryan Hickman writes tellingly about the importance of editing and the labor involved in the creation of "Taliban Bodies": "With as many as 30 unique images crammed into one second of audio in some spots, I had Premiere's timeline window zoomed in as far as it would go. It took try after try to get the timing right and countless previews before I was finished." He continues, "It took another week of work getting all the pictures to land on the beats of the song and to get the timing right for the intro."[9]

Hickman's own war music video sharing site, GrouchyMedia.com, situates editing and home computing technologies at the center of video creation and its concomitant meanings. In addition to numerous videos, the site also includes an FAQ section geared toward technologically savvy audience members. In it Hickman writes, "Then it was time to export the movie using Microsoft's Windows Media Tools, the Ligos LSX-MPEG encoder, and the export feature built into Premiere. I threw it all together in a web page using ColdFusion Studio 5.0 (I now use DreamWeaver), and posted it to the web."[10]

The fetishism of home studio technologies apparent here defines a central discourse for the kinds of videos found on GrouchyMedia and other combat music video sites. Through this highly technological language, the force (and implied success) of war representations is tied directly to the site of the home computer, aligning the power of war's soundtrack to technologies of mediation. Such accounts underscore the time, effort, and skill of video editors.

At stake for editor-producers like Hickman are conceptions of craftsmanship and claims about specific technological or artistic skills. For some individuals, war music video production has even opened doors to more professional opportunities as well. Video editor-producer Garrett Flynn, for example, was hired to create a "recruiting aid" video, "The Creed," for the New Jersey Army National Guard.[11] Interconnections like these between homemade war music video productions and armed forces recruitment advertising underscore the location these videos assume within what James Der Derian (2001) has called the "military-industrial-media-entertainment network," suggesting important crossovers between these videos and other forms of "militainment." It also underscores the complexity and diversity of the soundtrack to war.

In experiencing "Taliban Bodies," audiences enter a celebrated world of technological mediation, one in which militarism is realized through the discursive realm and editing potentials of Ligos LSX-MPEG encoders and ColdFusion Studio 5.0. The productive power of the home computer—that is, its ability to facilitate the creation of precise synch points through specific software and hardware configurations and the skill set of a knowledgeable and talented editor-producer to use them—cannot therefore be separated from the meanings and attendant pleasures of war music videos for creators and fans.

As such, it is useful to situate successful video creation vis-à-vis the kinds of accuracy lauded in military terms such as surgical precision or other forms of idealized, distanced killing. These are, of course, the exact technologies addressed in the text at the beginning of "Taliban Bodies," a text included on leaflets dropped on the Afghanistan Taliban. Through such ideological engagements with technologies, the representational and the real blur. In striking ways, the meticulousness of war music video editing is comparable to a kind of ideal military accuracy, and the development of the former pays tribute to the immanent brutalities of the latter. The video editor who arranges explosions (and the things exploded) to align with the regularity of a 4/4 beat is the representational reflection of the drone pilot who flies attack aircraft from halfway around the world. The technology that threatens to deliver bombs so accurately that "we can drop them right through your windows" morphs into the mimetic technologies of the home computer. Here citizen and soldier fuse through the technologies and practices of total war.

AUDIENCES, USES, AND DEPLOYMENTS

In general, audiences for war music videos tend to be young and male. Many are U.S. citizens, but I have corresponded with a sizable minority from other countries as well, specifically Canada, the United Kingdom, and Germany but also Iraq, the Maldives, and Mexico. Women are rarely either editor-producers or fans of combat videos, although they tend to be more represented as both in relation to another type of video genre, the tribute video. A discussion of these videos goes beyond the immediate scope of this chapter; it is worth noting that representations paying tribute to fallen soldiers (typical generalized depictions) tend to feature a broader range of slower music, from New Age artists to female singer-songwriters to country music stars. Synch points are virtually absent in these productions, suggesting an important difference in aesthetic intent and appeal.

Among combat video fans, many listener-viewers express interest in joining the military or have recently enrolled. It is quite common, for example, to see comments to this effect posted as video commentary on websites like YouTube. Enlisted soldiers are also often fans of war music videos, and I have yet to meet one who was unaware of their existence. Many trade videos while on deployment, and on more than one occasion I have been handed DVDs full of videos gathered in such ways when sitting down with soldiers for interviews. Other methods of distribution are typically online through sites like YouTube, as mentioned, but also in a number of tailor-made video-sharing websites. One of the largest video collections, for example, can be found on Military.com's entertainment section, titled "Shock and Awe," in which users can post their own videos and fans frequently comment on the merits of individual representations. Such methods of distribution are usually informal.

More formalized methods exist as well. For example, soldiers I have interviewed note that they are exposed to war music videos in official capacities throughout their deployments, particularly during the first few days after arrival, in which they sit through hours of video orientations that cover a variety of policies and often conclude with what one solider called "motivational videos."[12] Particularly well-known productions, like "Taliban Bodies," travel widely and are frequently shown at Basic Combat Training among all branches of the U.S. military. The marine combat correspondent quoted earlier noted that his video has been subsequently shown throughout all schools of the U.S. Marines.[13] War music videos, as such, are officially incorporated into the material realities of war and war-making bureaucracies, just as they define the aesthetic contours of global conflict and permanent war. In such instances, websites like Grouchy-Media.com, self-identified as the "place to find those pump-you-up-to-kill-the-bad-guys videos that everyone has been talking about," find their most explicitly direct use.[14]

Outside of these kinds of official scenarios, though, most audiences choose to watch and listen to videos because of the successful music selection and subsequent synch point creation. Successful war music videos—that is, those that are viewed often and circulate widely—are exactly those in which images of explosions, and the implied destruction of those people and things that are exploded, are arranged and rearranged to land directly on the beat of a song. A good war music video, as one audience member writes, includes "effective music, touching lyrics/tune. images and music should make the hairs on your back stand [up]." Another observes, "excellent editing; the cutaway to the dog eating, the one Marine shooting into the mirror, the bricks in the wall being shot down like a Tetris game . . . all right in tune to real hellraiser music. I was into the excitement of it but I managed to be grateful for their bravery as well."[15] The selection of specific musical content by editor-producers consequently helps define a video's affect, delineates its aesthetic forcefulness, and, in turn, contributes to a certain kind of feelingfulness of representation.

The virtuosity of video editors also works to conceal the ideological nature of many video creations. In watching and listening to well over three hundred videos, I can attest to the ways in which their grim reality can often be obscured by the skill of talented editors. During my research, I have found it hard to ignore the obvious time, energy, and expertise that goes into the creation of some productions. At such times, I have been equally implicated in the power of these videos and the ways they offer profound subjective engagements with war's aesthetic appeal. The power of military hardware, skillfully aligned to the contours of nu metal, creates a militarized audio-vision that is disturbingly compelling.

Much of the insidiousness of these videos can be explained through an analysis of their point of view as well as the limits in what they show. Whereas some certainly highlight the devastating aftermath of technologically enhanced killing—featuring the gruesome carnage left in its wake—a more sanitized version is more often present. (It is worth noting that graphic videos are typically removed from YouTube quickly, although such productions can easily be found on websites that cater to more extreme materials, notably LiveLeak.com.) Indeed, a majority of war music videos, as in the case of "Taliban Bodies," focus mostly on military technologies and their killing potentials.

The enemy, as such, is strikingly absent in a large amount of video productions, and the cameras and music that organize these representations primarily turn inward. The "us against them" Manichaeanism of war music videos importantly presents an enemy that is fundamentally interchangeable. This is a war machine, and it matters not who the enemy actually is. As such, combat music videos function to map not the Other but, rather, the Self. It is perhaps ironic that in countless representations set to Drowning Pool's "Bodies," the only bodies that are typically shown are those of U.S. soldiers. In important ways, therefore, these video representations function as the flip side to the Human Terrain System, the cultural group, here, being U.S. enlisted personnel. Such video self-fashioning provides U.S. armed forces with images of themselves in their imagined ideal. As the combat correspondent notes, "marines like watching marines do what marines do."[16]

War music videos, then, are ultimately inward facing, aligning military imagery with music to inspire, motivate, and deploy. For all the high-tech gadgetry that goes into their creation, the use of music here is as old as the premodern imaginations that began this chapter. What these videos offer to soldiers and sympathetic citizens alike, consequently, is a way of engaging with the profound history of the soundtrack to war. This history, as noted, is ultimately magical in its power and ability to crystallize community and solidify morale. It is devastating, too, in its pernicious appeal.

CONCLUSION: TOWARD AN EAR FOR WAR

The soundtrack to war is an important part of the imaginative and material conditions of war, and the anthropology of warfare would do well to theorize ways of effective listening. While a number of scholars have turned their attention to studies of war and visual culture (Virilio 1989; Kleinman and Kleinman 1997; Feldman 2000, among others), too often such work is carried out as if the world were without sound. The case of war music videos, I hope, suggests the importance of listening for our scholarship. For those interested in the contemporary deployment of music and sound in war, there is certainly no lack of opportunity for engagement, as I noted in the first part of this chapter. Whether studies address the reverberations of war music videos in combat scenarios, the use of music by soldiers in battle or in interrogation, or the increasing use of sonic cannons and other auralities of war, music and sound is now, and has long been, crucial to the ways war is fought, imagined, and made real. It is time we tune in to such sounds as we continue to explore the cultures and practices of the violence we call war. Only then will we be able to understand the full contours of war's sensorium.

NOTES

Earlier versions of this chapter were presented at the 2007 meeting of the Society for Ethnomusicology, the 2009 meeting of the Midwest Chapter of the Society for Ethnomusicology, and the 2009 meeting of the American Anthropological Association. Thanks to Scott Carter, Richard Floeckher, Ron Radano, and Fritz Schenker for extensive comments on earlier drafts. Thanks also to Neil Whitehead for continued support.

1. See http://bands.army.mil/bands.
2. Personal correspondence. All quotations in this chapter are reproduced verbatim, unless otherwise noted.
3. Originally posted at http://www.grouchymedia.com/about_grouchymedia.cfm. This page has since been taken down.
4. Phone interview, September 8, 2009.
5. Phone interview, September 8, 2009.
6. Interview, September 28, 2010.
7. Available at http://www.grouchymedia.com/videos/2001/10/taliban-bodies.html.
8. "U.S. Propaganda to Taliban: 'You Are Condemned,'" http://www.cnn.com/US.
9. Originally posted at http://www.grouchymedia.com/videos/taliban_bodies/makingof.cfm. This page has since been taken down.
10. Originally posted at http://www.grouchymedia.com/videos/taliban_bodies/makingof.cfm. This page has since been taken down.
11. Available at http://www.grouchymedia.com/videos/2006/04/creed.html.
12. Interview, September 28, 2010.
13. Phone interview, September 8, 2009.
14. See http://www.youtube.com/user/GrouchyMedia.
15. Anonymous posting at http://www.freerepublic.com.
16. Phone interview, September 8, 2009.

WAR AT LARGE

Miner Magic and the Carrion System

After terminating the Iraq occupation and Afghanistan-Pakistan (Af-Pak) war, there will be no ecstatic scenes of applauding gentlemen, admiring children, bouquets thrown about, and women dancing on tanks, like at the end of World War II, when an old continent with worn-out empires was liberated by its young, ambitious descendant. A romantic account of the cold war and its current successor, "the war on terror," would be that the United States has been addicted to reliving that historical moment when all eyes were fixed on it for living up to the highest expectations. Today it becomes ever more clear that another addiction has come into play. No multinational in the military industry or elsewhere can accept making less profit than was made the year before. By the time our troops have shaken the dust off their boots, there will be another war under way, probably in Africa (see Finnström's chapter in this volume) or in other regions poor enough in resources and communications means to be unable to credibly convey their side of the story.

Battles in deserts, mountains, and ruined cities are the surface signs of a more structural violence. The global political-economic system depends on profit—more precisely on the growth of profit, which since the days of colonization has meant occupying land and people on it to bear the brunt of our system.

A militarized concept of culture, in terms of human terrain systems, has been instrumental in separating us from them. The idea of separate terrains contributes to fencing off "our" democracies and declaring the rest as no-man's-land. Behind our fickle if sincere indignation at the misconduct of dictators of small countries stands our firm acquiescence in the conduct of the greater powers. We know whom to consider prey so that our profits magically grow. We know where the global rule of magic applies, where profits can be gained in proportion to the sacrifices made. The soldiers we send, the rebels they fight, and the many aspirers in between deserting their farms to try their luck elsewhere are battling over what in the end will never be more than carrion.

This final chapter presents a personal and somehow reflective account. It sketches an ethnography of rural Tanzania, and it will recapture and illustrate some of this book's arguments and their implications for ethnographic practice as I have come to experience them. More specifically, my chapter deals with aspirers who name themselves vultures. They dig for diamonds south of Lake Victoria. These are not "blood diamonds." That qualification illustrates all too well the dubious distinction invented by what Michael Hardt and Antonio Negri (2004) call Empire and which our anthropologies are part of (see also the critique by Kapferer and Bertelsen 2009). The phrase "blood diamonds" denounces one particular form of exploitation, the mining by rebel groups, and justifies another form of exploitation, the mining organized by the corporate state under the banner of the free market. The goal of this chapter is to recall the real and global war behind the moral wars our states engage in, which is precisely economic. The vultures reproduce a carrion system that specifies this global war. The chapter zeroes in on the magic employed by some of those artisanal miners. Its logic is frighteningly familiar to the motive of warfare in Iraq, Af-Pak, and Vietnam: making sacrifices to open the gates of freedom and fortune. Digging deeper into the profound affinity between global economic stress and local witchcraft-related violence allows us to fulfill the anthropological task, proposed in this volume's introduction, of transcending the culturalist divide, hardly resolved, between the modern and the primitive. That asymmetry, as argued throughout this book, lies at the heart of contemporary warfare. The best evidence against such asymmetrical anthropology is the strong resemblance between the new forms of magic in Africa and the rest of the world.

Vultures, they are called. *Babeshi*. They are six to eight people, mostly men but women too, digging for diamonds in a pit or *duara*, literally "circle" because of its often circular shape. Two dig and pile up the soil, which they throw into the sifting baskets of two other team members standing by their side in the pit with their feet in the water. Water is regularly fetched. The water permits one to submerge the basket and sift through the soil, throw away the pebbles, and look for something shiny.

The vultures take turns. Two rest on the side of the pit, but are never relaxed, it seems. They keep an eye on their colleagues in the pit. The team is ruled by suspicion. "Don't be mistaken," one man tells me, resting next to the pit on an old pile of surface soil. "If I catch any of my team members hiding a gem, he's dead. There is no place for friendship." They are vultures in the way they search for a catch, a diamond in the basket, but also in the way they peer down the pit at the other team members. Nothing I ever experienced during my years in Sukuma villages resembles this. Their invention of the epithet "babeshi" signals profound awareness of the anomaly.

Weeks pass, months pass, without a catch. Hunger sets in. The region I am talking of is Mwanza, Tanzania. The village is Mwanangwa. People came up to me begging for food. Not even in the slums of Mwanza have I seen this sense of need. Across the many hundreds of pits densely scattered over some twenty acres of land, split by the Mwanza–Shinyanga tarmac road, there were people shouting, chanting, joking, and also firmly addressing me, dozens at the verge of aggressing me as I passed them and tried to jest away their requests for food, something so basic any neighbor in a normal village would offer it to them. Anger and despair were visible on their faces. But for food and even water, one pays dearly here. Everything is calculated in Mwanangwa. Food, one meal a day ("like in prison" they joked to me), is the responsibility of the pit owner. So is medical care. But when he feels it has taken too long since the last catch, he may refuse to provide food. He may justify this by insinuating to the chief digger or "manager of the circle" (*msimamizi wa duara*, Swahili) that the diggers kept a gem from him. The pit owner is called *nsabi*, "the rich one," but that term should not be taken too literally. He is the employer. He usually does not dig. When a gem is found, he sells it, divides the profits, and keeps the largest share together with the owner of the field (*shamba*), an area of an acre or two with several dozen pits. One pit may yield no profit. Several can. So the winners are found higher up the ladder, starting with those field owners.

There are only six field owners. Officially they live on these fields as farmers. On each field a simple mud-brick house can be found surrounded by pits, but the owners actually live in fancier houses in nearby commercial centers such as Misungwi. They may rent out their mud-brick houses to diggers, although most diggers sleep in or around the pit. Here you pay for everything, miners say, evoking an extreme instance of the new reality they had begun to experience back home in the village as well. Given the acute lack of basic necessities, fights are frequent over theft, including suspicions of fraud or scam. The village vigilante group, Sungusungu, presided by the village head, is kept busy solving these issues. For every case the plaintiff will pay a sum of 20,000 Tanzanian shillings (TZS) (10 euros). A market has emerged for protection, suspicion, and accusation.

The diggers cannot provide food for themselves. They go weeks without income. Most often they are men from poor families, their oldest brother remaining with the land and the cattle but also with the duty to procure bride-wealth for his younger brothers. The female miners are single or divorced. The diggers may choose to invest the bit of savings they have in the private consultation of a diviner. For 100,000 TZS (about 50 euro, worth a year of food for one person), this diviner consults the spirits to determine where to start digging. The group of miners I stayed with had done this twice, once for a diviner who came all the way from Kahama, some one hundred kilometers farther south, afterward for a diviner from Bariadi, about the same distance east. They do not look like the diviners we are used to in the village, with their black garments, amulets, bracelets, and *luhanga* (the customary divination basket). They are smartly dressed with a suitcase in hand. True, the other diviners of the village may travel like this as well. And they sometimes help clients who want "to be divined for success," known as the practice of *kuhangilwa*. ("Kuhangilwa ku Ntuzu," the Sukuma used to say: "to get divined among the Ntuzu people," that is, in the east where the best diviners can be found, whereas in the west, *ng'weli*, in the direction of Burundi and Congo, black magic can be had.) But there is one difference. The spirits the artisanal miner's diviner addresses are not the souls of deceased ancestors. They are *majini*, spirits of Arab descent, believed to have served in the old days as protectors of Arab traders' treasures stored along the East African coast. To get the kind of wealth that diamonds stand for (as opposed to cattle, for example), it is no use bothering the Sukuma ancestral spirits (*masamva*). Arab spirits will listen, though. But their logic is quite different from kinship logic. Ancestors may feel responsible for their descendants and provide for them if the latter do good in the community and placate their ancestor with the proper attention through ritual, such as sacrificing beer at the altars and wearing bracelets in their honor. The sacrifice demanded by the majini spirits is somewhat different. They expect money, such as a considerable amount of cash left to rest for a night on someone's grave. In return, luck will be granted. So a market has emerged for magic adopting the straightforward logic of any market: the give-and-take of commodity exchange. What profits then would the taking of as much as a life not yield?

The mining village of Mwanangwa is a special case in Tanzania. Productive mines are exploited by international firms, mostly South African or Australian, after obtaining a license from the Tanzanian government. They work with a time limit and hence use enormous trucks and grinders as well as huge quantities of purifying chemicals in open air, all in the effort to get the most out of their stay and leave the area quickly, probably before the farmers in the vicinity have a clue of the effects on their natural environment. (A sad illustration recently is the gold mine of Tarime, over which ecological controversy has been growing in 2010, in response to which the responsible firm has dug a protective channel.) In April 2009 the head commissioner of Kwimba district visited Mwanangwa and granted Tanzanians the permission to mine at will and have free-market play in the sale of any diamonds found. He confirmed this on his return in February 2010. A large number of young prospectors and adventurers came flocking in at once. Yet district civil servants talked to me of Mwanangwa as an old, virtually exhausted mine.

The rich field nearby is secluded and kept off-limits for artisanal miners. The area lies a few kilometers away from the famous diamond mine in Mabuki, which has been exploited since 1936 by the geologist John Williamson (who, thanks to the diamond mine of Mwadui some fifty kilometers south, became one of the richest people in the world in the 1950s). During my first fieldwork in 1995, I lived in Nguge valley, close to Mabuki and Mwanangwa. The villagers were not concerned with the mines. Like now, the artisanal miners in the 1990s were landless immigrants coming from afar to try their luck. But one of the diviners in our village catered to them. This almost automatically implied that few of the villagers ever consulted her on common matters requiring divination, such as illness or bad harvests. Her name was Luhanga. She specialized in guiding miner activities in return for a considerable fee. After a decade of oracular guidance, she had acquired the means to build a guesthouse in the nearby commercial hub, Misungwi. Clients said they had accepted to pay her half of their profits if they were successful. Even if only few were successful, and even fewer kept their promise, the stream of clients had been steady. Whether or not her predictions worked, she was bound to get rich. Today some field owners from Mwanangwa are building in her guesthouse's street. People have come to realize that the biggest pieces of meat (*nyama*) end up among those feeding on the others' false hopes. But these pieces are merely carrion, too.

The real winners are not those specialized diviners or field owners, either. The winners, or rather their assistants, can be found in a couple of cars parked along the road. They are waiting for the lucky miner of the day. They wear sunglasses. Their skin happens to be much lighter, and they speak English. They are part of the global economic network interested in these stones. Buying an uncut diamond is to some extent a gamble, for its value is only known once it is cut. (Cutting also causes the diamond to diminish by 50 percent.) But there is little risk involved when the prices are as low as they are in Mwanangwa. A first-class stone of two carats, which as a cut diamond of one carat could fetch 30,000 euros in Europe, is sold for 3 million TZS at most (1,500 euros), about one twentieth of its potential value. One civil servant from Misungwi who had tried his luck for a few months in summer, told me that even these sums are rarely paid. For the bigger diamonds, the miners are happy to receive a small motorbike each. The more commonly found stones weigh up to 0.75 carat and make 100 euros at most, still a fraction of what they might be worth. The miners have come to speak of these smaller stones as "just money for food"—these same stones, after passing the invisible fence of the carrion system, are treated as treasures by Europeans.

To speak of miners seeking diamonds and spying on their colleagues as vultures, babeshi, peering down to look for dead prey, is evocative of the neoliberalist global world they have wound up in. It is a world we continue to reproduce. The endless stream of anthropological critiques since the 1990s on the neoliberalist turn in Africa has not changed that. The perpetual state of war of our respondents is telling of our system.

Babeshi is not a ludic metaphor used by contenders in dance competitions. Vultures feed on carrion. They anticipate the fall of the weakest. Three implications seem relevant here. First, vultures have to wait for the desired thing to happen. They have to be patient because they have no means to change the situation. Second, vultures cannot intervene with the more powerful players, such as the lions killing prey—in this case, the field owners and the buyers. The already-haves are never in danger, never threatened by a system that welcomes vultures. Third, for the vultures, competition is the main principle. They have nothing to fall back on. Taking those three elements together, I could not think of a better description to sum up the position of Africa within the global economic system.

There is another reason for distinguishing babeshi from dancers and users of magic. The violence and extroversion, very much contrasting with the subdued rhetorical style in the village and at home, is proper to the Sukuma dancer (and the user of magic). But dance takes place during a particular time of the year: in the dry season after the harvest. Moreover, dance competitions are held in a particular place, outside the village, just as markets are (with their commodity exchange). Yet the stress for a catch among artisanal miners in Mwanangwa seems constant. It is not one experiential state among several the miners can shift between. The condition coincides with the person. It is not one experiential state in a widely ranging palette, such as that of the dancer at night, next to that of the responsible elder he or she is at other times, a member of the village council (under the big tree); or that of the initiated member of a healing cult (outside the village at the pond); or that of the descendant honoring the ancestors at the altars in the central yard of the compound. More than social positions, these are ever so many experiences people travel between, permitting them to release the burden of one state as they enter another. The miners, though, seem reduced within the confines determined by the carrion system. Their food, their hopes, their fear, their status are all those of the vulture. If "Africa works" thanks to networks of patron–client relations (Chabal and Daloz 1999), we should acknowledge as well the extent to which these relations reflect a global structure of disempowerment. Hip hop stars such as Professor Jay voice people's awareness of sharp oppositions whereby the capitalist accumulation of patrons often collides with ancestral demands, ritual obligations, clan-based authority, unpredictable oracles, and initiatory cult membership.

Echoing the economic stress and global exploitation resulting from it, the miner's magic reveals the inner principle of the carrion system, I argue next. This magic differs from that which Sukuma are traditionally initiated into, and from the multiple and dynamically shifting experiences of the Sukuma user of magic. The miner's magic accords with the reductionism of the global economy. Rumor has it—a rumor later on spread by media across the world—that miners in Mwanangwa and in some other parts south of Lake Victoria believe their magic to require human sacrifice. The corpses of people with albinism would be the carrion the vulture-people need for their survival. The logic is straightforward. There is a thin line, it seems, between pure reason and madness. Before going into the logic of miners' magic, let us briefly reiterate what Westerners call rationality and the cultural basis for privileging one rationality as ever valid, irrespective of context. The interest in such rationality or reason stems from the search of a firm basis, a universal ground to act—in brief, "a" reason to act.

WAR AND DEADLY REASON

Because of the events of World War II, humanity will not be able to rid itself of one hypothesis, one that anthropologists in particular must keep in mind—and rest assured, they do, at least unconsciously. If a society situating itself at the height of "civilization" because of its progress in thought and art, for instance through its philosophers and composers, can resort to the massive and systematic atrocities that constituted the Holocaust, there might be something deeply problematic about the thing this society took pride in and invested so many resources and people in for centuries, in schools, academia, and salons. There might be something problematic about the process or historical scale of which it supposed itself to be the height. Reason, we know, was its name. How might we as anthropologists, reasoning along with our leaders, be complicit with the next global tragedy in the making?

A serious candidate for such tragedy is the U.S. war on terror, which refers to a series of wars, each democratically "sold" to the public with the purpose of gaining political influence and making money in other parts of the world. A postmodern brand of colonialism, serving a market with democratic institutions rather than one particular state, makes for a global war, barely sensed by the sponsors (that is us). David Keen (2007) has listed the advertising tricks—or what he calls magic—which the U.S. administration has been using to keep the war serial and endless. These tactics include scapegoating, wishful thinking, creating a demand for one's military supply, promising big gains, and lumping conflicts and opponents across the world into one war and one enemy. With the benefit of some distance, the tactics may strike one as the work of a creative sales-man. To be hardheaded, one may indeed ask why the United States should be any different from empires and warlords in the past, since power is the name of the game in politics.

What is overlooked in these descriptions of geopolitical struggles and the global war, I argue, is a more powerful element that has little to do with games in the strict sense and that we as social scientists have failed to address, although it is precisely the domain the state pays us to moni-tor: the domain of morality. By this I am not referring to values and com-mandments such as "Thou shalt not kill." I mean morality as a force, mostly presented in the form of what is "reasonable." It refers to a "reason" mobilizing masses to act. Why were the World Trade Center towers at-tacked? The way their construction was challenged and topped by towers in the Gulf and East Asia is telling enough. The twin towers were symbols of our imperialist arrogance, of our world domination by consent. Rather than just ruling the world, Empire wants to be legitimate. War in Africa or Asia should enter our souls as rational, namely, as a necessary sacrifice for these areas to obtain freedom and democracy and become part of the global market. The extent to which this reason of Empire is magical shows in our difficulty acknowledging the affinity with the magic of the miner counting on profit in return for the sacrifice of an albino's body part.

A transatlantic alliance is killing today in Afghanistan and Iraq for "a reason." The reason has been named democracy, more generally free-dom. Freedom is the magic expected to come from the violence. Why were thousands of Viet Cong killed and as many young compatriots sacri-ficed? Something magical was supposed to come from the sacrifice. Those bringing down the twin towers, from the other side of the fence, expected the same thing. They killed for magic to happen. The belief that it would happen is predicated on another belief—that of being on the side of the righteous. Their reason is the right reason. They believed to have history on their side. Maybe they did?

The magic we have learned to call reason is the mediating element that can persuade a social network into action in a fast, most contagious man-ner. There probably is no better lubricant for the machinery of systematic massive violence. The most ingeniously wicked administration still depends on the uncontrollable emergence of that go-ahead, the reason to act. That is what connects the different points constituting the cycle of war over the past century. The Iraq invasion was motivated by the terrorist attacks of September 11, 2011, which itself responded to the U.S. support for the Palestinian occupation by the state of Israel, the creation of which was justified earlier by the Nazi aggression, itself reacting to the burden of the Treaty of Versailles after World War I. The cycle probably goes back further and has parallel lines that I omit here, but we record the emergence of the same destructively absolute and nonnegotiable — "moral" — power or reason, which no other reason can reason away. It is a third force, equivalent to neither power nor authority. Outsiders may like to think of extremist insurgents as immoral (enemies) or amoral (adventurous rebels). Yet they have a reason, which in its logic is as lethally rigid as the military apparatus and other instruments of the state. So the question becomes, in what historical fact is this logic grounded? Empire is a reason, I argue next.

Like all technology (Feenberg 1999), the military apparatus is value-laden. When culture changes, it is materialized in technology. The recent change in military technology is alarming in that respect. What does it tell about our culture? Previously, weaponry served to scare the enemy, making the most out of every kill. The blood spilled, visible and manifold, would push to surrender. Today, victory and the other's capitulation seem of secondary concern. From the start the emphasis is on "stealth," hence clean killings. The high number of casualties during and after the invasion in Iraq in 2003, estimated at a total of over 600,000 (Burnham et al. 2006), is concealed by the absence of blood on TV and satellite images. The main intention, it seems, is to prolong military presence — war for the sake of war.

Many assume the industry to be behind it. Huge profits are made from every day of war. But that does not suffice as an explanation; there is also the general public acceptance. As the earlier chapters demonstrate, the technology of precision bombing, satellite images, drones, and so on has a culture of its own, grounded in a certain global politico-economic structure. The global structure reproduces itself in local variants on the belief that killing in itself will yield a magical outcome. The expected outcome is not surrender by the enemy. Anyone believing this has missed the point. The war on terror was never intended as a duel with winners and losers.

We can imagine the laughter of a U.S. general if a Taliban warrior would suddenly approach him brandishing a white flag. Nobody counts on surrender. No one counts on the war ending. The skirmishes in the desert and the mountains are telling signs of the real war, the (neo)colonial order imposed on the world.

According to Hardt and Negri (2004), the war between nations is a thing of the past. We must speak of a global war. The enemy is no longer an opponent in a battle but "banalized" (a criminal, says the left) as well as "absolutized" (a threat to the ethical order, says the right). War is no longer an interlude in a time of peace. It is part of what we do as members of the global economic system. We advertise and buy cell phones, cars, and jewelry that finance the killings over tantalite, oil, diamond, and gold in Africa and the Middle East. These wars are the sacrifice that we are not personally making but that we are willing to have our state make for our personal possession of the rare. Had it not been rare—so much so that it warranted killing—it would have lost its magic. That is the rule of Empire. It is very tempting to locate its origins in what Max Weber argued about the Protestant ethic. In our success of capitalist accumulation (and others' failure) we find proof of our predestination. For every insurgent defeated, our paradise comes nearer. The total sum of deaths at some point will give rise to a moment of magic, a growth of profit whose likelihood is proportional to the sacrifices made. In the logic of Empire, the magic will be called democracy or freedom. The belief in killing for magic is what connects various sites into one global war. The jihad martyr, a stronger believer than his ancestors were, detonates a bomb that will propel him straight into paradise. From the first drop of blood spilled, his sins are washed away and the end of the state of Israel comes one step closer. Likewise, extremists in Israel expect a magical outcome from a state purified of all non-Jews. In religion, economy, and politics, the kill for magic is Empire's just reason. Today, I argue next, it has reached the multifaceted world of Tanzanian healers.

MWANGA MAGIC AND VIOLENCE

It is hard not to notice these days how anthropological an issue violence has become. The United Nations refugee agency (UNHCR) issued a statement in September 2009 about millions of lives, especially women's and children's, jeopardized because of witchcraft beliefs and persecutions in Africa, primarily Congo, Tanzania, Nigeria, and Burundi, and also in

India, Nepal, Indonesia, and Melanesia.[1] In the past decade, BBC World and Al Jazeera have been reporting regularly about witch killings in Tanzania, often explicitly pointing to the largest cultural group of the country, Sukuma farmers living in a semi-arid region some one thousand kilometers to the west of Dar es Salaam. The spates of killings have been succeeded recently by a gruesome "new trend" in the same region, more than a decade after the media frenzy in South Africa about *muti* murders: the use of human organs for magical concoctions. So-called witch doctors from the Sukuma region would hire gangs to kill young people with albinism to sell bits of their bodies, especially their skin and bones, for magical recipes. The magic's purpose is not cure but good fortune. The ingredient's power would be proportional to the pain inflicted on the victim.

News agencies such as Reuters and international organizations such as the Red Cross have alerted the general public to the matter, which has featured in a growing list of documentaries (it suffices to search YouTube under the heading "Tanzania albino killings"). The horrific fate of "white black" Africans, their mortal fear, and indeed local discrimination has attracted attention in the media worldwide. Since James Ferguson (1990), among others, anthropologists have been wary of an emphasis on the culture-specific at the cost of the economic and political and hence the larger global processes of which cultures partake. Labeling the phenomenon as "occult," many explain magical murders in the anthropological terms of "challenge and riposte," which is an improvement in relation to the scheme domination/resistance (see Comaroff and Comaroff 1991:5). Occult violence would be a local response to the global reality of economic crisis and capitalism's oppression and war, thus emboldening traditions of magic (Sanders and West 2003). In my view, the microsociological challenge and riposte, which still separates action from reaction, prevents us from seeing the profound cultural affinity between capitalist economic stresses and witchcraft-related violence. The witchcraft is already in our system; it is integral to the carrion system, rather than a riposte from the African poor. How do we elicit the culture subtending witchcraft-related violence? I argue this "culture" not to be that of Sukuma, or any other group for that matter. Anyone participating in the game of the global economy is likely to resort to such violence. After the structural differentiation of society into functional subsystems with their own reasons such as economy, politics, and religion (Luhmann 1995), it seems that one reason has come to rule.

We may understand why someone would use secret means, magic (or poison), to get away with murder, but here we encounter the reverse: a kill to prepare magic. Killing someone in retaliation for having used magic or using magic in secrecy to kill are shocking, but maybe less so than killing for a magical thing to happen, which is to turn a human into an object instead of an enemy. It is predicated on the belief that the violent act itself gives access to sudden good. As in Aztec human sacrifice, such belief is most likely in political systems with a ruling caste and democratic deficit (more than in small communities whose members depend on each other for subsistence). An instance of such system is the neoliberal global economy sustained by international elite organizations such as the International Monetary Fund, which escape democratic control (Stiglitz 2002). These organizations have no enemy except the stagnation of profit on the market. They need a hinterland fenced off and regularly feeding the system with the most able-bodied who have proven their willingness to scavenge. The dehumanizing "culture" of this carrion system we find in the drone bombings and video-screen killings, discussed in earlier chapters, as well as in the practice of the *mwanga* buying miner from Mwanangwa. The only difference is that for the African artisanal miner mwanga magic represents a means of survival, whereas for us the magic of sponsored killings permitting consumption of the rare is a purpose in itself, the name of the game.

RATIONAL VIOLENCE: KILLING FOR MAGIC

Based on ethnographic research among Sukuma healers since 1995, I conclude that albinist fortune magic is not specific to any culture but a hyperrationalist type of violence that pops up when society becomes structurally undemocratic. Killing for magic does not accord well with the intuitivist culture of healers (*bafumu*) and their primary concern, which is quite simply to cure. Healers mainly cater to patients unattended to by hospital doctors. Convinced that many physical ailments have what scientists would call a psychiatric aspect, they treat patients with a combination of medicinal recipes, therapy management groups, rituals, and regular divinations monitoring the support of ancestral spirits. Recovery from illness results from initiation into an ancestrally sanctioned tradition of healing (*wa buhemba*). The initiated patient formally becomes a child of the healer, usually after a stay of two years. A second, very different task of healers is the sales of medicines (*bugota*). People who sell to anonymous clients on the market usually have no ritual tradition for treating people, because an essential element is the initiatory aspect, implying a personal bond, secrecy, and dependency on ancestral blessing.

The albinist fortune magic belongs to the noninitiatory category of medicine. In a nonmoralistic society such as that of Sukuma villages, where ancestors unpredictably bestow their blessings, it would be hard to classify any type of magic—besides that of the incurably envious witch— as illegitimate. Still, the albinist magic is sold to two categories of profession, which quite indicatively fall outside Sukuma village life: fishermen and artisanal miners. Many of these are emigrants, some living in more dire circumstances than the poorest farmers. Note that both professions have their livelihoods depending on, literally, a lucky catch.

It is true that Sukuma medicines contain (besides pharmacologically active plants) additives known as *shingila*, which establish a metaphorical link with the medicine's purpose. Thus we might deduce that the albinist fortune magic is called *mwanga*, the Swahili word for "light," because of the ingredient evoking the shining ray of hope sought daily by fishermen in the lake and by diggers in the dark of the pit. But those among them actually using the magic must be few, not only because of the high sums of money allegedly involved but also because of the peculiar belief such magic requires. Is not the possibility of such magic working remote? To think white skin will yield white fortune sounds like the improbable discovery of a natural law. We discover the limits of Stanley Tambiah's (1973) conventional definition of magic in terms of "persuasive analogies." It does not capture the margin of uncertainty my Sukuma informants integrated in their use of magic. The remote possibility of success seemed to them disproportional to the act of killing and torturing an innocent person.

Yet the phenomenon exists, and with the governmental awareness campaigns it set in motion (among others on the radio), its institutionalization has grown (Green and Mesaki 2005). As far as viewers and listeners can tell from all the hassle created and the strong prohibitions on the belief in and use of mwanga, we are dealing with the infliction of a form of violence that is unfortunate but rational from the perspective of the clients. So how do we explain the rise of mwanga?

A major obstacle to its diffusion disappeared as magic became marketed and "purified" from the demands of tradition and ancestral spirits and from the societal approval mediating cultural creativity in initiatory cults. An indication of that process is the choice for the name *mwanga* in the national commercial language of KiSwahili, instead of the local KiSukuma language normally used for magic.

There is another way of concluding on the hyperrationality of mwanga magic. In these peasant communities with a history of famines and epidemics, death is a feasible prospect, and every helping hand under the burning sun (and each belly to feed) makes a difference. In this context we may comprehend why albinist life expectancy is low, and the care their condition requires can hinder the group's welfare. Such pragmatism could explain the derogatory term reserved for sufferers of albinism: *zeru zeru*, "worth zero," a name they have learned to call themselves. The elimination, killing, of albinos may thus have a history in Sukuma villages, showing the community at its most rational. It may be illustrated by the fate of the mentally handicapped boy I had seen for months, running around naked in the neighborhood where I lived, until his corpse was found in a field nearby, painted with hued dots appropriately suggestive of the occult, hence diverting suspicion away from the family. At the same time as speaking of rational violence, I insist on the limited domain it occupies in Sukuma life. The possible drift of this violence toward the center is the alarming part of mwanga magic. It introduces a cultural change that puts an end to the initiatory dimension of magic and ritual.

The straight link between ingredient and purpose, their shared brightness, struck one of my Sukuma friends as incredibly naive. By signaling that nobody needs to summon ancestral support (*lubango*) to get lucky, that an ingredient or spell could do the trick, mwanga magic conflicts with initiation in at least two medicinal cults, Bunamhala and Cwezi. Such type of magic occupies a peripheral position in Sukuma cosmology, which is populated by unpredictable ancestral spirits (masamva) as well as witches (*balogi*) trying to corrupt the ancestors. But is that naiveté not what marks capitalist industry and the scientific search for natural laws? If we go deeper into the violently rational culture of mwanga, we learn something about the global economy—a reversal of and variant on the anthropological habit George Marcus and Michael Fischer (1986) coined "cultural critique." The rational violence of mwanga magic actually resembles the pure reason determining a Sukuma patient's construction of the witch. The figure constructed in the healer's compound is a product of imagination that is cathartic, and extremely telling in that sense, yet not at all representative of ordinary discourse. As I have explicated elsewhere, it takes a complete disregard of traditions, such as the distinction between commercial transaction and clan duty, to suppose that clan members can lay claim to your life on the basis of the debt their gifts created (Stroeken 2010). The execution of the indebted by the witch is imagined to be inevitable, following a strict rationality—a moral reason. The killer of witches, then, retaliates according to the same morality as the witch. A cycle of violence has begun without any sure way of ending. This morality is the magic that perpetuates and globalizes war. Crucial in the continuation of the deadly cycle is what the witch killer does. He does not retort ritually, such as with countermagic. He does not want the success or failure of his act to depend on the unknown of ancestral blessing. The killing of the witch is done with the sure blow of the machete. The original violence is transmitted in all its contagion and with the same certainty as the retaliation that legitimated the wars in the wake of 9/11. The ancestral world, still at the center of Sukuma cosmology, has been squarely bypassed. That is the truth of witch killing. The economic, the religious, and the political converge in its moral reason.

Witch killing used to be an exceptional activity organized by kings (*batemi*). The supra- or subhuman king, secluded in his court and scrupulously obeying a list of prohibitions, had the ritual means to absorb and end the cycle of violence, to terminate its dangerous morality, its frighteningly purity of reason. The witch killer today cuts the corpse in parts, like a sacrificed cow. The cut body parts dehumanize the victim so as to keep the morality of the act intact. This is the same dehumanizing operation we recognize in remote bombings on targets speaking another language, worshiping another God, and representing vectors on a radar screen ceasing to bleep. Those victims are deplored but in the end serve the higher good of Empire's interests. The carrion system has an unspoken hierarchy of morally lower categories of people on which to scavenge. Tanzanian miners chose sufferers of albinism. Witch killers focused on elderly women, as did European inquisitors just prior to the birth of the imperialist structures we know today. What is historically new is not the deadly cycle but the incapacity of ending it, ritually or in other ways. The role played by the military industry and the larger economic structures as well as our international institutions populated by social scientists in this incapacity is what causes concern and has set anthropologists thinking. There seems to be no experiential shift possible toward another rationality than the one moral reason in which our economy, religions, science, and politics converge. We have tried to explain this from a certain alliance of structures, which can be historically determined in terms such as imperialism and the new corporate class spanning from Washington over Paris and Moscow to Mumbai and Beijing. The growth of its profits is guaranteed by a carrion system, which fences off a no-man's-land embracing the system's magic and providing a constant influx of cheap lives.

Ending the occupation in Iraq and Afghanistan will only give the false impression of war being over. The real war will rage on in the slums of our new nascent metropoles and on the shrinking arable land of farmers in Africa, for instance, south of Lake Victoria, where this chapter's account was situated. We cannot dissociate conflict and civil war from structural inequality and the carrion system; the despair poignantly pictured on this book's cover is that of the miner too. The war rages on as long as we ignore the global significance of the local processes we study.

NOTE

1. The statement was accessed January 5, 2010, from http://www.reuters.com /article/worldNews/idUSTRE58M4Q820090923.

REFERENCES

Acuna, Claudia. 2007. Militares Observaron Detencion de Victimas. *El Periodico*,
  September 27. Accessed April 1, 2010, from http://www.elperiodico.com.gt
  /es/20070927/actualidad/44107.

Agamben, Giorgio. 2005. *State of Exception*. Chicago: University of Chicago Press.

Albro, Robert (chair), James Peacock, Carolyn Fluehr-Lobban, Kerry Fosher, Laura
  McNamara, George Marcus, Laurie Rush, Jean Jackson, Monica Schoch-Spana,
  and Setha Low. 2009. AAA Commission on the Engagement of Anthropology
  with the U.S. Security and Intelligence Communities (CEAUSSIC). Final Report
  on the Army's Human Terrain System Proof of Concept Program. Submitted
  to the American Anthropological Association Executive Board, October 2009.
  http://www.aaanet.org/cmtes/commissions/CEAUSSIC/upload/CEAUSSIC
  _HTS_Final_Report.pdf.

Alleg, Henri. 1958. *The Question*. New York: G. Braziller.

Allen, Lori A. 2009. Martyr Bodies in the Media: Human Rights, Aesthetics, and
  the Politics of Immediation in the Palestinian Intifada. *American Ethnologist*
  36(1):161–80.

Allen, Robertson. 2009. The Army Rolls through Indianapolis: Fieldwork at the Virtual Army Experience. *Transformative Works and Cultures* 1(2). Accessed February 21, 2011, from http://journal.transformativeworks.org/index.php/twc/article
  /view/80/97.

———. 2011. The Unreal Enemy of America's Army. *Games and Culture* 5(3):38–60.

Allen, Tim, and Koen Vlassenroot. 2010a. Introduction. In *The Lord's Resistance
  Army: Myth and Reality*, edited by T. Allen and K. Vlassenroot. London: Zed
  Books.

———, eds. 2010b. *The Lord's Resistance Army: Myth and Reality*. London: Zed
  Books.

Alrich, Amy. 2008. *Framing the Cultural Training Landscape: Phase 1 Findings*.
  Alexandria, Va.: Institute for Defense Analysis.

Alston, Philip. 2007. *Civil and Political Rights, Including the Questions of Dis-*

appearances and Summary Executions. Mission to Guatemala. February 19.
A/HRC/4/20/Add.2,11. United Nations: Human Rights Council.

Altendorf, Guido. n.d. ISAF Joint Command Information Dominance Center.
Accessed April 3, 2010, from https://www.cimicweb.org/Documents/PRT%20
CONFERENCE%202010/Information_Dominance_Center_Overview.pdf.

Amnesty International. 1997. "Breaking God's Commands": The Destruction of
Childhood by the Lord's Resistance Army. Amnesty International Country
Report, AFR 59/01/97. Accessed September 10, 2002, from http://www.web
.amnesty.org/ai.nsf/index/AFR590011997.

————. 1999. Uganda Breaking the Circle: Protecting Human Rights in the Northern War Zone. Amnesty International Report, AFR 59/01/99. Accessed September 10, 2002, from http://www.web.amnesty.org/ai.nsf/index/AFR590011999.

Andrade, Dale, and James H. Willbanks. 2006. CORDS/Phoenix: Counterinsurgency
Lessons from Vietnam for the Future. Military Review (March/April):9–23.

Appy, Christian G. 1993. Working-Class War: American Combat Soldiers and Vietnam. Chapel Hill: University of North Carolina Press.

Arens, William. 1980. The Man-Eating Myth: Anthropology and Anthropophagy.
New York: Oxford University Press.

Armitage, John. 2003. Militarized Bodies: An Introduction. Body & Society 9(4):1–12.

Arquilla, John. 2010. The New Rules of War. Foreign Policy (March/April). Accessed
April 6, 2010, from http://www.foreignpolicy.com/articles/2010/02/22/the_new
_rules_of_war.

Arquilla, John, and David Ronfeldt. 2001. The Advent of Netwar (Revisited). In Networks and Netwars: The Future of Terror, Crime, and Militancy, edited by John
Arquilla and David Ronfeldt. Santa Monica, Calif.: RAND.

Asad, Talal, ed. 1973. Anthropology and the Colonial Encounter. London: Ithaca
Press.

Asher, Thomas. 2008. Making Sense of Minerva Controversy and the NSCC.
Accessed February 19, 2009, from http://www.ssrc.org/minerva/wp-content
/upload/2008/10/asher.pdf.

Astore, William. 2009. Déjà Vu All Over Again in Afghanistan. Mother Jones
(April 17). http://www.motherjones.com/print/23133.

Atkinson, Ronald R. 2009. From Uganda to Congo and Beyond: Pursuing the Lord's
Resistance Army. New York: International Peace Institute. Accessed December 20, 2010, from http://www.ipacademy.org.

————. 2010. The Roots of Ethnicity: The Origins of the Acholi of Uganda before 1800,
2nd ed. Kampala: Fountain.

Axe, David. 2010. Social Scientists under Fire. Miller-McCune (March–April):
58–69.

Bacevich, Andrew J. 2008. The Petraeus Doctrine. Atlantic Online (October).
Accessed March 4, 2009, from http://www/theatlantic.com/doc/print/200810
/petraeus-doctrine.

BAE. 2009. Senior Human Terrain Analyst, BAE Systems Information Technology

(Job Posting). Accessed February 10, 2009, from http://www.applyhr.com
/12560533.

Baker, Aryn. 2009. Backlash from Afghan Civilian Deaths. *Time*, June 23. http://
www.time.com/time/world/article/0,8599,1636551,00.html.

Batson, Douglas. 2008. *Registering the Human Terrain: A Valuation of Cadastre.*
Washington: National Defense Intelligence College.

Baudrillard, Jean. 1994. The Precession of Simulacra. In *Simulacra and Simulation.*
Ann Arbor: University of Michigan Press.

———. 1995. *The Gulf War Did Not Take Place.* Bloomington: Indiana University
Press.

BBC News. 2010. Call of Duty: Modern Warfare 2 Takes $1bn in Sales. January 13.
Accessed March 23, 2011, from http://news.bbc.co.uk/2/hi/technology/8457335
.stm.

Behrend, Heike. 1991. Is Alice Lakwena a Witch? The Holy Spirit Movement and
Its Fight against Evil in the North of Uganda. In *Changing Uganda: The Dilem-
mas of Structural Adjustment and Revolutionary Change*, edited by Holger Bernt
Hansen and Michael Twaddle. London: James Currey.

Ben-Ari, Eyal. 1998. *Mastering Soldiers: Conflict, Emotions, and the Enemy in an
Israeli Military Unit.* New York: Berghahn Books.

———. 2003. Sleep and Night-Time Combat in Contemporary Armed Forces:
Technology, Knowledge and the Enhancement of the Soldier's Body. In *Night-
Time and Sleep in Asia and the West: Exploring the Dark Side of Life*, edited by
Brigitte Steger and Lodewijk Brunt. London: Routledge Curzon.

Berardi, Franco ("Bifo"). 2009a. *The Soul and Work: From Alienation to Autonomy.*
Los Angeles: Semiotext(e).

———. 2009b. *Precarious Rhapsody: Semiocapitalism and the Pathologies of the
Post-alpha Generation.* London: Minor Compositions.

Bergen, Peter, and Peter Tiedemann. 2010. The Year of the Drone. New American
Foundation. Accessed on February 25, 2010, from http://www.humansecurity
gateway.com/documents/NAF_YearOfTheDrone.pdf.

Bergerud, Eric M. 1993. *Red Thunder, Tropic Lightning: The World of a Combat Division in Vietnam.* Boulder: Westview Press.

Besteman, Catherine. 2009. Counter AFRICOM. In *The Counter-Counterinsurgency
Manual: Or, Notes on Demilitarizing American Society*, edited by Network of
Concerned Anthropologists. Chicago: Prickly Paradigm Press.

Beyerstein, Lindsey. 2007. Anthropologists on the Front Lines. *These Times*,
November 30.

Bickford, Andrew. 2009. Anthropology and HUMINT. In *The Counter-
Counterinsurgency Manual: Or, Notes on Demilitarizing American Society*, edited
by Network of Concerned Anthropologists. Chicago: Prickly Paradigm Press.

Binnendijk, Hans, and Patrick Cronin. 2008. *Civilian Surge: Key to Complex Operations: A Preliminary Report.* Washington: National Defense University, Center for
Technology and National Security Policy.

Bloch, Maurice. 2008. Truth and Sight: Generalizing without Universalizing. *Journal of the Royal Anthropological Institute* 14(suppl. 1):S22–32.

Boas, Franz. 1928. *Anthropology and Modern Life*. New York: W. W. Norton.

Bodley, John. 2008. *Victims of Progress*. New York: McGraw-Hill.

Boellstorff, Tom. 2006. A Ludicrous Discipline? Ethnography and Game Studies. *Games and Culture* 1(1):29–35.

———. 2008. *Coming of Age in Second Life: An Anthropologist Explores the Virtually Human*. Princeton, N.J.: Princeton University Press.

Bolter, Jay David, and Richard Grusin. 2000. *Remediation: Understanding New Media*. Cambridge, Mass.: MIT Press.

Branch, Adam. 2005. Neither Peace nor Justice: Political Violence and the Peasantry in Northern Uganda, 1986–1998. *African Studies Quarterly: The Online Journal for African Studies* 8(2):1–31.

———. 2008. Against Humanitarian Impunity: Rethinking Responsibility for Displacement and Disaster in Northern Uganda. *Journal of Intervention and Statebuilding* 2(2):151–73.

———. 2011. *Displacing Human Rights: War and Intervention in Northern Uganda*. Oxford: Oxford University Press.

Bremen, Jan van. 1998. *Anthropology and Colonialism in Asia: Comparative and Historical Colonialism*. London: Routledge.

Bricmont, Jean. 2006. *Humanitarian Imperialism: Using Human Rights to Sell War*. New York: Monthly Review Press.

Brown, Keith, and Catherine Lutz. 2007. Grunt Lit: The Participant Observers of Empire. *American Ethnologist* 34(2):322–28.

Brown, Michael F., and Eduardo Fernández. 1991. *War of Shadows: The Struggle for Utopia in the Peruvian Amazon*. Berkeley: University of California Press.

Bumiller, Elisabeth. 2010. We Have Met the Enemy and He Is PowerPoint. *New York Times*, April 27, A1.

Burden, Matthew Currier. 2006. *The Blog of War: Front-Line Dispatches from Soldiers in Iraq and Afghanistan*. New York: Simon and Schuster.

Burleigh, Nina. 2007. McFate's Mission: Can a Former Punk Rocker Raised on a Houseboat Change the Way America Fights? *MORE* (September):122, 124, 126, 128.

Burnham, Gilbert, R. Lafta, S. Doocy, and L. Roberts. 2006. Mortality after the 2003 Invasion of Iraq: A Cross-sectional Cluster Sample Survey. *Lancet* 368:1421–28.

CAE (Centers of Academic Excellence). n.d. Intelligence Community Centers of Academic Excellence (CAE) Program. Accessed April 25, 2010, from http://www.dni.gov/cae.

Cakaj, Ledio. 2010. The Lord's Resistance Army of Today. Washington: The Enough Project. Accessed November 26, 2010, from http://www.enoughproject.org.

———. 2011. Too Far from Home: Demobilizing the Lord's Resistance Army. Washington: The Enough Project. Accessed February 15, 2011, from http://www.enoughproject.org.

Campbell, Donovan. 2009. *Joker One: A Marine Platoon's Story of Courage, Leadership, and Brotherhood*. New York: Random House.

Capuzzo, Jill. 2007. When Troops Need More Than Knowledge of War. *New York Times*, October 17, B4.

Carlough, Montgomery Cybele. 1994. Pax Britannica: British Counterinsurgency in Northern Ireland, 1969–1982. Ph.D. dissertation, Yale University.

Casas-Zamora, Kevin. 2009. Guatemalastan: How to Prevent a Failed State. Opinion, Brookings Institution, May 22. Accessed April 2, 2010, from http://www .brookings.edu/opinions/2009/0522_guatemala_casaszamora.aspx.

Castresana, Carlos. 2009. International Peace Institute Policy Forum on CICIG. New York, July 7.

CBS Interactive Staff. 2009. Drones: America's New Air Force. Accessed May 11, 2009, from http://news.cnet.com/8301-11386_3-10237404-76.html.

CEH (Comisión para el Esclarecimiento Histórico). 1999. *Memoria del Silencio*, vols. 1–12. Guatemala City: CEH.

Center for a New American Security. n.d. Dr. John A. Nagl. Center for a New American Security. Accessed April 11, 2010, from http://www.cnas.org/node/57.

Cereser, Leonardo. 2006. 293 conclusiones entrega PDH a la CIDH. *Prensa Libre*, July 20. Accessed September 1, 2012, from http://www.prensalibre.com/noticias /conclusiones-entrega-PDH-CIDH_0_130188884.html.

———. 2007. Extorsiones a la orden del día. *Prensa Libre*, April 1. Accessed September 1, 2012, from http://www.prensalibre.com/noticias/Extorsiones -orden-dia_0_146986754.html.

Chabal, Patrick, and Jean-Pascal Daloz. 1999. *Africa Works: The Political Instrumentalization of Disorder*. Bloomington: Indiana University Press.

Chagnon, Napoleon A. 1968. *Yanomamö. The Fierce People*. New York: Holt, Rinehart and Winston.

———. 1974. *Studying the Yanomamö*. New York: Holt, Rinehart and Winston.

Chion, Michel. 1994. *Audio-Vision: Sound on Screen*. Edited and translated by Claudia Gorbman. New York: Columbia University Press.

Clastres, Pierre. 1989. *Society against the State: Essays in Political Anthropology*. New York: Zone Books.

———. 1998. *Chronicle of the Guayaki Indians*. New York: Zone Books.

Clifford, James, and George E. Marcus. 1985. *Writing Culture: The Poetics and Politics of Ethnography*. Santa Fe: School of Advanced Research Press.

Cole, Juan. 2009. Empire's Paranoia about the Pashtuns. *Truthout*, July 27. http:// truthout.org/072709T.

Comaroff, Jean, and John L. Comaroff. 1991. *Of Revelation and Revolution: Christianity, Colonialism, and Consciousness in South Africa*. Chicago: University of Chicago Press.

———. 1993. *Modernity and its Malcontents: Ritual and Power in Postcolonial Africa*. Chicago: University of Chicago Press

Cone, Robert W. 2006. NTC: The Changing National Training Center. *Military*

Review (May–June). http://www.army.mil/professionalwriting/volumes/volume4
/august_2006/8_06_3.html.

Connable, Ben. 2009. All Our Eggs in a Broken Basket: How the Human Terrain
System Is Undermining Sustainable Military Cultural Competence. *Military
Review* (March–April):57–64.

Cook, Nicholas. 2001. Theorizing Musical Meaning. *Music Theory Spectrum*
23:170–95.

Cork, Jeff. 2009. Modern Warfare 2 Sells Close to 5 Million in First Day. November 12. Accessed March 23, 2011, from http://gameinformer.com/b/news/archive
/2009/11/12/modern-warfare-2-sells-close-to-5-million-in-first-day.aspx.

Corn, Tony. 2009. Toward a Kilcullen-Biden Plan? Bounding Counterinsurgency
in Afghanistan. *Small Wars Journal*. Accessed October 13, 2009, from http://
smallwarsjournal.com/blog/journal/docs-temp/312-corn.pdf.

Cowan, Jane K., Marie-Bénédicte Dembour, and Richard A. Wilson, eds. 2001. *Culture and Rights: Anthropological Perspectives*. Cambridge: Cambridge University
Press.

Cox, Ana Marie. 2006. The YouTube War. *Time*, July 19 (online edition). Accessed
May 2007, from http://www.time.com.

Cusick, Suzanne G. 2006. Music as Torture/Music as Weapon. *Revista Transcul-
tural de Música/Transcultural Music Review* 10:1–18.

———. 2008. "You Are in a Place That Is Out of the World . . .": Music in the De-
tention Camps of the "Global War on Terror." *Journal of the Society of American
Music* 2(1):1–26.

DARPA (Defense Advanced Research Projects Agency). 2006. Hybrid Insect MEMS
(Hi-MEMS): Presolicitation Notice. Accessed April 29, 2010, from http://www
.darpa.mil/MTO/solicitations/baa06–22/index.html.

———. 2007. DARPA-BAA07–56. Deep Green. Accessed April 4, 2011, from https://
www.fbo.gov/index?print_previews=1&s=opportunity&mode=form&id=4276c2
5fd2ed23a00a6e7.

———. 2008. DARPA-BAA-09-03 Machine Reading Broad Agency Announcement.
Accessed April 20, 2010, from https://www.fbo.gov/download/edb/edbaaf9dad2c
b7d11d47ee265a71f94b/Machine-Reading-BA-14Nov08_final-.pdf.

Dartmouth Laboratory for Human Terrain. 2009. Laboratory for Human Terrain.
http://www.dartmouth.edu/~humanterrain.

Deleuze, Gilles, and Félix Guattari. 1987. *A Thousand Plateaus: Capitalism and
Schizophrenia*. Minneapolis: University of Minnesota Press.

De Luce, Dan. 2009. No Let-Up in US Drone War in Pakistan. *Truthout*, July 22.
Accessed July 22, 2009, from http://www.truthout.org/072209B?n.

de Peuter, Greig, and Nick Dyer-Witheford. 2005. A Playful Multitude? Mobilising
and Counter-Mobilising Immaterial Game Labour. *Fibreculture* 5. Accessed
February 3, 2010, from http://www.journal.fibreculture.org/issue5/depeuter
_dyerwitheford.html.

Der Derian, James. 2001. *Virtuous War: Mapping the Military-Industrial-Media-
Entertainment Network*. Boulder: Westview Press.

DeYoung, Karen. 2009. Civilians to Join Afghan Surge. *Washington Post*, March 19. http://www.washingtonpost.com/wp-dyn/content/article/2009/03/18 /AR2009031802313.html.

DIA (Defense Intelligence Agency). n.d. Pat Roberts Intelligence Scholars Program. Accessed April 20, 2010, from http://www.dia.mil/employment/student/2008 _PatRoberts_Intelligence_Scholar_Program_Final.pff.

Dick, Philip K. 2002 [1956]. *The Minority Report*. New York: Pantheon.

DOA (Department of the Army). 2006. FM 3-24 Counterinsurgency. Washington: Headquarters, Department of the Army.

———. 2008. FM 3-0 Operations. Washington: Headquarters, Department of the Army.

———. 2009a. FM 3-24.2 Tactics in Counterinsurgency. Washington: Headquarters, Department of the Army.

———. 2009b. FM 3-07.1 Security Force Assistance. Washington: Headquarters, Department of the Army.

Dodge, Robert. 2009. Rethinking Afghanistan: Alternatives to War. *Truthout*, November 8. http://archive.truthout.org/110809C.

Dolan, Chris. 2009. *Social Torture: The Case of Northern Uganda, 1986–2006*. Oxford: Berghahn Books.

Doom, Ruddy, and Koen Vlassenroot. 1999. Kony's Message: A New Koine? The Lord's Resistance Army in Northern Uganda. *African Affairs* 98(390):5–36.

Dowie, Mark. 2009. *Conservation Refugees. The Hundred Years Conflict between Global Conservation and Native Peoples*. Cambridge, Mass.: MIT Press.

Downs, Frederick. 1978. *The Killing Zone: My Life in the Vietnam War*. New York: W. W. Norton.

DSB (Defense Science Board). 2009. Report of the Defense Science Board Task Force on Understanding Human Dynamics. Washington: Washington Office of the Under Secretary of Defense for Acquisition, Technology, and Logistics.

DuBois, Page. 1991. *Torture and Truth*. New York: Routledge.

Duffy, Jill. 2007. The Game Industry Salary Survey 2007. September 3. Accessed March 23, 2011, from http://www.gamecareerguide.com/features/416/the_game _industry_salary_survey_2007.php?page=1.

Edgerton, Robert B. 1992. *Sick Societies: Challenging the Myth of Primitive Harmony*. New York: Free Press.

EFE. 2007. Asesinato de fiscal guatemalteco estaría vinculado a caso de salvadoreños. Accessed July 15, 2008, from http://www.panamaamerica.com.pa.

Eisenlohr, Patrick. 2009. Technologies of the Spirit: Devotional Islam, Sound Reproduction and the Dialectics of Mediation and Immediacy in Mauritius. *Anthropological Theory* 9(3):273–96.

El Periodico. 2012. Erwin Sperisen es arrestado en Suiza. August 31. Accessed August 31, 2012, from http://www.elperiodico.com.gt/es/20120831/pais/217250/.

Engelhardt, Tom 2008a. The Value of One, the Value of None: An Anatomy of Collateral Damage in the Bush Era. *Truthout*, September 11. http://www .tomdispatch.com/post/174975.

———. 2008b. Catch 2,200: Nine Propositions on the US Air War for Terror. *Truthout*, April 10. http://www.truthout.org/docs_2006/printer_041008S.shtml.

———. 2009a. What Are Afghan Lives Worth? *Truthout*, July 7. http://www.truthout.org/070709B?n.

———. 2009b. Too Big to Fail? Why All the President's Afghan Options Are Bad Ones. *Truthout*, November 1. http://www.truthout.org/1102092.

———. 2009c. Drone Race to a Known Future: Why Military Dreams Fail—and Why It Doesn't Matter. *Truthout*, November 10. http://www.truthout.org/1111095.

———. 2009d. Terminator Planet: Launching the Drone Wars. *Truthout*, April 7. http://truthout.org/040809K?.

———. 2009e. Killing Civilians: How Safe Do You Actually Want to Be? *Truthout*, April 24. http://truthout.org/042409D?.

Engstrom, Nicholas. 2003. The Soundtrack for War. *Columbia Journalism Review* 42:45–47.

Enloe, Cynthia. 2007. *Globalization and Militarism: Feminists Make the Link*. New York: Rowman and Littlefield.

Ephron, Dan, and Silvia Spring. 2008. A Gun in One Hand, a Pen in the Other. *Newsweek*. Accessed April 28, 2008, from http://www.newsweek.com/id/131752/output/print.

ERIC (Equipo de Reflexion, Investigacion y Comunicación), Instituto de Encuestas y Sondeo de Opinion (IDESCO), Instituto de Investigaciones Economicas y Sociales (IDIES), and Instituto Universitario de Opinion Publica (IUDOP). 2001. *Maras y Pandillas en Centroamerica*, vol. 1. Manaugua: UCA; ERIC, IDESCO, IDIES, and IUDOP.

———. 2004. *Maras y Pandillas en Centroamerica*, vols. 2 and 3. San Salvador: UCA.

Erwin, Sandra I. 2007. Mathematical Models: The Latest Weapons against Urban Insurgencies. *National Defense Magazine* (December). http://www.national defensemagazine.org/archive/2007/December/Pages/Mathematical2412.aspx.

Evans-Pritchard, E. E. 1937. *Witchcraft, Oracles and Magic among the Azande*. Oxford: Clarendon Press.

———. 1940. *The Nuer: A Description of the Modes of Livelihood and Political Institutions of a Nilotic People*. Oxford: Clarendon Press.

———. 1976. Some Reminiscences and Reflections on Fieldwork. Appendix IV in *Witchcraft, Oracles and Magic among the Azande*, abridged with an introduction by Eva Gillies. Oxford: Clarendon Press.

Fabian, Johannes. 1983. *Time and the Other: How Anthropology Makes Its Object*. New York: Columbia University Press.

Farinacci, Prospero. 1676. *Praxis, et theoricae criminalis*. Nuremberg: W. M. Endteri and J. A. Endteri.

FAS (Federation of American Scientists). 2002. Land Information Warfare Activity (LIWA) / Information Dominance Center. Accessed April 3, 2010, from http:www.fas.org/irp/agency/inscom/liwa/index.html.

Faylor, Chris. 2009. America's Army Devs Laid Off following Launch. June 18. Accessed March 23, 2011, from http://www.shacknews.com/onearticle.x/59202.

FDPL (Fundación para el Debido Proceso Legal). 2007. Controles y decontroles dela corrupcion judicial. Washington: FDPL.

Featherstone, Steve. 2008. Human Quicksand for the U.S. Army, a Crash Course in Cultural Studies. *Harper's Magazine* (September).

Feenberg, Andrew. 1999. *Questioning Technology*. New York: Routledge.

Feffer, John 2009. Our Suicide Bombers: Thoughts on Western Jihad. *Truthout*, August 6. http://www.truthout.org/080609K.

Feinstein, Andrew. 2011. *The Shadow World: Inside the Global Arms Trade*. New York: Farrar, Straus and Giroux.

Feitlowitz, Marguerite. 1998. *A Lexicon of Terror: Argentina and the Legacies of Torture*. New York: Oxford University Press.

Feldman, Allen. 2000. Violence and Vision: The Prosthetics and Aesthetics of Terror. In *Violence and Subjectivity*, edited by Veena Das, Arthur Kleinman, Mamphela Ramphele, and Pamela Reynolds. Berkeley: University of California Press.

Ferguson, James. 1990. *The Anti-politics Machine: "Development," Depoliticization, and Bureaucratic Power in Lesotho*. Cambridge: Cambridge University Press.

Ferguson, R. Brian. 1999. A Paradigm for the Study of War and Society. In *War and Society in the Ancient and Medieval Worlds*, edited by Kurt Raaflaub and Nathan Rosenstein. Cambridge, Mass.: Harvard University Press and the Center for Hellenic Studies.

———. 2011. Plowing the Human Terrain: Toward Global Ethnographic Surveillance. In *Dangerous Liaisons: Anthropology of the National Security State*, edited by Laura McNamera and Robert A. Rubinstein. Santa Fe: School of Advanced Research Press.

Ferguson, R. Brian, and Neil L. Whitehead, eds. 1992a. *War in the Tribal Xone: Expanding States and Indigenous Warfare*. Santa Fe: School of Advanced Research Press.

———. 1992b. The Violent Edge of Empire. In *War in the Tribal Zone*, edited by R. Brian Ferguson and Neil L. Whitehead. Santa Fe: School of American Research Press.

———, eds. 2000. *War in the Tribal Zone: Expanding States and Indigenous Warfare*, rev. ed. Santa Fe: School of American Research Press.

Fick, Nathaniel. 2006. *One Bullet Away: The Making of a Marine Officer*. Boston: Houghton Mifflin.

Filkins, Dexter. 2008. *The Forever War: Dispatches from the War on Terror*. London: Bodley Head.

Finney, Nathan. 2008. *Human Terrain Team Handbook*. Ft. Leavenworth, Kan.: U.S. Army.

Finnström, Sverker. 2008. *Living with Bad Surroundings: War, History, and Everyday Moments in Northern Uganda*. Durham: Duke University Press.

———. 2009. Rumors of War and Saddam Hussein in Uganda. *Anthropology and Humanism* 34(1):61–70.

———. 2010a. An African Hell of Colonial Imagination? The Lord's Resistance

Army in Uganda, Another Story. In *The Lord's Resistance Army: Myth and Reality*, edited by T. Allen and K. Vlassenroot. London: Zed Books.

———. 2010b. Reconciliation Grown Bitter? War, Retribution, and Ritual Action in Northern Uganda. In *Localizing Transitional Justice: Interventions and Priorities after Mass Violence*, edited by Rosalind Shaw and Lars Waldorf, with Pierre Hazan. Stanford, Calif.: Stanford University Press.

Flynn, Michael T., Matt Pottinger, and Paul Batchelor. 2010. *Fixing Intel: A Blueprint for Making Intelligence Relevant for Afghanistan*. Washington: Center for a New American Security.

Forte, Maximilian C. 2008. Suspect Media: Making Propaganda for the Human Terrain System. *Zero Anthropology Blog*. Accessed February 3, 2011, from http://zeroanthropology.net/2008/09/25/suspect-media-making-propaganda-for-the-human-terrain-system.

———. 2011. The Human Terrain System and Anthropology: A Review of Ongoing Public Debates. *American Anthropology* 113(1):149–53.

Foucault, Michel. 1972. *Power/Knowledge*. New York: Pantheon Books.

Freeman, Derek. 1999. *The Fateful Hoaxing of Margaret Mead: A Historical Analysis of Her Samoan Research*. New York: Basic Books.

Friedland, LeeEllen, Gary Shaeff, and Jessica Glicken Turnley. 2007. *Socio-cultural Perspectives: A New Intelligence Paradigm*. Mitre Technical Report MTR070244. Bedford, Mass.: Mitre Center for National Security Programs. Accessed April 25, 2010, from http://www.mitre.org/work/tech_papers/tech-paper_08/07_1220/07_1220.pdf.

Gall, Carlotta. 2008. Evidence Points to Civilian Toll in Afghan Raid. *New York Times*, September 8.

Gates, Robert. 2008. U.S. Department of Defense: Speech to the Association of American Universities (Washington, D.C.), April 14. Accessed March 4, 2009, from http://www.defenselink.mil/speeches/speech.aspx?speechid=1228.

Gebauer, Gunter, and Christoph Wulf. 1995. *Mimesis: Culture-Art-Society*. Berkeley: University of California Press.

Geertz, Clifford. 1980. *Negara: The Theatre State in Nineteenth-Century Bali*. Princeton, N.J.: Princeton University Press.

Geschiere, Peter. 1997. *The Modernity of Witchcraft: Politics and the Occult in Postcolonial Africa*. Charlottesville: University Press of Virginia.

Gill, Lesley. 2004. *The School of the Americas: Military Training and Political Violence in the Americas*. Durham: Duke University Press.

Glenn, David. 2008. Pentagon Announces First Grants in Disputed Social-Science Program. *Chronicle of Higher Education*, December 23.

Goldstein, Daniel M. 2003. "In Our Own Hands": Lynching, Justice, and the Law in Bolivia. *American Ethnologist* 30(1):11–43.

Goldstein, Harry. 2006. Modeling Terrorists. *IEEE Spectrum* 43(9):26–34. http://www.spectrum.ieee.org/sep06/4424.

González, Roberto. 2007. We Must Fight the Militarization of Anthropology. *Chronicle Review* 53(22):B20.

————. 2008. "Human Terrain": Past, Present, and Future Applications. *Anthropology Today* 24(1):21–26.

————. 2009. *American Counterinsurgency: Human Science and the Human Terrain*. Chicago: Prickly Paradigm Press.

Goodman, Steve. 2009. *Sonic Warfare: Sound, Affect, and the Ecology of Fear*. Cambridge, Mass.: MIT Press.

Gopal, Anand. 2008. The Surge That Failed: Afghanistan under the Bombs. *Truthout*. Accessed October 10, 2008, from http://www.truthout.org/100908U?.

Gordon, Lewis R. 2007. *Disciplinary Decadence: Living Thought in Trying Times*. Boulder: Paradigm.

Graham, David. 2009. Weapons Porn: The Greatest, Weirdest, Coolest Hardware in the American Arsenal. *Newsweek*, September 23. http://www.newsweek.com/id/215823.

Green, Maiah, and Simeon Mesaki. 2005. The Birth of the "Salon": Poverty, "Modernization," and Dealing with Witchcraft in Southern Tanzania. *American Ethnologist* 32(3):371–88.

Green, Matthew. 2008. *The Wizard of the Nile*. London: Portobello.

Gregory, Derek. 2006. The Death of the Civilian? *Environment and Planning D: Society and Space* 24:633–38.

Grossman, Dave. 1995. *On Killing: The Psychological Cost of Learning to Kill in War and Society*. Boston: Little, Brown.

Gusterson, Hugh. 2007. Anthropology and Militarism. *Annual Review of Anthropology* 36:155–75.

————. 2008. The Minerva Controversy. Social Science Research Council. Accessed February 19, 2009, from http://www.ssrc.org/essays/minerva/2008/10/09/gusterson.

————. 2009. The Uses and Abuses of Anthropology. Presentation at "Reconsidering American Power" conference, University of Chicago, April 24.

Gusterson, Hugh, and Catherine Besteman, eds. 2009. *The Insecure American: How We Got Here and What We Should Do about It*. Berkeley: University of California Press.

Gutmann, Matthew, and Catherine Lutz. 2010. *Breaking Ranks: Iraq Veterans Speak Out against the War*. Berkeley: University of California Press.

Guyer, Sarah. 2007. *Romanticism after Auschwitz*. Stanford, Calif.: Stanford University Press.

Hajjar, Remi. 2006. The Army's New TRADOC Culture Center. *Military Review* (November–December):89–92.

Hallpike, Christopher R. 1977. *Bloodshed and Vengeance in the Papuan Mountains: The Generation of Conflict in Tauade Society*. Oxford: Clarendon Press.

Halpern, Sue. 2008. Virtual Iraq: Using Simulation to Treat a New Generation of Traumatized Veterans. *New Yorker*, May 19.

Halter, Ed. 2006. *From Sun Tsu to Xbox: War and Video Games*. New York: Thunder's Mouth.

Hamacher, Heath. 2007. "Americas Army" Contractors Take Basic Training.

November 15. Accessed March 23, 2011, from http://www.army.mil/-news/2007/11/15/6131-americas-army-contractors-take-basic-combat-training.

Handelman, Don. 2009. What Is Happening to the Anthropological Monograph? *Social Anthropology* 17(2):218–23.

Hannerz, Ulf. 1981. The Management of Danger. *Ethnos* 46(1–2):19–46.

Hardt, Michael, and Antonio Negri. 2004. *Multitude: War and Democracy in the Age of Empire*. New York: Penguin.

Hartley, Jason Christopher. 2005. *Just Another Soldier: A Year on the Ground in Iraq*. New York: Harper Collins.

Hashim, Ahmed S. 2006. *Insurgency and Counter-insurgency in Iraq*. Ithaca, N.Y.: Cornell University Press.

Hayden, Tom. 2009. Kilcullen's Long War. *The Nation*, November 2, 22–24.

Hedges, Chris. 2008. Pouring Gas on the Afghanistan Bonfire. *Truthdig*, August 25. http://www.truthdig.com/report/item/20080825_hedges_afghanistan_worsening.

Hedges, Chris, and Laila Al-Arian. 2007. The Other War. *The Nation*, July 30, 11–31.

Hedges, Michael. 2006. Iraq Videos on Web Offer Soldier's Eye View of War. *Houston Chronicle*, August 12, 1.

Herlihy, Peter, Jerome Dobson, Miguel Aguilar Robledo, Derek Smith, John Kelly, and Aida Ramos Viera. 2008. A Digital Geography of Indigenous Mexico: Prototype for the American Geographical Society's Bowman Expeditions. *Geographical Review* 98:395–415.

Herr, Michael. 1991. *Dispatches*. New York: Vintage Books.

Herrera, O., and G. Galeano. 2012. Víctor Soto, ex jefe del Dinc se entrega ante Fiscalía de la Cicig. *El Periodico*, August 12, 1.

Herskovits, Melville J. 1938. *Acculturation: The Study of Culture Contact*. New York: J. J. Augustin.

Hickman, Ryan. 2001. Taliban Bodies. Music video, 2 min, 29 sec. Accessed March 2010 from http://www.grouchymedia.com/videos/2001/10/taliban-bodies.html.

Hinton, Alexander Laban. 2005. *Why Did They Kill? Cambodia in the Shadow of Genocide*. Berkeley: University of California Press.

————. 2010. "Night Fell on a Different World": Dangerous Visions and the War on Terror, a Lesson from Cambodia. In *Iraq at a Distance: What Anthropologists Can Teach Us about the War*, edited by A. C. G. M. Robben. Philadelphia: University of Pennsylvania Press.

Hobsbawm, Eric. 2000. *Bandits*. New York: New Press.

Hodge, Nathan. 2009. Help Wanted: "Human Terrain" Teams for Africa. *Danger Room* (Wired blog). Accessed February 10, 2009, from http://blog.wired.com/defense/2009/01/help-wanted-hum.html.

————. 2011. *Armed Humanitarianism: The Rise of the Nation Builders*. New York: Bloomsbury.

Hoffman, Danny. 2011. *The War Machines: Young Men and Violence in Sierra Leone and Liberia*. Durham: Duke University Press.

Holladay, Kathleen. 2009. Bringing Communication Theory and Research to Bear on Problems of Terrorism. *Human Social Culture Behavior Newsletter* 3(16).

Honan, Joseph. 2003. Riding the Whirlwind: Command and Control of Swarms Using the Public Safety Model. Accessed November 12, 2009, from http://www.comdig.de/Conf/C4ISR/Honan.ppt.

Huggins, Martha K. 1991. *Vigilantism and the State in Modern Latin America: Essays on Extralegal Violence*. New York: Praeger.

Huizinga, Johan. 2002 [1949]. *Homo Ludens: A Study of the Play-Element in Culture*. London: Routledge.

Human Rights Watch. 1997. *The Scars of Death: Children Abducted by the Lord's Resistance Army in Uganda*. New York: Human Rights Watch.

———. 2003a. Abducted and Abused: Renewed Conflict in Northern Uganda. Accessed July 11, 2003, from http://www.hrw.org/reports/2003/uganda0703.

———. 2003b. *Hearts and Minds: Post-war Civilian Deaths in Baghdad Caused by U.S. Forces*. New York: Human Rights Watch.

———. 2005. Uprooted and Forgotten: Impunity and Human Rights Abuses in Northern Uganda. Accessed November 1, 2006, from http://www.hrw.org.

———. 2008. Afghanistan: Civilian Deaths from Airstrikes. September 8. http://www.hrw.org/en/news/2008/09/07/afghanistan-civilian-deaths-airstrikes.

———. 2009. The Christmas Massacres: LRA Attacks on Civilians in Northern Congo. Accessed February 2009, from http://hrw.org.

———. 2010. Trail of Death: LRA Atrocities in Northeastern Congo. Accessed November 4, 2010, from http://hrw.org.

Ignatieff, Michael. 2000. *Virtual War: Kosovo and Beyond*. London: Chatto and Windus.

Institoris, Heinrich. 1588. *Malleus maleficarum*. Frankfurt: Nicolai Bassaei.

Jackson, Michael. 1989. *Paths toward a Clearing: Radical Empiricism and Ethnographic Inquiry*. Bloomington: Indiana University Press.

———. 2002. The Exterminating Angel: Reflections on Violence and Intersubjective Reason. *Focaal: European Journal of Anthropology* (39):137–48.

Jaschick, Scott. 2008a. A Pentagon Olive Branch to Academe. *Inside Higher Ed*. Accessed May 12, 2008, from http://www.insidehighered.com/news/2008/04/16/minerva.

———. 2008b. Pentagon Provides Details on "Minerva." *Inside Higher Ed*. Accessed May 12, 2008, from http://www.insidehighered.com/news/2008/05/12/minerva.

Jelinek, Pauline. 2009. US Lacks Civilians for Afghan "Civilian Surge." *USA Today*, April 23. http://www.usatoday.com/news/washington/2009-04-23-afghanistan-surge_N.htm.

Johnson, Bruce, and Martin Cloonan. 2008. *Dark Side of the Tune: Popular Music and Violence*. Hampshire, U.K.: Ashgate.

Johnson, Chris W. 2004. The Role of Night Vision Equipment in Military Incidents and Accidents. In *Human Error, Safety and Systems Development*, edited by Chris W. Johnson and Philippe Palanque. Boston: Kluwer Academic Press.

Joint Forces Command. 2008. The JOE 2008: Joint Operating Environment. U.S. Joint Forces Command. Accessed June 29, 2009, from https://us.jfcom.mil/sites/J5/j59/default.aspx.

Jones, Ann. 2009. Meet the Afghan Army: Is It a Figment of Washington's Imagination? *Truthout*, September 21. http://truthout.org/092109H?.

Kafka, Franz. 1977. *The Penal Colony: Stories and Short Pieces*. New York: Schocken Books.

Kamps, Louisa. 2008. Army Brat: How Did the Child of Peace-Loving Bay Area Parents Become the New Superstar of National Security Circles? *Elle* (April):309–11, 360–62.

Kapferer, Bruce. 1997. *The Feast of the Sorcerer: Practices of Consciousness and Power*. Chicago: University of Chicago Press.

———. 2002. Introduction: Outside All Reason—Magic, Sorcery and Epistemology in Anthropology. In *Beyond Rationalism: Rethinking Magic, Witchcraft and Sorcery*, edited by Bruce Kapferer. New York: Berghahn Books.

Kapferer, Bruce, and Bjørn Enge Bertelsen. 2009. Introduction: The Crisis of Power and Reformations of the State in Globalizing Realities. In *Crisis of the State: War and Social Upheaval*, edited by Bruce Kapferer and Bjørn Enge Bertelsen. New York: Berghahn.

Kapferer, Bruce, and Angela Hobart. 2005. Introduction: The Aesthetics of Symbolic Construction and Experience. In *Aesthetics in Performance: Formations of Symbolic Construction and Experience*, edited by Bruce Kapferer and Angela Hobart. New York: Berghahn Books.

Kaplan, Fred. 2009. Attack of the Drones. *Newsweek*, September 28.

Keen, David. 2007. How to Sell an Endless War: Buy Hard. *Counterpunch*, July 21/22. Accessed January 1, 2010, from www.counterpunch.org/keen07212007.html.

Kelly, Kathy. 2009. Now We See You, Now We Don't. *Truthout*, June 26. http://truthout.org/062609R?.

Key, Joshua, as told to Lawrence Hill. 2007. *The Deserter's Tale: The Story of an Ordinary Soldier Who Walked Away from the War in Iraq*. New York: Grove Press.

Kilcullen, David J. 2000. The Political Consequences of Military Operations in Indonesia 1945–99: A Fieldwork Analysis of the Political Power-Diffusion Effects of Guerilla Conflict. Ph.D. dissertation, University of New South Wales, Australian Defence Force Academy.

———. 2006. Twenty-Eight Articles: Fundamentals of Company-Level Counterinsurgency. *Military Review* (May–June):103–8.

———. 2009a. *Counterinsurgency*. Oxford: Oxford University Press.

———. 2009b. *The Accidental Guerrilla: Fighting Small Wars in the Midst of a Big One*. New York: Oxford University Press.

Kilcullen, David, and Andrew McDonal Exum. 2009. Death from Above, Outrage Down Below. *New York Times*, May 16. Accessed June 7, 2009, from http://www.nytimes.com/2009/05/17/opinion/17exum.html.

Kipp, Jacob, Lester Grau, Karl Prinslow, and Don Smith. 2007. The Human Terrain System: A CORDS for the 21st Century. *Military Review* (September–October):8–15.

Kittler, Friedrich A. 1999. *Gramophone, Film, Typewriter*. Stanford, Calif.: Stanford University Press.

Kitts, Jeff, and Brad Tolinski. 2002. *Guitar World Presents: Nu-Metal*. Milwaukee: Hal Leonard.

Klein, Naomi. 2007. *The Shock Doctrine*. New York: Metropolitan Books.

Kleinman, Arthur, Veena Das, and Margaret Lock, eds. 1997. *Social Suffering*. Berkeley: University of California Press.

Kleinman, Arthur, and Joan Kleinman. 1997. The Appeal of Experience; the Dismay of Images: Cultural Appropriations of Suffering in Our Times. In *Social Suffering*, edited by Arthur Kleinman, Veena Das, and Margaret Lock. Berkeley: University of California Press.

Kline, Stephen, Nick Dyer-Witherford, and Greig De Peuter. 2003. *Digital Play: The Interaction of Technology, Culture, and Marketing*. Montreal: McGill-Queen's University Press.

Krepinevich, Andrew F. 1986. *The Army and Vietnam*. Baltimore: Johns Hopkins University Press.

Kwon, Heonik. 2006. *After the Massacre: Commemoration and Consolation in Ha My and My Lai*. Berkeley: University of California Press.

Kyle, James H. 1995. *The Guts to Try: The Untold Story of the Iran Hostage Rescue Mission by the On-Scene Desert Commander*. New York: Ballantine Books.

Lal, Amit. 2006. Hybrid Insect MEMS Proposer's Day. Accessed April 30, 2010, from http://www.darpa.mil/MTO/solicitations/baa06–22/pdf/lol_proposerday.pdf.

Landay, Jonathan. 2009. Do US Drones Kill Pakistani Extremists or Recruit Them? *Truthout*, April 7. http://www.truthout.org/040809S?.

Landay, Jonathan, and Saeed Shah. 2009. Seven Years Later: Al-Qaeda Gaining Ground. *Truthout*, September 10. http://truthout.org/article/911-seven-years-later-al-qaeda-gaining-ground?.

Landers, Jim. 2009. Anthropologist from Plano Maps Afghanistan's Human Terrain for Army. *Dallas Morning News*, April 8. http://www.dallasnews.com/shared content/dws/news/world/stories/DN-afghanculture_08int.ART.State.Edition 2.48b1d26.html.

Langer, Lawrence L. 1982. *Versions of Survival: The Holocaust and the Human Spirit*. Albany: State University of New York Press.

Lanning, Michael Lee. 1988. *Inside the LRRPS: Rangers in Vietnam*. New York: Ballantine Books.

Latour, Bruno. 1993. *We Have Never Been Modern*. Cambridge, Mass.: Harvard University Press.

Lawyers' Rights Watch Canada. 2009. *Guatemala Attacks on Jurists*. Vancouver: Lawyers' Watch Canada.

Lazreg, Marnia. 2008. *Torture and the Twilight of Empire: From Algiers to Baghdad*. Princeton, N.J.: Princeton University Press.

Lazzarato, Maurizio. 1996. Immaterial Labour. In *Radical Thought in Italy Today*, edited by Michael Hardt and Paolo Virno. Minneapolis: University of Minnesota Press.

Leach, Edmund. 1977. *Custom, Law, and Terrorist Violence*. Edinburgh: Edinburgh University Press.

Lenoir, Timothy. 2000. All but War Is Simulation: The Military-Entertainment Complex. *Configurations* 8(3):289–335.

———. 2003. Programming Theaters of War: Gamemakers as Soldiers. In *Bombs and Bandwidth: The Emerging Relationship between Information Technology and Security*, edited by Robert Latham. New York: New Press.

Leon, Wilmer III. 2009. Afghanistan/Pakistan a New Vietnam? *Truthout*, September 10. http://www.truthout.org/091009D?.

Longley, Kyle. 2008. *Grunts: The American Combat Soldier in Vietnam*. Armonk, N.Y.: M. E. Sharpe.

Lubkemann, Stephen. 2008. *Culture in Chaos: An Anthropology of the Social Condition in War*. Chicago: University of Chicago Press.

Luhmann, Niklas. 1995. *Social Systems*. Stanford, Calif.: Stanford University Press.

Lutz, Catherine. 2001. *Homefront: A Military City and the American 20th Century*. Boston: Beacon Press.

———. 2002a. Making War at Home in the United States: Militarization and the Current Crisis. *American Anthropologist* 104:723–35.

———. 2002b. Wars Less Known. *South Atlantic Quarterly* 101(2):285–96.

———. 2008. The Perils of Pentagon Funding for Anthropology and the Other Social Sciences. Accessed February 19, 2009, from http://essays.ssrc.org.minerva/2008/11/08'/lutz.

———. 2009. The Military Normal: Feeling at Home with Counterinsurgency in the United States. In *The Counter-Counterinsurgency Manual: Or, Notes on Demilitarizing American Society*, edited by Network of Concerned Anthropologists. Chicago: Prickly Paradigm.

Maček, Ivana. 2009. *Sarajevo under Siege: Anthropology in Wartime*. Philadelphia: University of Pennsylvania Press.

MacKenzie, Jea, and Mustafa Saber. 2009. Did a US "Hit" Create an Afghan Hero? *Truthout*, October 15. http://www.truthout.org/1015093?.

Malinowski, Bronislaw. 1948. *Magic, Science and Religion*. New York: Free Press.

———. 1979. The Role of Magic and Religion. In *Reader in Comparative Religion: An Anthropological Approach*, 4th ed., edited by William A. Lessa and Evon Z. Vogt. New York: Harper Collins.

Malkin, Elisabeth. 2010. 2 Top Guatemalan Police Officials Are Arrested on Drug Charges. *New York Times*, March 3, A11.

Mansoor, Peter R. 2008. *Baghdad at Sunrise: A Brigade Commander's War in Iraq*. New Haven, Conn.: Yale University Press.

Marcus, George, and Michael Fischer. 1986. *Anthropology as Cultural Critique: An Experimental Moment in the Human Sciences*. Chicago: University of Chicago Press.

Masellis, Nick. 2009. Human Terrain: A Strategic Imperative on the 21st Century Battlefield. *Small Wars Journal*. Accessed October 12, 2009, from http://smallwarsjournal.com/blog/journal/docs-temp/250-marsellis.pdf.

Matlary, Janne, and Øyvind Østerud. 2007. *Denationalisation of Defence: Convergence and Diversity*. Aldershot, U.K.: Ashgate.

McBratney, John. 2005. Racial and Criminal Types: Indian Ethnography and Sir Arthur Conan Doyle's "The Sign of Four." *Victorian Literature and Culture* 33(1):149–67.

MCCDC (Marine Corps Combat Development Command). 2006. *A Tentative Manual for Countering Irregular Threats: An Updated Approach to Counterinsurgency*. Quantico, Va.: U.S. Marine Corps Headquarters.

McChrystal, Stanley. 2009. *Commander's Initial Assessment*. Kabul, Afghanistan: Headquarters, International Security Assistance Force.

McFarland, Maxie. 2005. Military Cultural Education. *Military Review* (March–April):62–69.

McFate, Montgomery. 2005a. Anthropology and Counterinsurgency: The Strange Story of their Curious Relationship. *Military Review* (March–April):24–38.

———. 2005b. The Military Utility of Understanding Adversary Culture. *Joint Force Quarterly* (July):42–48.

———. 2008. Cultural Knowledge and Common Sense. *Anthropology Today* 24(1): 27.

McFate, Montgomery, and Andrea Jackson. 2005. An Organizational Solution for DOD's Cultural Knowledge Needs. *Military Review* (July–August):18–21.

McGivering, Jill. 2009. Afghan People "Losing Confidence." *BBC News*, February 9. http://news.bbc.co.uk/2/hi/south_asia/7872353.stm.

McGray, Douglas. 2003. The Marshall Plan. *Wired*, November 2. Accessed May 10, 2010, from http://www.wired.com/wired/archive/11.02/marshall_pr.html.

McNally, Richard J. 2003. *Remembering Trauma*. Cambridge, Mass.: Harvard University Press.

McNeill, William H. 1995. *Keeping Together in Time: Dance and Drill in Human History*. Cambridge, Mass.: Harvard University Press.

Melillo, Michael. 2006. Outfitting a Big-War Military with Small-War Capabilities. *Parameters* (Autumn):22–35.

Melman, Seymour. 1970. *Pentagon Capitalism: The Political Economy of War*. New York: McGraw-Hill.

———. 1974. *The Permanent War Economy*. New York: Simon and Schuster.

———. 1984. The End of War. In *Warfare, Culture, and Environment*, edited by R. Brian Ferguson. Orlando: Academic Press.

Mentore, George. 2004. The Glorious Tyranny of Silence and the Resonance of Shamanic Breath. In *In Darkness and Secrecy: The Anthropology of Assault Sorcery and Witchcraft in Amazonia*, edited by Neil L. Whitehead and Robin Wright. Durham: Duke University Press.

Merleau-Ponty, Maurice. 1962. *Phenomenology of Perception*. London: Routledge and Kegan Paul.

Metz, Steven. 2007. *Learning from Iraq: Counterinsurgency in American Strategy*. Carlisle, Pa.: Strategic Studies Institute.

Meyer, Birgit, and Peter Pels, eds. 2003. *Magic and Modernity: Interfaces of Revelation and Concealment*. Stanford, Calif.: Stanford University Press.

Mills, C. Wright. 1956. *The Power Elite*. New York: Oxford University Press.

———. 1961. *The Sociological Imagination*. Oxford: Oxford University Press.

Minerva Initiative. n.d.a. Funded Research. Accessed March 16, 2010, from http://minerva.dtic.mil/funded.html.

———. n.d.b. Frequently Asked Questions. Accessed April 25, 2010, from http://minerva.dtic.mil/faqs.html.

MINUGUA (United Nations Mission in Guatemala). 2004. Ninth Report of the United Nations Verification Mission in Guatemala. Accessed September 1, 2012, from http://en.wikisource.org/wiki/MINUGUA_-_Ninth_report.

Mitchell, W. J. T. 1986. *Iconology: Image, Text, Ideology*. Chicago: University of Chicago Press.

Moncrieff, Virginia. 2008. Taliban Support Increasing, Holds 72% of Afghanistan: Report. *Huffington Post*, March 17.

Mondzain, Marie-José. 2000. Can Images Kill? *Critical Inquiry* 36:20–51.

Morgan, David. 2005. *The Sacred Gaze: Religious Visual Culture in Theory and Practice*. Berkeley: University of California Press.

Morris, Andrew N. 1985. *Night Combat Operations*. Combat Studies Institute report no. 10. Ft. Leavenworth, Kan.: U.S. Army Command and General Staff College. Accessed December 18, 2009, from http://cgsc.leavenworth.army.mil/carl/resources/csi/morris/morris.asp.

Moseley, Alexander. 2002. *A Philosophy of War*. New York: Algora.

Mujahid, Abdul Malik. 2009. Aerial Bombing Makes Terrorists. *Truthout*, May 24. http://www.truthout.org/052409Y?.

Mulrine, Anna. 2008. Targeting the Enemy: Inside the Air Force's Control Center for Iraq and Afghanistan. *US News and World Report*, June 9, 26–28.

Museveni, Yoweri K. 1992. *What Is Africa's Problem?* Kampala: NRM Publications.

Mychalejko, Cyril, and Ramor Ryan. 2009. U.S. Military Funded Mapping Project in Oaxaca. *Z Magazine*, April 1. Accessed September 9, 2009, from http://www.zmag.org/zmag/viewArticle/21044.

Nabokov, Vladimir. 1955. *Lolita*. New York: Vintage.

Nagl, John. 2005. *Learning to Eat Soup with a Knife: Counterinsurgency Lessons from Malaya and Vietnam*. Chicago: University of Chicago Press.

———. n.d. The Evolution and Importance of Army/Marine Corp Field Manual 3-24, Counterinsurgency. Accessed August 28, 2009, from http://www.press.uchicago.edu/Misc/Chicago/841519foreword.html.

Naiman, Robert. 2009. Stopping Pakistan Drone Strikes Suddenly Plausible. *Truthout*. May 7. http://www.truthout.org/050709A?.

Nash, June. 1993. *We Eat the Mines and the Mines Eat Us*. New York: Columbia University Press.

Nelson, Diane M. 1999. *A Finger in the Wound: Body Politics in Quincentennial Guatemala*. Berkeley: University of California Press.

Ninh, Bao. 1993. *The Sorrow of War*. London: Secker and Warburg.

Nonviolent Peaceforce. 2007. CICIG Opens Dialogue to Establish Its Priorities. Accessed June 3, 2009, from http://nonviolentpeaceforce.org/en/guatemalaOct07.

Nordstrom, Carolyn. 1997. *A Different Kind of War Story*. Philadelphia: University of Pennsylvania Press.

———. 2002. Terror Warfare and the Medicine of Peace. In *Violence: A Reader*, edited by Catherine Besteman. New York: Palgrave Macmillan.

———. 2004a. *Shadows of War: Violence, Power, and International Profiteering in the Twenty-First Century*. Berkeley: University of California Press.

———. 2004b. The Tomorrow of Violence. In *Violence*, edited by Neil L. Whitehead. Santa Fe: School of American Research Press.

O'Brien, Tim. 1991. *The Things They Carried*. New York: Penguin Books.

———. 2006 [1973]. *If I Die in a Combat Zone*. London: Harper Collins.

Overwatch Systems. 2011. MAP-HT: Mapping the Human Terrain. http://www.overwatch.com/products/mapht.php.

Packer, George. 2006. Knowing the Enemy: Can Social Scientists Redefine the "War on Terror?" *New Yorker*, December 18. http://www.newyorker.com/archive/2006/12/18/061218fa_fact2?printable=true.

———. 2008. Kilcullen on Afghanistan: "It's Still Winnable, but Only Just." *New Yorker*, November 14. http://www.newyorker.com/online/blogs/georgepacker/2008/11/kilcullen-on-af.html.

Pantano, Ilario. 2006. *Warlord: No Better Friend, No Worse Enemy*. New York: Threshold Editions.

Patai, Raphael. 1976. *The Arab Mind*. New York: Scribners.

Patai, Raphael, with Norwell B. De Atkine. 2007. *The Arab Mind*. New York: Red Brick Press.

p'Bitek, Okot. 1971. *Religion of the Central Luo*. Nairobi: East African Literature Bureau.

PDH (Procuraduria de Derechos Humanos de Guatemala). 2006. *Informe de Las Caracteristicas de las Muertes Violentas en el Pais, February*. Guatemala City: PDH.

Peisner, David. 2006. Music as Torture: War Is Loud. *Spin*, November 16. http://www.spin.com/articles/music-torture-war-loud.

Peteet, Julie. 2010. The War on Terror, Dismantling, and the Construction of Place: An Ethnographic Perspective from Palestine. In *Iraq at a Distance: What Anthropologists Can Teach Us about the War*, edited by Antonius C. G. M. Robben. Philadelphia: University of Pennsylvania Press.

Pieslak, Jonathon. 2009. *Sound Targets: American Soldiers and Music in the Iraq War*. Bloomington: Indiana University Press.

Poffenberger, Michael. 2011. Groundbreaking News. Email newslist message, October 18. Available from http://www.theresolve.org.

Polk, William. 2009. An Open Letter to President Obama. *The Nation*, October 19, 12–14.

Popp, Robert. 2005. Utilizing Social Science Technology to Understand and Counter the 21st Century Strategic Threat. DARPA Information Exploitation Office. Accessed April 4, 2010, from http://webext2.darpa.mil/darpatech2005/presentations/ixo/popp.pdf.

Prensa Libre. 2008a. Asesinato del Fiscal. July 14. Accessed March 5, 2010, from http://www.prensalibre.com/pl/2008/julio/14/250617.html.

Prensa Libre. 2008b. Colom teme que narcos mexicanos tomen territorio nacional. December 2. Accessed September 1, 2012, from http://www.prensalibre.com /noticias/Colom-narcos-mexicanos-territorio-nacional_0_169783178.html.

Prensa Libre. 2008c. Video difundido en Youtube muestra escenas de matanza en Huehuetenango. December 12. Accessed September 1, 2012, from http://www .prensalibre.com/noticias/Video-difundido-Youtube-matanza-Huehuetenango _0_169784454.html.

Price, David. 2004. *Threatening Anthropology: McCarthyism and the FBI's Surveillance of Activist Anthropologists*. Durham: Duke University Press.

———. 2005a. The CIA's Campus Spies: Exposing the Pat Roberts Intelligence Scholars Program. *CounterPunch*, March 12/13. Accessed April 19, 2010, from http://www.counterpunch.org/price03122005.html.

———. 2005b. Carry on Spying (or Pay Us Back at the Rate of 2,400 Per Cent): CIA Skullduggery in Academia. *Counterpunch*, May 21/22. Accessed April 20, 2010, from http://www.counterpunch.org/price05212005.html.

———. 2008a. *Anthropological Intelligence: The Deployment and Neglect of American Anthropology in the Second World War*. Durham: Duke University Press.

———. 2008b. The Leaky Ship of Human Terrain Systems: First Read of a Leaked Handbook. *CounterPunch*, December 12. http://www.counterpunch.org /price12122008.html.

———. 2009a. Problems with Counterinsurgent Anthropological Theory: Or, by the Time a Military Relies on Counterinsurgency for a Foreign Military Victory It Has Already Lost. Presented at University of Chicago, Department of Anthropology Conference, Reconsidering American Power, Chicago, Ill., April 24.

———. 2009b. Anthropology, Human Terrain's Prehistory, and the Role of Culture in Wars Waged by Robots. *CounterPunch*, October 1–15, 16(17):1, 4–6.

———. 2010a. Soft Power, Hard Power and the Anthropological "Leveraging" of Cultural "Assets": Distilling the Politics and Ethics of Anthropological Counterinsurgency. In *Anthropology and Global Counterinsurgency*, edited by John Kelly, Sean Mitchell, Bea Jauregui, and Jeremy Walton. Chicago: University of Chicago Press.

———. 2010b. On Rendering Cultural Complexities as Stereotype: Anthropological Reflections on the Special Forces Advisor Guide. *Anthropology Now* 2(1):57–63.

———. 2010c. Silent Coup: How the CIA Is Welcoming Itself Back onto American University Campuses. *CounterPunch*, January 16–31, 17(2):1–5.

———. 2010d. Human Terrain Systems Dissenter Resigns, Tell Inside Story of Training's Heart of Darkness. *CounterPunch*, February 15. Accessed March 16, 2010, from http://www.counterpunch.org/price02152010.html.

QDR (Quadrennial Defense Review). 2010. Report. Secretary of Defense, Washington, D.C.

Redaccion El Faro 2007. *Asesor de Vielman tenia estructuras paralelas en El Salva-*

dor. San Salvador: El Faro. Accessed April 2, 2010, from http://archivo.elfaro.net
/secciones/Noticias/20070305/noticias11_20070305.asp.

Redaccion Prensa Libre. 2009. Recomienda Retirar la Imunidad. February 20, A4.

Reger, Greg M., Kevin M. Holloway, Colette Candy, Barbara O. Rothbaum, JoAnn
Difede, Albert A. Rizzo, and Gregory A. Gahn. 2011. Effectiveness of Virtual
Reality Exposure Therapy for Active Duty Soldiers in a Military Mental Health
Clinic. *Journal of Traumatic Stress* 24(1):93–96.

Renzi, Fred. 2006a. The Military Cooperation Group. Master's thesis, Naval Postgraduate School.

———. 2006b. Networks: Terra Incognita and the Case for Ethnographic Intelligence. *Military Review* (September–October):16–23.

Reyes, Kenia. 2009. A prisión dos acusados de plagio de Fernando García. El Periodico, April 7. Accessed April 2, 2010, from http://www.elperiodico.com.gt/es
/20090307/pais/93737.

———. 2010. CICIG da dos hipótesis del plan contra Montenegro. El Periodico,
March 11. Accessed April 2, 2010, from http://www.elperiodico.com.gt/es
/20100311/pais/141755/?cat=5.

Richards, Paul. 1996. *Fighting for the Rain Forest: War, Youth and Resources in Sierra
Leone.* Oxford: James Curry.

———, ed. 2005. *No Peace No War: An Anthropology of Contemporary Armed Conflicts.* Athens: Ohio University Press.

Riches, David. 1986. The Phenomenon of Violence. In *The Anthropology of Violence,*
edited by David Riches. Oxford: Basil Blackwell.

———. 1991. Aggression, War, Violence: Space/Time and Paradigm. *Man*
26(2):281–97.

Ricks, Thomas E. 2007. *Fiasco: The American Military Adventure in Iraq.* New York:
Penguin Books.

Rieckhoff, Paul. 2007. *Chasing Ghosts. Failures and Facades in Iraq: A Soldier's Perspective.* New York: NAL Caliber.

Robben, Antonius C. G. M. 2009. Anthropology and the Iraq War: An Uncomfortable Engagement. *Anthropology Today* 25(1):1–3.

———. 2010a. Chaos, Mimesis and Dehumanisation in Iraq: American Counterinsurgency in the Global War on Terror. *Social Anthropology* 18(2):138–54.

———, ed. 2010b. *Iraq at a Distance: What Anthropologists Can Teach Us about the
War.* Philadelphia: University of Pennsylvania Press.

Roig-Franzia, Manuel. 2007. Linked Killings Undercut Trust in Guatemala Culture
of Corruption, Impunity Exposed. *Washington Post* Foreign Service, March 23,
A10.

Roitman, Janet. 2004. *Fiscal Disobedience: An Anthropology of Economic Regulation
in Central Africa.* Princeton, N.J.: Princeton University Press.

Roxborough, Ian. 2008. The Minerva Controversy: The Military-Social Science
Interface. Social Science Research Council. Accessed February 19, 2009, from
http://www.ssrc.org/essays/minerva/2008/10/29/roxborough.

Russolo, Luigi. 1989. *The Art of Noise*. Translated with an introduction by Barclay Brown. New York: Pendragon Press.

Sacks, Oliver. 2007. *Musicophilia: Tales of Music and the Brain*. New York: Vintage Books.

Salemink, Oscar. 1999. Ethnography as Martial Art: Ethnicizing Vietnam's Montagnards, 1930–1954. In *Colonial Subjects: Essays on the Practical History of Anthropology*, edited by Peter Pels and Oscar Salemink. Ann Arbor: University of Michigan Press.

Saletan, William. 2008. Ghosts in the Machine: Do Remote-Control War Pilots Get Combat Stress? *Slate*, August 11. http://www.slate.com/id/2197238.

Sanders, Todd, and Harry G. West. 2003. Power Revealed and Concealed in the New World Order. In *Transparency and Conspiracy: Ethnographies of Suspicion in the New World Order*, edited by Harry G. West and Todd Sanders. Durham: Duke University Press.

Sanford, Victoria. 2003a. *Violencia y Genocidio en Guatemala*, Guatemala City: F&G Editores.

———. 2003b. *Buried Secrets: Truth and Human Rights in Guatemala*. New York: Palgrave Macmillan.

———. 2003c. The "Gray Zone" of Justice: NGOs and Rule of Law in Post-war Guatemala. *Journal of Human Rights* 2(3):393–405.

———. 2004. Contesting Displacement in Colombia: Citizenship and State Sovereignty at the Margins. In *Anthropology in the Margins of the State*, edited by Veena Das and Deborah Poole. Santa Fe: School of American Research, 2004.

———. 2008a. Si Hubo Genocidio—Yes, There Was a Genocide in Guatemala. In *The Historiography of Genocide*, edited by Dan Stone. New York: Palgrave Macmillan.

———. 2008b. From Genocide to Feminicide: Impunity and Human Rights in 21st Century Guatemala. *Journal of Human Rights* 7(2):104–22.

Sanford, Victoria, and Asale Angel-Anjani, eds. 2006. *Engaged Observers: Anthropology, Advocacy, and Activism*. News Brunswick, N.J.: Rutgers University Press.

Sanford, Victoria, and Martha Lincoln. 2010. Body of Evidence: Feminicide, Local Justice and Rule of Law in "Peacetime" Guatemala. In *Transitional Justice: Global Mechanisms and Local Realities in the Aftermath of Genocide and Mass Atrocity*, edited by Alex Hinton. New Brunswick, N.J.: Rutgers University Press.

Sartre, Jean-Paul. 1958. Preface. In *The Question*, by Henri Alleg. New York: G. Braziller.

Sas, Luis Angel. 2007. Aprehenden a dos escoltas del director policiaco. *El Periodico*, September 25, 3.

———. 2008. La hora de la muerte de Víctor Rivera ex asesor de la cartera del interior. *El Periodico*, April 9. Accessed April 2, 2010, from http://www.elperiodico.com.gt/es/20080409/pais/52137.

Satia, Priya. 2009. Attack of the Drones. *The Nation*, November 9, 14, 16.

Scales, Robert. 2004. Statement of Major General Robert Scales, USA (ret.): Testifying before the House Armed Services Committee on July 15, 2004. Accessed

April 10, 2010, from http://www.au.af.mil/au/awc/awcgate/congress/04-07
-15scales.pdf.

Scarry, Elaine. 1987. *The Body in Pain: The Making and Unmaking of the World*. New
York: Oxford University Press.

Schaner, Eric. 2008. The Human Terrain System: Achieving a Competitive Advantage through Enhanced "Population-Centric" Knowledge Flows. Master's thesis,
Naval Postgraduate School.

Schnepel, Burkhard, and Eyal Ben-Ari. 2005. Introduction: "When Darkness
Comes . . .": Steps toward an Anthropology of the Night. *Paideuma* 51:153–63.

Schomerus, Mareike. 2007. *The Lord's Resistance Army in Sudan: A History and
Overview*. Geneva: Small Arms Survey, Graduate Institute of International Studies.
Accessed September 22, 2007, from http://www.smallarmssurveysudan.org.

———. 2010a. Chasing the Kony Story. In *The Lord's Resistance Army: Myth and
Reality*, edited by Tim Allen and Koen Vlassenroot. London: Zed Books.

———. 2010b. "A Terrorist Is Not a Person Like Me": An Interview with Joseph
Kony. In *The Lord's Resistance Army: Myth and Reality*, edited by Tim Allen and
Koen Vlassenroot. London: Zed Books.

Schwark, Stuart. 2009. HSCB: How We Got Here and the Next Steps. *Human Social
Culture Behavior Newsletter* 1(Spring):9–10.

Scot, Reginald. 1584. *The Discoverie of Witchcraft*. London: William Brome.

Scott, James C. 1985. *Weapons of the Weak: Everyday Forms of Peasant Resistance*.
New Haven, Conn.: Yale University Press.

Sedillo, Simon. 2009. The Demarest Factor: The Ethics of U.S. Department of Defense Funding for Academic Research in Mexico. Accessed September 9, 2009,
from http://www.elenemigocomun.net/2255.

Sepp, Kalev. 2007. From "Shock and Awe" to "Hearts and Minds": The Fall and Rise
of US Counterinsurgency Capability in Iraq. *Third World Quarterly* 28:217–30.

Shachtman, Noah. 2007a. "Sim Iraq" Sent to Battle Zone. *Danger Room* (Wired
blog). Accessed November 19, 2009, from http://blog.wired.com/defense/2007
/11/mathematicalmo.html.

———. 2007b. Navy: Let's Play "Sim Iraq." *Danger Room* (Wired blog). Accessed
November 20, 2009, from http://blog.wired.com/defense/2007/11/culture
-modelli.html.

Siddiqi, Shibil. 2009. Pakistan's Ideological Blowback. *Truthout*, June 30. http://
www.truthout.org/063009D.

Silliman, Stephen W. 2008. The "Old West" in the Middle East: U.S. Military
Metaphors in Real and Imagined Indian Country. *American Anthropologist*
110(2):237–47.

Silverman, Barry. 2007. Human Terrain Data: What Should We Do with It? In *Pro-
ceedings of 2007 Winter Simulation Conference*, edited by S. G. Henderson et al.
http://repository.upenn.edu/cgi/viewcontent.cgi?article=1330&context=ese
_papers.

Singer, P. W. 2009. *Wired for War: The Robotics Revolution and Conflict in the 21st
Century*. New York: Penguin.

————. 2010. Meet the Sims . . . and Shoot Them. *Foreign Policy* (March/April). Accessed April 6, 2010, from http://www.foreignpolicy.com/articles/2010/02/22/meet_the_sims_and_shoot_them.

Sluka, Jeffrey. 2009. Losing Hearts and Minds in the War against Terrorism. In *Iraq at a Distance: What Anthropologists Can Teach Us about the War*, edited by Antonius C. G. M. Robben. Philadelphia: University of Pennsylvania Press.

Smith, Linda Tuhiwai. 1999. *Decolonizing Methodologies: Research and Indigenous Peoples*. London: Zed Books.

Society for Modeling and Simulation International. 2009. Modeling and Simulation in Human Terrain Systems: Call for Papers. Accessed April 4, 2010, from http://www.scs.org/specialissues?q=node/101.

Solomon, Norman. 2009. Going for Broke: Six Ways the Af-Pak War Is Expanding. *Truthout*, May 21. http://www.truthout.org/052109T?.

Stannard, Matthew B. 2007. Montgomery McFate's Mission: Can One Anthropologist Possibly Steer the Course in Iraq? *San Francisco Chronicle*, April 29. http://www.sfgate.com/cgi-bin/article.cgi?f=/c/a/2007/04/29/CMGHQP19VD1.DTL.

Stanton, John. 2009. *General David Petraeus' Favorite Mushroom: Inside the US Army's Human Terrain System*. Arlington, Va.: Wiseman Publishing.

————. 2010. Human Terrain Systems' MAP-HT Failure. *Inteldaily.com*, May 31. http://inteldaily.com/2010/05/human-terrain-systems-map-ht-failure-people-not-being-paid-map-ht-cost-overrruns.

Stanton, Shelby L. 1992. *Rangers at War: Combat Recon in Vietnam*. New York: Ballantine Books.

Stein, Rebecca L. 2008. Souvenirs of Conquest: Israeli Invasions as Tourist Events. *International Journal of Middle East Studies* 40:647–69.

Stewart, Pamela J., and Andrew Strathern. 2002. *Violence: Theory and Ethnography*. London: Continuum.

Stiglitz, Joseph. 2002. *Globalization and Its Discontents*. New York: Penguin.

Stocking, George W. 1992. *The Ethnographer's Magic and Other Essays*. Madison: University of Wisconsin Press.

Stroeken, Koen. 2010. *Moral Power: The Magic of Witchcraft*. Oxford: Berghahn Books.

Sun-Tzu. 2007. *The Art of War*. New York: Filiquarian Press.

Swofford, Anthony. 2005. *Jarhead: A Marine's Chronicle of the Gulf War and Other Battles*. New York: Scribner's.

Tambiah, Stanley. 1973. Form and Meaning of Magical Acts: A Point of View. In *Modes of Thought*, edited by Robin Horton and Ruth Finnegan. London: Faber.

Taussig, Michael T. 1987. *Shamanism, Colonialism, and the Wild Man: A Study in Terror and Healing*. Chicago: University of Chicago Press.

Tax, Sol. 1950. Action Anthropology. *América Indígena* 12:103–9.

Taylor, Glenn. 2009. Target Audience Simulation Kit for Influence Operations. *Human Social Culture Behavior Newsletter* 1(Spring):3, 6.

Taylor, Glenn, and Ed Sims. 2009. Developing Believable Interactive Cultural Char-

acters for Cross Cultural Training. *HCI International 2009*. http://www.soartech
.com/images/uploads/file/taylor-HCI2009-paper-FINAL-marked.pdf.

Thompson, Mark. 2008. Collateral Tragedies. *Time*, September 15, 34–35.

Tierney, Patrick. 2002. *Darkness in El Dorado: How Scientists and Journalists Devastated the Amazon*. New York: W. W. Norton.

Tishkov, Valery. 2004. *Chechnya: Life in a War-Torn Society*. Berkeley: University of California Press.

Tomlinson, Gary. 1993. *Music in Renaissance Magic: Toward a Historiography of Others*. Chicago: University of Chicago Press.

Turner, Victor. 1979. Frame, Flow, and Reflection: Ritual and Drama as Public Liminality. *Japanese Journal of Religious Studies* 6(4):465–99.

Turse, Nick. 2011. Does the Pentagon Really Have 1,180 Foreign Bases? Accessed March 16, 2011, from http:www.lewerockwell.com/engelhardt415.html.

University of Texas at Dallas. 2010. Game Trains Soldiers in a Virtual Iraq or Afghanistan. Accessed February 23, 2010, from http://www.utdallas.edu/news/2010/2/23-1251_Game-Trains-Soldiers-in-a-Virtual-Iraq-or-Afghanis_article.html.

U.S. Africa Command. 2011. Transcript: General Ham Discusses "AFRICOM Perspectives" at CSIS Military Strategy Forum, October 4, 2011. Accessed April 18, 2012, from http://www.africom.mil/getarticle.asp?art=7306.

U.S. Bureau of Labor Statistics. 2010. Local Area Unemployment Statistics. Accessed March 23, 2011, from http://data.bls.gov/PDQ/servlet/SurveyOutput Servlet?data_tool=latest_numbers&series_id=LASST06000003.

U.S. Department of Defense. 2006. Interim Progress Report on DOD Directive 3000.05 Military Support for Stability, Security, Transition, and Reconstruction (SSTR) Operations. http://www.defenselink.mil/policy/sections/policy_offices/solic/stabilityOps/assets/refdocs/DODD%203000%2005%20REPORT%20TO%20SECDEF%202006%20(unclass).pdf.

———. 2009a. Introduction to the HSCB Program. *Human Social Culture Behavior Newsletter* 1(Spring): 1.

———. 2009b. A Dynamic Socio-cultural Network Lens. *Human Social Culture Behavior Newsletter* 2(2009):13.

U.S. Department of State. 2001. Statement on the designation of 39 organizations on the USA Patriot Act's "Terrorist Exclusion List" as of December 5, 2001. Accessed March 4, 2002, from http://www.state.gov/r/pa/prs/ps/2001/6695.htm.

———. 2010. Bureau for International Narcotics and Law Enforcement Affairs, International Narcotics Control Strategy Report, Volume 1: Drug and Chemical Control. March. Accessed February 29, 2012, from http://www.state.gov/documents/organization/137411.pdf.

———. n.d. Office of the Coordinator for Reconstruction and Stabilization. http://www.state.gov/s/crs.

U.S. Secretary of Defense. 2007. RDT&E Project Justification (R2a Exhibit). http://www.defenselink.mil/comptroller/defbudget/fy2008/budget_justification/pdfs/rdtande/Vol_3_OSD/BA-3.pdf.

────. 2008. RDT&E Budget Item Justification (R2 Exhibit), PE Number 0602670D8Z, Human, Social and Culture Behavior Modeling Applied Research. http://www.dtic.mil/descriptivesum/Y2009/OSD/0602670D8Z.pdf.

────. 2009. RDT&E Budget Item Justification (R2 Exhibit), PE Number 0602670D8Z, Human, Social and Culture Behavior Modeling Applied Research. http://www.dtic.mil/descriptivesum/Y2009/OSD/0602670D8Z.pdf.

Valentin, Karen, and Lotte Meinert. 2009. The Adult North and the Young South: Reflections on the Civilizing Mission of Children's Rights. *Anthropology Today* 25(3):23–28.

Valentine, Douglas. 1990. *The Phoenix Program*. New York: William Morrow.

Vanasco, Jeannie. 2011. Why Is the US Government Interested in Storytelling? *New Yorker Online*, March 22. http://www.newyorker.com/online/blogs/books/2011/03/why-is-the-us-government-interested-in-storytelling.html.

Vasquez, Jose N. 2009. Seeing Green: Visual Technology, Virtual Reality, and the Experience of War. In *An Anthropology of War: Views from the Frontline*, edited by Alisse Waterston. New York: Berghahn Books.

Vayda, Andrew P. 1979. Review of *Bloodshed and Vengeance in the Papuan Mountains: The Generation of Conflict in Tauade Society* by C. R. Hallpike. *American Anthropologist* 81(2):424–25.

Vernallis, Carol. 2004. *Experiencing Music Video: Aesthetics and Cultural Context*. New York: Columbia University Press.

Vidal, Silvia, and Neil L. Whitehead. 2004. Dark Shamans and the Shamanic State: Sorcery and Witchcraft as Political Process in Guyana and the Venezuelan Amazon. In *Darkness and Secrecy: The Anthropology of Assault Sorcery and Witchcraft in Amazonia*, edited by Neil L. Whitehead and Robin Wright. Durham: Duke University Press.

Virilio, Paul. 1989. *War and Cinema: The Logistics of Perception*. London: Verso.

────. 2002. *Desert Screen: War at the Speed of Light*. New York: Continuum.

Virno, Paolo. 2004. *A Grammar of the Multitude*. Los Angeles: Semiotext(e).

Walt, Stephen. 2009. High Cost, Long Odds. *The Nation*, November 9, 11–12.

West, Bing. 2009. Counterinsurgency Lessons from Iraq. *Military Review* (March/April):2–12.

West, Harry G., and Todd Sanders, eds. 2003. *Transparency and Conspiracy: Ethnographies of Suspicion in the New World Order*. Durham: Duke University Press.

Whitehead Neil L. 2002. *Dark Shamans: Kanaimà and the Poetics of Violent Death*. Durham: Duke University Press.

────. 2004a. Introduction. In *Violence*, edited by Neil L. Whitehead. Santa Fe: School of American Research Press.

────. 2004b. On the Poetics of Violence. In *Violence*, edited by Neil L. Whitehead. Santa Fe: School of American Research Press.

────. 2007. Violence and the Cultural Order. *Daedalus* (Winter):1–11.

Whitehead, Neil L., and Michael Harbsmeier, eds. 2008. *Hans Staden's True History: An Account of Cannibal Captivity in Brazil*. Durham: Duke University Press.

Whitehead, Neil L., and Michael Wesch 2012. *Human No More: Digital Subjectivities, Un-human Subjects and the End of Anthropology*, edited by Neil L. Whitehead and Michael Wesch. Boulder: University of Colorado Press.

Whitehead, Neil L., and Robin Wright, eds. 2004. *Darkness and Secrecy: The Anthropology of Assault Sorcery and Witchcraft in Amazonia*. Durham: Duke University Press.

Wilcox, John. 2007. Precision Engagement: Strategic Context for the Long War. PowerPoint presentation to the Precision Strike Winter Roundtable. http://www.dtic.mil/ndia/2007psa_winter/wilcox.pdf.

Williams, Sarah. 2011. "A Swearing and Blaspheming Wretch": Representations of Witchcraft and Excess in Early Modern English Broadside Balladry and Popular Song. *Journal of Musicological Research* 30(4):309–56.

Winans, Edgar. 1992. Hyenas on the Border. In *The Paths to Domination, Resistance and Terror*, edited by Carolyn Nordstrom and JoAnn Martin. Berkeley: University of California Press.

Winter, Bronwyn, Denise Thompson, and Sheila Jeffreys. 2002. The UN Approach to Harmful Traditional Practices. *International Feminist Journal of Politics* 4(1):72–94.

Wolf, Eric. 1982. *Europe and the People without History*. Berkeley: University of California Press.

Wright, Evan. 2004. *Generation Kill: Devil Dogs, Iceman, Capitan American, and the New Face of American War*. New York: G. P. Putnam's Sons.

Yenne, Bill. 2004. *Attack of the Drones: A History of Unmanned Aerial Combat*. Osceola, Wisc.: Zenith Press.

Young, Allan. 1995. *The Harmony of Illusions: Inventing Post-traumatic Stress Disorder*. Princeton, N.J.: Princeton University Press.

Yousafzai, Sam, and Mark Hosenball. 2009. Predators on the Hunt in Pakistan. *Newsweek*, February 9, 35.

Youssef, Nancy. 2009. US Airstrike in Afghanistan Tests McChrystal's New Order. *Truthout*, July 17. Accessed July 18, 2009, from http://www.truthout.org/071809E?n.

Zaidi, Mosharraf. 2009. The Best Wall of Defense. *The Nation*, November 9, 18–19.

Zaloga, Steven. 2008. *Unmanned Aerial Vehicles: Robotic Air Warfare 1917–2007*. Buffalo, Minn.: Osprey Press.

CONTRIBUTORS

ROBERTSON ALLEN is an instructor in interdisciplinary arts and sciences at the University of Washington, Bothell. He received his doctorate in anthropology from the University of Washington in 2012. His dissertation research explored the interconnections between the U.S. military, interactive media, and high-tech labor by focusing on the production, marketing, and deployment of the official U.S. Army video game, *America's Army*. His articles on this topic have appeared in the journals *Transformative Works and Cultures* and *Games and Culture*.

R. BRIAN FERGUSON is professor of anthropology at Rutgers University, Newark. He has studied war for more than thirty years, trying to keep up as a generalist in a field that is expanding in different directions at increasing speed. He is currently working on a book called *Chimpanzees, War, and History: Are Men Born to Kill?*

SVERKER FINNSTRÖM is associate professor of cultural anthropology at Uppsala University, Sweden. Since 1997 he has conducted recurrent fieldwork in northern Uganda, with a focus on how young adults, born into civil war, understand and attempt to control their moral and material circumstances. Besides his articles, both popular and academic, he is the author of *Living with Bad Surroundings: War, History, and Everyday Moments in Northern Uganda* (2008), published by Duke University Press, for which he was honored with the Margaret Mead Award in 2009.

ROBERTO J. GONZÁLEZ is professor of anthropology at San Jose State University. He is the author of several books, including *Zapotec Science: Farming and Food in the Northern Sierra of Oaxaca* (2001), *American Counterinsurgency: Human Science and the Human Terrain* (2009), and most recently *Militarizing Culture: Essays on the Warfare State* (2010). He is a founding member of the Network of Concerned Anthropologists.

DAVID PRICE is associate professor of anthropology at Saint Martin's University in Lacey, Washington. He is the author of *Threatening Anthropology: McCarthyism and the FBI's Surveillance of Activist Anthropologists* (2004) and *Anthropological Intelligence: Deployment and Neglect of American Anthropology during the Second*

World War (2008), also published by Duke University Press. He was a member of the American Anthropological Association's 2006–2007 Ad Hoc Commission on the Engagement of Anthropology with the U.S. Security and Intelligence Communities.

ANTONIUS C. G. M. ROBBEN is professor of anthropology at Utrecht University, the Netherlands. He has recently published the edited volume *Iraq at a Distance: What Anthropologists Can Teach Us about the War* (2010).

VICTORIA SANFORD is professor of anthropology at Lehman College and the Graduate Center, City University of New York. She is the author of *Buried Secrets: Truth and Human Rights in Guatemala* (2003), *Violencia y Genocidio en Guatemala* (2003), *Guatemala: Del Genocidio al Feminicidio* (2008), and *La Masacre de Panzos: Etnicidad, Tierra y Violencia en Guatemala* (2009). She is currently writing *The Land of Pale Hands: Feminicide, Social Cleansing and Impunity in Guatemala.*

JEFFREY A. SLUKA earned his doctorate from the University of California, Berkeley, and is associate professor in the Social Anthropology Programme at Massey University, New Zealand. A political anthropologist with extensive fieldwork experience in Northern Ireland, he is an expert on political violence and the cultural dynamics of armed conflicts involving ethnonationalist movements and indigenous peoples. He is the author of *Hearts and Minds, Water and Fish: Popular Support for the IRA and INLA in a Northern Irish Ghetto* (1989) and edited *Death Squad: The Anthropology of State Terror* (2000) and (with Antonius C. G. M. Robben) *Ethnographic Fieldwork: An Anthropological Reader* (2007).

KOEN STROEKEN is associate professor of Africanist anthropology at the Department of African Languages and Cultures, Ghent University. He has recently published the monograph *Moral Power: The Magic of Witchcraft* (2010) analyzing the informal medico-political system of peacemaking and violence in rural Tanzania.

MATTHEW SUMERA is a Ph.D. candidate in ethnomusicology at the University of Wisconsin, Madison. His work addresses the intersections of war, music, aesthetics, and representation. His primary interest is in developing approaches to studying the ubiquity of musical use as a powerful tool through which to examine cultural and political formations.

NEIL L. WHITEHEAD was professor of anthropology at the University of Wisconsin, Madison. He was the author of *Dark Shamans: Kanaimà and the Poetics of Violent Death* (2002) and the editor of *Terror and Violence: Imagination and the Unimaginable* (with Andrew Strathern and Pamela J. Stewart, 2005); *In Darkness and Secrecy: The Anthropology of Assault Sorcery and Witchcraft in Amazonia* (with Robin Wright, 2004); *Histories and Historicities in Amazonia* (2003); and *The Discoverie of the Large, Rich and Bewtiful Empire of Guiana by Sir Walter Raleigh* (1998). *Dark Shamans* and *In Darkness and Secrecy* are both also published by Duke University Press.

INDEX

carrion system, 235–41; principles of, 240; witchcraft and, 245

casualty avoidance, 181. *See also* civilians

Center for Computational Analysis of Social and Organizational Systems, 73

Center for Terrorism and Intelligence Studies, 70

Central American Parliament (PARLA-CEN), 208; killings, 208–19

Central Intelligence Agency (CIA), 32, 36, 44n9, 91, 96, 102, 174

chaos, 4, 7–8, 16, 135–39, 141, 146, 150, 195, 224

checkpoint, 67, 141, 175, 199; flash, 137–38, 141

children: growing up with war, 145, 186; rights of, 29, 118; soldiering, 15, 118; targets of war, 124, 127, 138, 148, 244

Chion, M., 224, 227

choiceless choices, 118; of life or death, 142, 144

cinematographic eye, 145–46, 149–50

civilians: as casualties, 15, 55, 68, 79, 120–25, 132, 134, 141, 148, 171, 188; CIVCAS, 175; as collateral damage, 66, 175

civilization, 5, 14, 29, 241

coalition forces/troops, 75, 89, 97, 172–73, 189; casualties of, 181

Cockburn, B., 186

coercion, 177, 189, 217

cognitariat, 155, 157–58

COIN. *See* counterinsurgency

collateral damage, 15, 21, 60, 175, 186, 190

collateral disaster, 172

colonialism/colonization, 31, 47, 55, 58, 234; anthropology/ethnography and, 12, 18, 27, 41, 43n3, 54–55, 60; colonial mirror, 24; epistemology of, 12, 28, 41; human terrain/enemy mapping and, 60, 85, 114; legacy/complicity, 8, 11, 28; postmodern brand of, 241. *See also* imperialism

combat air patrols, 178, 180

Combined Action Platoons, 136

Combined Air and Space Operations Center, Middle East, 181

commodity exchange, 238, 240

computers: avatars, 71; games for (*see* digital games); magic of, 7, 58, 66, 68, 145, 149; mapping and modeling on, 69, 75, 97–98; music and videos on, 228–29

computer science, 67, 69–70

computer simulation, 23, 145, 148; virtual Iraq, 148; virtual Vietnam, 68, 148

conspiracy theories/thinking, 4, 11, 20–21

Control-Alt-Delete (Ctrl-Alt-Del), 178

convoys, military, 140, 175

corruption: of government, 80, 92, 198; mass violence and, 115; narcotraffickers and, 199; police and, 203

counterinsurgency, 7, 16, 28, 46–64, 111–12, 125, 131, 172–74; advocates of, 63, 80; anthropology and, 62; against Black Panthers, 67; COIN, 85–87, 91, 93, 107–8; *Counterinsurgency Field Manual*, 61; culture of, 61; in Iraq, 134, 136–37, 150; as magic, 83; pseudoscience, 191; tactics, 92, 134, 137, 150, 188; as theology/cult, 80, 93; theory of, 86, 177; in Vietnam, 134, 136; virtual, 171

counterterrorism (CT), 68, 73, 107–8, 169, 181–82

crime: against humanity, 114, 124, 207; genocidal, 195; organized, 195–97, 199–200, 203, 205–6, 208; war, 114, 185

culture: the anthropological product vs., 100; in computer games, 155; concept of, 2, 13, 17, 30, 61, 72, 88; culturalism, 28; immersion in, 95, 106; of impunity, 212; militarized concept of, 85–86, 187, 235; models of (human terrain), 13, 47, 65–67, 86–87; musical, 216, 218; operational idea of, 87–88; of the other, 29, 46, 55, 69, 73; Pentagon idea of, 75, 86–87; of terror, 212; as uncultured wilderness, 115; violence and, 13; to visualize, 132–33, 143;

weaponization of, 7, 27–28, 169, 187, 243; of witchcraft, 245

cybernetics, 9, 11, 19, 65, 68–69, 82–83

cyberspace, 2, 20, 191

D'Andrade, R., 66, 107

dark matter of global war, 21

Dartmouth Laboratory for Human Terrain, 70–71, 73

death: by assault sorcery, 24n2; bargain with, 37; civilian, 134, 140, 172–73, 175, 178, 186–87; combat, 16, 55; at a distance, 19, 56, 186; grievous or tragic, 122–23, 147–48; humanitarian, 123–26; as last freedom, 130; magical, 20, 56, 112, 128, 218, 244; as powerful stories, 129; space of, 13, 19–20, 112, 128; spectacular, 119; spirits of the dead, 147–48; squads of, 4, 196, 199, 206–9; trails of, 111, 114

Defense Advanced Research Projects Agency (DARPA), 83n1, 96–98

dehumanization, 9, 10, 53, 134, 141–44, 150, 156, 201, 246, 249; as animal, 126; culture of, 246; as depersonalization, 73, 143; of enemy, 155; hostile gaze of, 22; human terrain as, 10; magic of, 9, 134; virtualization of, 187; visual isolation as, 141–43; witchcraft as, 73, 249

Deleuze, G., and F. Guáttari, 4–5

democracy, violence and, 3, 14, 23–24, 39, 43n2, 93, 130–31, 242, 244, 246

demonstrations, 175, 185

Der Derian, J., 10, 25n8, 155, 163, 181, 229

desensitization, 143, 148, 187

diamonds, 235–41; non-blood, 44n9, 235; price of, 239

digital games, 7, 15, 22–23, 56, 65–66, 72, 76, 78, 145, 152–54, 187, 216, 231; industry of, 158–59; first-person shooting games, 154; liminality/magic circle, 156, in PTSD treatment, 149; sim games, 78; war reality as, 181

divide and conquer, 18, 82, 112, 177

divination, 237–38, 246

DNA, 100, 117

domination: anthropology/ethnography and, 18, 28–29, 40, 59, 61, 191, 245; counterinsurgency as, 131; Western, 17, 48, 217, 221, 242, 246

drones (unmanned aerial vehicles, UAVS), 1, 9, 16–17, 50, 55–62, 67, 132, 143, 145, 171, 181–91; culture of, 243, 246; hunter-killer, 178, 185, 187; kill ratio/hit rate, 183; MQ-1 Predator, 55–56, 58, 178–80, 183, 192; MQ-9 Reaper, 178–79; strikes of, 60, 174–76, 182–83, 185

Drowning Pool (music band), 221–23, 226, 227, 232

economy: 2008 crisis, 204, 214, 216–18; as global, 10, 13, 20, 241–44; permanent arms economy, 14

El Salvador, U.S. intelligence in, 94, 186, 200

empire, 8, 82, 99–100, 234–35, 242–44, 249

Engelhardt, T., 175–76, 178, 181–82, 184–85, 188, 190

engineering: armed social, 93; computerized behavioral models and, 69; social, 10, 16, 23, 61–63, 67, 78, 80, 82

epistemology, 27, 219; colonial, 8, 12, 28, 41; of confidence, 80; flawed, 3, 12, 18–19, 26–27, 30, 36, 38, 79

ethics, research, 8, 11, 28, 47–48, 52–53, 57, 59–60. See also American Anthropological Association

ethnography: legitimate, 8–9, 12, 17–18; of military, 18–19, 30–31; as power/domination, 28–29, 40; as practice, 26, 42, 78–79; torturous epistemology of, 19, 27, 31, 36–38, 40, 61, 79, 169

Evans-Pritchard, E. E., 11–12, 18, 78, 99; on witchcraft, sorcery, and magic, 24n2

evil, as moral category, 24, 114, 127, 129–30, 131, 144

Exum, A., 60, 183

improvised explosive device (IED), 90, 135, 140, 145, 149

impunity, 195, 199, 202; culture of, 212; humanitarian, 125; magic and, 195; murder and, 196; rule of law and, 213

indigenous peoples, 31, 43n2, 176–77, 199; human terrain mapping and, 96, 100; insurgents and, 51

insurgency, 57–58; prediction of, 9, 64–84, 137; production of, 16, 135, 177, 182–83, 188–89

insurgents, 8, 9, 16, 17, 22, 30, 39, 46, 48, 51, 65, 67, 76–80, 90, 94, 108, 115, 125, 133, 135–38, 146, 149, 171–93, 243–44. *See also* guerrilla warfare; rebels

International Criminal Court (ICC), 111–12, 114–15, 117, 119, 122, 124, 126, 131

international forces, 176

International Monetary Fund (IMF), 4–5, 246

Internet, 6, 25n5, 96; online worlds/realities and, 3, 6, 7, 10, 17, 18, 21, 101–2, 153–54, 162–63, 178, 218, 230

intersubjectivity, experiencing violence, 3, 36

Iraq: 2003 U.S. invasion of, 206; veterans of, 149

Irish Republican Army (IRA), 49, 51–52; Provisional IRA (PIRA), 51–52

Israel, 6, 23, 185, 243–44

Jackson, A., 51

jihad, 68, 244; cyber, 10

kanaimà. See magic; sorcery: assault

Kapferer, B., 4–5, 111, 191, 219, 235

Kilcullen, D., 48–49, 59–60, 63, 84n2, 86, 90, 183, 185

Kosovo, 178

labor: affective, 156; cognitive, 156–57; forced, 124; immaterial, 156; military as a market of, 167; non-labor and, 157; precarious, 158

Lansdale, E., 46

La Violencia, 196–97, 199

Lawrence, T. E., 58

Leach, E., 111, 127

legitimacy, 63, 188, 194, 202

liminality, 157, 202; magic circle and, 202; public, 7, 156

Lincoln Group, 51

Lockheed Martin, 68

long-range acoustic devices (sound cannons), 217

long-range arms, 149

long-range reconnaissance patrol, 139

Lord's Resistance Army/Movement (LRA), 13, 111–31

Loyd, P., 47

L-3 Communications, 68

Lutz, C., 104, 109, 141, 153, 155, 163, 215

magic, 2–25, 77, 132–33, 80–81, 83, 111–12, 126–31, 132–34, 138–39, 191, 194–95, 200, 202–3, 213, 216, 234–50; advertising war, 241–42; albino killings (*mwanga* magic), 241–48; circles of, 156; death by, 56, 112; de-magicalization, 16, 119–20, 131; ethnographer's, 26; Evans-Pritchard on, 24n2, 99; as illusion of control, 99; initiation, 246–47; of *kanaimà*, 32; magico-primitive vs. techno-modern, 2–3, 6, 20, 68–69, 82–83, 98, 156, 217–18, 223, 238; rationality, reason, and, 242; sacrifice, 237–38, 244–46; of the state, 42; technology, 243, 247; traditional, 246–48; the virtual and, 3. *See also* Malinowski, B.

Malinowski, B.: legacy of, 12, 26; magic and, 21, 99, 128; *Magic, Science, and Religion*, 83

Manichaean worldview, 3, 112, 126, 144, 231

Mapping the Human Terrain (MAP-HT), 9–11, 17, 68, 75–76, 79, 88, 90, 121–22, 156, 168

Marcus, G., 27, 34, 248

martyrs, 184, 244

massacres, 120–21, 148, 195, 208, 212

mathematics. *See* human terrain

McChrystal, S. A., 91, 188, 190

McFate, M., 47, 49–64, 85, 88, 95, 97

McNeil, W. H., 215–16

media, 1, 6–7, 20–21, 74, 106, 111–12, 131, 144, 153, 163, 183, 245; as magical, 126–31, 156, 241; mainstream, 16, 50, 181, 187, 216; military-entertainment/militainment, 15, 22–23, 25n8, 153, 169n3, 181, 186–87, 229; multimedia, 78, 138, 143, 150; propaganda, 117–18, 122–23, 125, 126; social, 22, 114, 164; spectacle, 117, 126–27; virtual, 23. *See also* military; YouTube

mediation, 6, 12, 15, 17, 22, 64n1, 133, 141–44. *See also* hypermediation; immediation

militants, 67, 93, 174–75, 177, 183–84, 186

military: contracting, 10, 43n4, 47, 53, 66, 80, 83, 106, 158, 162, 164–69, 197, 212–14; industry, 10, 187, 234, 243, 249; intervention, 16–17, 111–12, 115, 120, 189; militarization, 12, 100–101, 157, 168, 177, 187, 216–17; military-industrial complex, 14, 79–80, 187; military-industrial-media-entertainment network/complex, 181, 229; military-industrial-robotics complex, 181; recruitment to, 26, 145, 149, 153, 156, 197–98, 216, 228

Mills, C. W., 81, 187

mimesis, 6, 21, 23, 40, 144, 229

Minerva Initiative, 31, 42, 102, 104–5

mining, 235, 238; artisanal, 235–38, 246–48

modeling and simulation, 9, 65–71, 77, 83, 96–97, 106–7

moral reason. *See* rationality

Mosely, A., 172

music: esprit de corps and, 215–16; magic and, 217–218; military normal and, 215; torture and, 217; war and, 214–33. *See also* war music videos

muti (mutilation) murders, 20, 24n2, 244. *See also* sorcery: assault

Mwanangwa (Tanzania), 236–41

mwanga. See magic

Nabokov, V., 59

Nagl, J., 47, 80, 84n2, 86, 92

narco-traffickers, 6, 197, 199, 203

narrative, 40, 44n5, 50–52, 63, 67, 75, 80, 112, 128, 130, 154, 156, 159, 163, 169n10, 224

National Training Center (NTC), 76–77

Negri, A. *See* Hardt, M.

neoliberalism, 80, 92, 99, 201, 206, 239–41, 246

netwar, 136

Network of Concerned Anthropologists, 11

New York Times, 60, 118, 150n1, 171

night vision: equipment (image intensifiers) for, 132–51; goggles for (NVGs), 67, 139–41, 145, 149; magic and, 3, 132–34, 138–39; nocturnal combat and, 132–35, 138, 140, 150; starlight scopes for, 139; thermal imaging devices for, 132, 139, 143

9/11. *See* September 11, 2001

North Atlantic Treaty Organization (NATO), 172, 178, 182

North Waziristan (Pakistan), 184

Nuer, the (of Sudan), 12, 18, 79

nu metal, 220–22. *See also* war music videos

Obama, B., 45n12, 82, 114, 186, 190; administration of, 46, 173; overseas contingent operations (war on terror) of, 190

occult, 2, 4–5, 13, 20–21, 26, 133, 165, 191, 217, 248, 254

occupation, enforced, 18, 31, 34, 46–48, 50–56, 60, 63, 67, 74, 80–82, 169, 173, 175, 187, 189, 234, 243, 250

Operation Enduring Freedom, 172, 179

Shock and Awe (music video website), 230
siege mentality, 60, 183
Silverman, B., 69–70
simulation. *See* computer simulation; modeling and simulation; Synthetic Environment for Analysis and Simulation
Singer, P. W., 56, 181–82, 185
social cleansing, 16, 194–95, 203–5, 208–9, 211–12; ethnic, 82
social forecasting, 65, 67, 73–74, 76, 79, 83
social network analysis, 70, 78
soft sell, 158, 163
soldiers: anthropologists as, 103, 107; causalities, 55, 124; child, 15; as cultural experts, 87; ethnic, 21; ghost, 147–48; invisible, 141; as killing machines, 144; as laborers, 156, 167, 215–16; by remote, 56; self-fashioning, 15; soldier/civilian blur, 8, 10, 21, 88, 156, 163, 199, 229; virtual, 21, 153–55, 157, 159, 162, 164, 167–69, 199
sonic warfare, 216–17, 232
sorcery, 7, 15, 19–21, 24, 27, 115, 191; assault, 2–3, 5, 24n2, 32, 34, 44n9; Evans-Pritchard on, 24n2; global, 17; *kanaimà*, 20, 21, 32–34, 44n9; by remote, 2, 4, 9, 17, 55–56, 60, 74, 171, 175, 186, 188, 191–92, 216, 247, 249
South Waziristan (Pakistan), 182
Soviets, 100, 177, 186, 193
special forces, 166, 188; manuals/advisor guides, 13, 61
spectacide, 22–23, 44n11, 117, 121, 125–26, 144, 150, 215; definitions of, 25n8, 192
stability operations, 54, 82, 87, 90–92, 94, 97, 107–9
stealth warfare, 1, 149, 243
Stewart, P., and A. Strathern, 112, 129
strategic hamlets, 67, 173
Strathern, A. *See* Stewart, P., and A. Strathern
suicide attacks, 135, 137, 176, 182, 189

Sukuma (Tanzania), 236, 244–46; language of, 248
Sunni, awakening of (Iraq), 177
suspicion, 4, 20, 32, 181, 236–38, 248
swarming operations, 133–34, 136–37, 141, 150
Swat District (Pakistan), 174
Synthetic Environment for Analysis and Simulation (Purdue University), 71

Taliban, 172–78; as drone targets, 181–82; growing support for, 43n3, 49, 186, 188–89
"Taliban Bodies" (music video), 223–31. *See also* war music videos
Tanzania, 4, 13, 16–17, 115, 235–36, 245–46
Tax, S., action anthropology and, 62
Taylor, G., 66, 71–72
technology: culture and, 243; global politics and, 2, 91, 153; human terrain modeling and, 70, 72; as magical, 7; military, 4, 15, 136, 143–44, 149–50, 186, 229; nature of, 6; substituting strategy, 183; virtual war and, 172. *See also* military
three-finger salute. *See* Control-Alt-Delete
torture: counterinsurgency and, 124; ethnography as, 18–19, 26–45, 79; music and, 217; social, 17, 205, 211
trauma, 23; psychic, 147, 150; traumatic memories, 147–49. *See also* post-traumatic stress disorder
tribal, as label, 2, 21, 43n2, 82
tribal zones, 13, 171–93; human terrain of, 78, 106
truth: claim to, 123; creation of, 4, 38–39, 45n13, 129, 212; idea of, 26–27, 38, 45n15, 128, 142

Uganda, 15, 16, 17, 22, 111–31
United Nations (UN), 29, 119, 176, 203; in Guatemala, 206; High Commission for Refugees (UNHCR), 244

United States Air Force (USAF), 19, 56, 77–78, 101, 104, 178, 181, 192

United States Department of Defense (DOD), 24n1, 25n3, 65, 74, 86, 103, 105

United States Department of Homeland Security, 10

United States Office of Naval Research, 73, 78, 79

unmanned aerial vehicles (UAVs). *See* drones

USS *Vincennes*, 141–42

video games. *See* digital games

Viet Cong, 68, 135, 242

Vietnam War, 21, 55, 59, 68, 107, 132–51, 235, 242; veterans of, 147–48

visual culture, 132–34, 143, 232

vulture people, 236–41

war: asymmetrical, 2, 15, 47; definition of, 7; drug wars, 10, 16, 197, 201; long war, 85, 190–91; machine, 5, 58, 232; on the poor, 234, 247, 250; psychological warfare, 21, 53, 54, 67, 222; on terror, 5, 30, 39, 97, 113, 115, 171, 174–76, 181–82, 188, 190, 201, 216, 232, 234, 241–44. *See also* global war; war music videos

Wardynski, C., 160, 169n2

war music videos: audiences and deployment of, 229–32; editing technologies and, 228–29; musical mediation and, 219–22; synch points and, 224, 226–31; "Taliban Bodies," 223–31

weapons of mass destruction, 7

West, H. G., and T. Sanders, 2, 4–6, 11, 16, 245

WikiLeaks, 16

witchcraft, 2, 3, 13, 17, 19–20, 22, 37–38, 45n13, 69, 73, 112–15, 127–30, 191, 244–46; replacing magic, 248. *See also* Evans-Pritchard, E. E.

World War I, 142, 149, 243

World War II, 14, 46, 59, 106, 149, 234, 241–43

Yankovic, A., 178

YouTube, 15, 44n11, 200, 219, 220, 230, 231

NEIL L. WHITEHEAD was professor of anthropology at the University of Wisconsin. His books include *Of Cannibals and Kings: Primal Anthropology in the Americas* (2011) and *Dark Shamans: Kanaimà and the Poetics of Violent Death* (Duke, 2002). He was the editor of numerous works, including (with Michael Wesch) *Human No More: Digital Subjectivities, Unhuman Subjects, and the End of Anthropology* (2012); (with Michael Harbsmeier) *Hans Staden's True History: An Account of Cannibal Captivity in Brazil*, by Hans Staden (Duke, 2008); and (with Robin Wright) *In Darkness and Secrecy: The Anthropology of Assault Sorcery and Witchcraft in Amazonia* (Duke, 2004). He was a former editor of *Ethnohistory*.

SVERKER FINNSTRÖM is associate professor of cultural anthropology at Uppsala University, Sweden. He is the author of *Living with Bad Surroundings: War, History, and Everyday Moments in Northern Uganda* (Duke, 2008), winner of the Margaret Mead Award (American Anthropological Association and the Society for Applied Anthropology).

Library of Congress Cataloging-in-Publication Data
Virtual war and magical death : technologies and imaginaries for terror and killing / Neil L. Whitehead and Sverker Finnström, eds.
p. cm.—(The cultures and practice of violence series)
Includes bibliographical references and index.
ISBN 978-0-8223-5435-2 (cloth : alk. paper)
ISBN 978-0-8223-5447-5 (pbk. : alk. paper)
1. War and society. 2. War and civilization. 3. War—Technological innovations. 4. Technology—Anthropological aspects. I. Whitehead, Neil L. II. Finnström, Sverker. III. Series: Cultures and practice of violence series.
GN497.V578 2013
303.6'6—dc23   2012044778